Murray

19

GRAND PRIX YEAR

Foreword by Nigel Mansell

Photography
JOHN TOWNSEND

PUBLISHED IN ASSOCIATION WITH

AUTOGLASS

ACKNOWLEDGEMENTS

This book means a great deal to me. It has been my pleasure and privilege to talk to the world about motor sport in general and Grand Prix racing in particular on television and radio for some 42 years now, and I have enjoyed every second of it. Four years ago my friend Roger Chown persuaded me to write — not talk — about my Grand Prix year and he published the result which went a whole lot better than either of us had expected. It seemed that the format, style and content were satisfying a need and it gave me a great deal of satisfaction that my recording of and views on the sport that means so much to me were apparently giving pleasure to so many people.

"Murray Walker's Grand Prix Year 1987" was followed by similar reviews of '88 and '89 and I looked forward to writing about 1990. But then, almost too late, came the realisation that it would not be possible for Roger and his company to publish it. Last year I said "It's not easy writing a book. Not for me anyway." I can tell you that writing one is a lot easier than finding a new publisher — especially when you don't start until March for a book to appear in November! To have got Richard Poulter's Hazleton Publishing to take it on was beyond my wildest dreams, but they did and you are holding the result. Everybody at Hazleton is a motor sport enthusiast. As the people who produce those prestige publications "Autocourse", "Motocourse" and "Rallycourse" they know what their readers want and they see that they get it. I am proud to be associated with them and profoundly grateful to Richard and his colleagues.

So thank you indeed to Richard for rescuing the book, to Simon Arron for editing it, to George Greenfield for producing it, to Clive and Chrissie Wylie for designing it, to Liz Le Breton for promoting it, to the inimitable Maurice Hamilton for the statistics and to Deirdre Fenney for co-ordinating it. Thank you too to Autoglass for sponsoring it and, of course, to the photographer's photographer John Townsend for the great pictures. Without them, no book. With them, a lot of fun and a happy sense of achievement.

Finally, thank you for buying it. Hope you enjoy reading it as much as I've enjoyed writing it!

MURRAY WALKER

Murray Walker's 1990 Grand Prix Year is published by Hazleton Publishing, 3 Richmond Hill, Richmond, Surrey TW10 6RE, in association with Autoglass Ltd.
Designed by Clive Wylie and Associates, London SW15.
Typeset by Surrey Typesetters Ltd, Stoneleigh, Surrey.
Colour reproduction by Masterlith Ltd, Mitcham, Surrey.
Printed in England by The Nuffield Press Ltd, Oxford.

DISTRIBUTORS
UK & OTHER MARKETS
Osprey Publishing Limited
59 Grosvenor Street, London W1X 9DA

AUSTRALIA
Universal Motor Publications
c/o Automoto Motoring Bookshop
152-154 Clarence Street
Sydney 2000, New South Wales

NEW ZEALAND
David Bateman Limited
"Golden Heights", 32-34 View Road
Glenfield, Auckland 10

PUBLISHER: Richard Poulter

EXECUTIVE PUBLISHER: Elizabeth Le Breton

EDITOR: Simon Arron

PRODUCTION MANAGER: George Greenfield

PUBLISHING CO-ORDINATOR: Deirdre Fenney

GRAND PRIX STATISTICS: Maurice Hamilton

PHOTOGRAPHER: John Townsend

Title page photograph by Nigel Snowdon.

Having left McLaren at the end of 1989, with a third World Championship in his pocket, Alain Prost didn't take long to introduce his winning ways at Ferrari.

The colourful photograph of Ivan Capelli on the back cover is by Mark Karp.

CONTENTS

Nigel Mansell's second season with Ferrari brought about more tribulations than triumphs, much to the chagrin of his adoring home crowd. Nigel will join Williams-Renault in 1991.

I am very happy to be opening Murray's 1990 year book, and it seems appropriate that I should have the opportunity to have my say before he gets his teeth into the ups and downs of my final season with Ferrari.

I actually have a lot to thank him for. Not only has he commentated on all but a handful of my F1 races with Lotus, Williams and Ferrari, bringing my various triumphs and disappointments into countless living rooms as only he knows how, but he has also done plenty more besides. Murray it was who interviewed me in sweltering Brazilian heat, with his microphone switched off, necessitating a rerun in conditions reminiscent more of a sauna than a motor racing paddock. And with the TV cameras very definitely switched on, he managed to score a direct hit on a very painful bruise during the Austrian Grand Prix press conference in 1987, his forefinger going out of control at precisely the wrong moment after I'd clouted my head on a stout girder!

Such useful contributions aside, he has supported me throughout my career. He quizzed me when I was struggling to make a name for myself in Formula Ford, hosted an F3 sponsorship announcement for me and has pursued me with enthusiasm ever since. As I know Derek Warwick, Martin Donnelly and countless others will testify, I'm certainly not the sole subject of his relentless enthusiasm.

Murray's passionate fervour, much in evidence throughout this perceptive annual review, is a rare constant in a Formula 1 world where most things change by the minute. I know it'll stay that way, and that he'll have the same zealous interest in the up and coming generation of British drivers as he did in my early days. For that, I salute him.

My advice to them is to make sure he always switches his microphone on before an interview, and to stand well back if you have a headache …

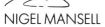

NIGEL MANSELL

AUTOGLASS

Dear Readers

Another season gone, and what a season it has proved to be! If you can't remember who did what, or where, when etc, then read the book!

AUTOGLASS (and in certain markets CARGLASS) are actively involved in many aspects of motor sport in Europe, but for the past couple of seasons Formula 1 has been a new stage on which to appear, and to be associated with the "finest Formula 1 scriptwriter in the business" as well is a bonus.

The previous Murray Walker Year Books have allowed countless fans to relive the season, and at the same time be privy to much of the "way of life" surrounding the enthralling world of Formula 1.

Sit back and enjoy Murray's journey through the 1990 season with us.

Mike Cornwell

Mike Cornwell
European Marketing Director
AUTOGLASS

1990 DRIVERS

Driver	Country	Team	No. GPs
Michele Alboreto	I	Footwork Arrows	144
Jean Alesi	F	Tyrrell	23
Philippe Alliot	F	Ligier	93
Paolo Barilla	I	Minardi	8
Gerhard Berger	A	McLaren	99
Eric Bernard	F	Larrousse Lola	18
Thierry Boutsen	B	Williams	121
David Brabham	AUS	Brabham	8
Gary Brabham	AUS	Life	0
Alex Caffi	I	Footwork Arrows	54
Ivan Capelli	I	Leyton House	64
Andrea de Cesaris	I	Dallara	150
Yannick Dalmas	F	AGS	20
Martin Donnelly	GB	Lotus	13
Gregor Foitek	CH	Brabham, Monteverdi Onyx	7
Bertrand Gachot	B	Coloni	5
Bruno Giacomelli	I	Life	69
Olivier Grouillard	F	Osella	21
Mauricio Gugelmin	BR	Leyton House	42
Johnny Herbert	GB	Lotus	8
Stefan Johansson	S	Monteverdi Onyx	78
Claudio Langes	I	Eurobrun	0
Nicola Larini	I	Ligier	35
J.J. Lehto	SF	Monteverdi Onyx	7
Nigel Mansell	GB	Ferrari	149
Pier-Luigi Martini	I	Minardi	54
Stefano Modena	I	Brabham	42
Gianni Morbidelli	I	Dallara, Minardi	3
Roberto Moreno	BR	Eurobrun, Benetton	10
Satoru Nakajima	J	Tyrrell	58
Alessandro Nannini	I	Benetton	77
Riccardo Patrese	I	Williams	208
Nelson Piquet	BR	Benetton	188
Emanuele Pirro	I	Dallara	24
Alain Prost	F	Ferrari	168
Bernd Schneider	D	Footwork Arrows	9
Ayrton Senna	BR	McLaren	110
Aguri Suzuki	J	Larrousse Lola	16
Gabriele Tarquini	I	AGS	19
Derek Warwick	GB	Lotus	131

1990 GRANDS PRIX

Race	Winner	Pole Position	Fastest Lap
USA	A. Senna	G. Berger	G. Berger
Brazil	A. Prost	A. Senna	G. Berger
San Marino	R. Patrese	A. Senna	A. Nannini
Monaco	A. Senna	A. Senna	A. Senna
Canada	A. Senna	A. Senna	G. Berger
Mexico	A. Prost	G. Berger	A. Prost
France	A. Prost	N. Mansell	N. Mansell
Great Britain	A. Prost	N. Mansell	N. Mansell
Germany	A. Senna	A. Senna	T. Boutsen
Hungary	T. Boutsen	T. Boutsen	R. Patrese
Belgium	A. Senna	A. Senna	A. Prost
Italy	A. Senna	A. Senna	A. Senna
Portugal	N. Mansell	N. Mansell	R. Patrese
Spain	A. Prost	A. Senna	R. Patrese
Japan	N. Piquet	A. Senna	R. Patrese
Australia	N. Piquet	A. Senna	N. Mansell

1990 WORLD CHAMPIONSHIP

Drivers		Pts	Teams	Pts
1.	Ayrton Senna	78	1. McLaren-Honda	121
2.	Alain Prost (73)	71	2. Ferrari	110
3.	Nelson Piquet (44)	43	3. Benetton-Ford	71
	Gerhard Berger	43	4. Williams-Renault	57
5.	Nigel Mansell	37	5. Tyrrell-DFR	16
6.	Thierry Boutsen	34	6. Lola-Lamborghini	11
7.	Riccardo Patrese	23	7. Leyton House-Judd	7
8.	Alessandro Nannini	21	8. Lotus-Lamborghini	3
9.	Jean Alesi	13	9. Brabham-Judd	2
10.	Roberto Moreno	6	Arrows-DFR	2
	Ivan Capelli	6		
	Aguri Suzuki	6		
13.	Eric Bernard	5		
14.	Derek Warwick	3		
	Satoru Nakajima	3		
16.	Alex Caffi	2		
	Stefano Modena	2		
18.	Mauricio Gugelmin	1		

Prost and Piquet totals count best 11 results only. Drivers' full scores shown in brackets.

DURING 1990 ...

* Australia hosted the 500th World Championship Grand Prix.
* McLaren lost more Grands Prix than they won for the first time since 1987.
* Ayrton Senna became the most successful Grand Prix driver from South America, the first man to achieve 50 pole positions, led the most laps, negotiated Grand Prix racing's most lucrative contract, resolved his 18-month feud with Alain Prost in Italy, then revived it in Japan after winning his second World Championship in contentious circumstances.
* In France, Ferrari (Alain Prost) won a record 100th Grand Prix.
* Claudio Langes (Eurobrun) and Bruno Giacomelli (Life) failed to pre-qualify for all the Grands Prix they entered. Giacomelli replaced Gary Brabham, whose two attempts to pre-qualify the same car also drew a blank.
* Phoenix was generally criticised as being an unsuitable venue for a Grand Prix, because of its point-and-squirt configuration.
* The Onyx team became Monteverdi, but eventually withdrew from the World Championship in disarray.
* Silverstone held its last British Grand Prix before extensive reconstruction.
* At the British Grand Prix, Riccardo Patrese became the first driver to compete in 200 World Championship events.
* Martin Donnelly and Alessandro Nannini suffered serious injuries in separate accidents, the latter victim of a bizarre helicopter crash.
* David Brabham became the first son of a World Champion to compete in a Grand Prix (and in a car bearing his father's name).
* Alain Prost and Nelson Piquet both won for their third different constructor (Prost: Renault/McLaren/Ferrari; Piquet: Brabham/Williams/Benetton).
* Brazil's new Interlagos circuit was adjudged to be a great success (but Sao Paulo wasn't).
* At the British Grand Prix meeting, Nigel Mansell announced his decision to retire at the end of 1990. He then reversed it after the Spanish race.
* Andrea de Cesaris increased to 150 his record number of non-winning GP drives.
* At Suzuka, Aguri Suzuki became the first Japanese driver to finish a Grand Prix in the first three places.
* Porsche announced their intention to re-enter Grand Prix racing in 1991, powering the Arrows team which was to be renamed Footwork-Porsche.
* Alain Prost became the first driver to score over 600 World Championship points (and 650!).
* Jean Alesi signed to drive for Ferrari in 1991 after only one full season of Grand Prix racing.
* Alain Prost finished in the top five of the World Championship for the tenth successive year.
* Roberto Moreno (Benetton) finished second in Japan, having failed to pre-qualify for ten of the previous 14 races (Eurobrun).

1990 DRIVERS
Who have won a GP,
been on pole or set fastest lap

Grand Prix Wins		Races Contested	Pole Positions	Fastest Laps
44	Alain Prost	168	22	34
26	Ayrton Senna	110	52	15
22	Nelson Piquet	188	24	23
16	Nigel Mansell	149	15	16
5	Gerhard Berger	99	6	12
5	Michele Alboreto	144	2	4
3	Riccardo Patrese	208	3	8
3	Thierry Boutsen	121	1	1
1	Alessandro Nannini	77	0	2
0	Andrea de Cesaris	150	0	1
0	Derek Warwick	131	0	2
0	Mauricio Gugelmin	42	0	1
0	Satoru Nakajima	58	0	1

PREFACE

Harmony restored? With Prost having moved on, to be replaced by Berger, McLaren started the year with the happy knowledge that its two drivers would at least talk to each other.

1989, the first year without turbo engines since 1976, had been good. McLaren had again deservedly won both the drivers' (Alain Prost) and constructors' World Championships, but this time without quite the crushing dominance they had enjoyed the previous year. For Ferrari had won three of the 16 races, Williams two and Benetton one. But if the racing had been satisfying, the accompanying politics had been bitter, contentious and no credit to the sport. Mansell was excluded from Spain and heavily fined, Senna disqualified from Japan and, subsequently, fined even more heavily and given a suspended six-month ban for "consistent dangerous driving." And if 1989 had ended in discord and strife, the winter months before the new season were no better.

The legal saga of McLaren and Senna versus the governing body, FISA, dragged on until the latest possible moment and ended with McLaren paying their driver's $100,000 fine and Ayrton producing a retraction of his allegation that FISA had manipulated the 1989 drivers' championship. As a result of his debatably sincere "apology", he was granted his superlicence and had his ban lifted. FISA had thus won on every count and there were fervent hopes that the feuding was over. But after such acrimony, it seemed unlikely.

Meantime, as ever, there had been an enormous amount of work and movement amongst the contestants preparing to enter a new decade of Grand Prix racing. There were

to be 19 teams and 35 drivers (down from 20 and 39 in 1989), but this year there were only two constructors with the same drivers that they had used throughout 1989 — Williams (Patrese/Boutsen) and Leyton House (Gugelmin/Capelli).

The volatility of life at the top in Formula 1 was demonstrated by the fact that there were an astounding 15 driver moves from team to team, the appearance of five new signings and 14 departures of drivers who had been part of the scene during 1989. Seems hard to believe? Count them!

The most significant moves were of triple World Champion Alain Prost, fed up with life at McLaren next to Senna, to Ferrari, to be replaced by Ferrari's Gerhard Berger. Triple World Champion Nelson Piquet went from Lotus to Benetton and was replaced by Derek Warwick (ex-Arrows). But when the music stopped, 11 other seats were occupied by new backsides. Satoru Nakajima moved to Tyrrell from Lotus, Gregor Foitek to Brabham (his third Grand Prix team in two seasons), Michele Alboreto (ex-Lola) and Alex Caffi to the new-look Arrows team (now owned by the Japanese Footwork concern), Olivier Grouillard from Ligier to drive the sole Osella and Emanuele Pirro from Benetton to replace Caffi at Dallara. Ligier had two new drivers in Nicola Larini and Philippe Alliot, from Osella and Lola, whilst Japan's Aguri Suzuki had thankfully left Zakspeed to join Gérard Larrousse's Lola team. And after a nail-biting winter wondering whether they were to get Grand Prix drives, Bertrand Gachot and Roberto Moreno transferred from Rial and Coloni to Subaru-Coloni and Eurobrun.

With Onyx and AGS enjoying some stability, by keeping the same drivers as they had

Disillusioned with the power politics that plagued his last season with McLaren, Prost was looking forward to the challenge of Ferrari under Cesare Fiorio's leadership.

employed at the end of 1989 (Johansson/Lehto and Tarquini/Dalmas), there were major changes in five of the other teams. Martin Donnelly joined Derek Warwick to make a powerful, all-new driver pairing at Lotus. Paolo Barilla signed on for a full season (he hoped!) with Minardi, and Eric Bernard did likewise for Lola. And finally there were to be two completely new faces, promoted from Formula 3000 — Italy's Claudio Langes to Eurobrun and Australia's Gary Brabham (Sir Jack's second son) to the new Life team.

They were the lucky ones. From 1989, there were an amazing 14 failures to make the entry list — including some true notables.

Unhappy with Brabham's prospects, 1988 World Sports-Prototype Champion Martin Brundle had returned to Jaguar. Jonathan Palmer had also returned to Sports-Prototype racing (but kept in touch as McLaren's Formula 1 test driver). Eddie Cheever was out and so were Piercarlo Ghinzani, Johnny Herbert (back to Japanese Formula 3000, but still the Lotus F1 test driver), Luis Sala, René Arnoux, Pierre-Henri Raphanel, Oscar Larrauri, Bernd Schneider, Christian Danner, Joachim Winkelhock, Volker Weidler and Enrico Bertaggia. It's tough at the top!

There were major changes amongst the teams too. No entries from Rial and Zakspeed (who sadly took Yamaha with them into oblivion). The Italian Life concern, who had tried but failed to compete in 1989, were back again. Tyrrell seemed set to continue their

Those who thought Nelson Piquet had done little to merit a Benetton contract, on the basis of his two years with Lotus, would soon be made to eat their words.

revival with impressive new sponsorship, a new management structure and a switch from Goodyear to Pirelli tyres. Brabham had gone through a miserable and disrupting winter of non-stop litigation about their future. Eurobrun, Coloni and Life were to use new 12-cylinder engines, although Eurobrun subsequently failed to do so. And, a sign of the times, ten teams were now owned or heavily backed by Japanese companies. So, with eight teams now to be powered by V10 or V12 engines, what were the prospects for the 1990 season? In a

Political machinations at Brabham followed the takeover by Middlebridge Engineering. David Brabham took over as Stefano Modena's team-mate at Imola, and became the first son of a former World Champion to start a Grand Prix when he qualified in Monaco.

word — stimulating!

For it seemed that things were going to be much more competitive than they had been the previous year (particularly as the gap between McLaren and Ferrari, reduced in 1989, looked now to be non-existent). Surely McLaren, having lost Prost and top designer/engineer Steve Nichols to Ferrari were going to be

weakened? And would Senna get on any better with Berger than he had with Prost? Ferrari, on the other hand, were now much stronger with the acquisition of a rejuvenated and fiercely motivated Prost joining his friend Nigel Mansell — plus the recruitment of another of Alain's mates, the more than competent Nichols. Add to that a new V12 engine that allegedly matched McLaren's V10 Honda power and a dramatically improved development of their innovative semi-automatic gearbox, and Ferrari looked to be in great shape — a fact strongly underlined by their record-breaking winter testing times. Williams too looked to be much stronger. Their FW13 design, which had won in Australia, had been vigorously developed and was now to be propelled by a virtually all-new version of 1989's successful (two wins in its first season) Renault V10, lower, lighter, shorter and with more power. Were Patrese and Boutsen quite good enough in comparison with the McLaren and Ferrari superstars? Debatable, but both had been consistently capable in 1989 (third and fifth in the drivers' championship),

Onyx was apparently reprieved when Swiss Peter Monteverdi took the reins. By mid-season, however, the once promising British team had a new Swiss base and an inexperienced crew. Monteverdi's first F1 venture since the early '60s was to be a brief one.

Satoru Nakajima (left) switched from Lotus to Tyrrell, joining budding superstar Jean Alesi. The fact that Uncle Ken's team would get Honda V10 engines in 1991 was not unrelated . . .

Larrousse Lola maintained the brightest overalls in the business, but had two new recruits to wear them. Formula 3000 graduate Eric Bernard (left) became a full-time team member, after a couple of drives in 1989, while Aguri Suzuki moved from the now defunct Zakspeed operation.

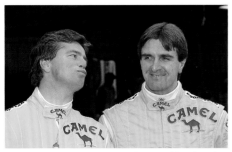

The blend of experience (Derek Warwick) and youth (Martin Donnelly) promised much for Lotus, with its new Lamborghini-engined chassis. Smiles would become something of a rarity over the course of the season.

Pasta heir Paolo Barilla, a former winner of the Le Mans 24 Hours, joined Minardi for his first season of Grand Prix racing.

Having assisted both McLaren and Ferrari to the fore in recent seasons, John Barnard had now moved to Benetton, as an integral part of the Witney team's ambitious long-term plans.

and over 16 races consistency pays.

Benetton's sole win in 1989 had been by default, but a win is a win. With John Barnard, founder of McLaren's success and designer of the Ferrari 640, now in charge, we could expect the revised Witney car, driven by a motivated Nelson Piquet and Alessandro Nannini, to be even more competitive. Whether the improved Ford V8 horsepower would be enough to overcome its V10 and V12-engined rivals was another story, but time would tell. And one of those V12 teams was a new-look and significantly stronger Lotus. Lamborghini power for Derek Warwick and Martin Donnelly, two very gritty chargers, allied to a new Frank Dernie-designed car and strong management were expected to put this once-great team back on the podium.

So the competition during 1990 was expected to be razor sharp. Especially taking into account the fact that the ''second division'' teams had all been working equally hard over the winter. Leyton House (né March), Dallara, AGS, Minardi, Tyrrell, Arrows, Brabham, Ligier, Onyx and Lola had all been in the points in 1989 and that's where they'd be aiming to be in the new season — but higher. For Lola, AGS and the rest — Osella, Subaru-Coloni, Eurobrun, and Life — things were going to be made even harder by the need to pre-qualify, but for the onlooker that was a bonus. An extra hour of highly concentrated action at every meeting.

So all in all it looked unpredictably exciting and there was eager anticipation for the first race of the new season — the Phoenix Grand Prix!

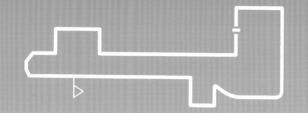

Togetherness: Alesi refused to be intimidated by the ominous presence of Senna in his mirrors. The Brazilian eventually squeezed through to win, but the Frenchman's brilliant second place earned him most of the rave notices.

Every Grand Prix year begins with a long-haul flight, and in that respect 1990 was just the same as its predecessors. But this time the destination was different — very different. For instead of the 12-hour drag south to the marrow-bubbling heat and vibrant atmosphere of Rio de Janeiro in Brazil, the teams travelled west to the staider, high-rise modernity of Phoenix, Arizona in the USA. The change was motivated by the fact that during last year's first-ever street race there was too much of a good thing in terms of temperature. For the point-and-squirt Phoenix Grand Prix had been held in high summer, 100-degree plus conditions that were plain unacceptable. So 1990 saw America's position in the World Championship calendar move from June to March.

In 1989 the Phoenicians had demonstrated their indifference to Formula 1 by largely ignoring it. Would the earlier date and cooler conditions make any difference this year? And after the turmoil of the politics-ridden winter, were all the teams who had registered with FISA actually going to be in Arizona?

Things were looking good when the contestants unpacked in their garages on Washington Street. Against all expectations everyone was there, for both Brabham and Onyx had seemingly resolved their ownership problems. And Ayrton Senna had been given his superlicence after "apologising" to FISA for accusing them of manipulating the 1989 championship. Great! But, to sound a dull note, the welcome presence of Gary Brabham with the new W12-engined Life entry meant that there were 35 cars trying to compete, so the dreaded pre-qualifying session at 08.00 on Friday morning would be necessary. Never mind, the weather was excellent with clear blue skies and a pleasant 75-degree temperature. "Am I going right for the pits and garages?" I asked a policeman as I walked in two blocks from the track.

"The what?"

"The garages — for the Grand Prix."

"Oh, the Gran Pree. Don't know." So much for any hopes of heightened local awareness and interest in 1990.

After five months of development, no one knew what to expect. Ferrari had been tremendously impressive in the winter testing sessions but McLaren's Ron Dennis was unimpressed. "They've undoubtedly won the winter championship but now we'll have to see how they get on in the summer series!" We soon got the answer, and it wasn't at all what we expected. For after Friday's qualifying session Alain Prost was in seventh position and Nigel Mansell a disastrous 17th. Both were suffering from a repetition of the semi-automatic gearbox unpredictability that had plagued the team in 1989, and both were more than bothered by engines which continued to drive them into the corners after they had lifted off. Not at all what you need at Phoenix! So it was situation normal with a McLaren heading the times. With Senna in a very abnormal fifth place due to an engine problem, it was Gerhard Berger in provisional pole position for his first race drive in a McLaren.

No great surprise there, then, but what followed most certainly was. Pirelli's hard work over the winter had clearly done the trick. Second fastest was Pier-Luigi Martini (Minardi), third Andrea de Cesaris (Dallara), fourth — and fastest of all in the morning's "free" session — Jean Alesi (Tyrrell) and eighth Olivier

Gerhard Berger started his McLaren career in stirring style. James Hunt congratulates him on taking pole position.

Grouillard (Osella). In fact eight of the top 16 were Pirelli shod — and all of them in "underpowered" V8 cars. But would they be able to hold their positions in Saturday's timed session, when everyone was expected to go a lot faster?

Yes they would! Because on March 10 arid Arizona had only its third day of rain in 1990 and Martin Donnelly, fastest in his Lotus-Lamborghini, was over 20 seconds slower than Berger's Friday time. So for the start of the season's first Grand Prix there was a very different and really exciting grid, with the mischievously inclined relishing the prospect of Ayrton Senna trying to get past Andrea de Cesaris!

Go! For a few yards Berger took the lead but, before Turn One, Alesi audaciously thrust his Tyrrell in front of the McLaren and, with a spellbinding display of car control at the limit, calmly and coolly pulled away from the Austrian. This was incredible, and just what Grand Prix racing needed. Something new! By lap four the Frenchman was four seconds ahead of Berger, with Senna up to third ahead of de Cesaris (no problem), Martini fifth, Piquet a fighting sixth and looking good, Boutsen seventh and Prost eighth — in a smoking Ferrari. Riccardo Patrese had hit Olivier Grouillard's

Against the city backdrop typical of so many American street circuits, Satoru Nakajima heads for sixth place to complete Tyrrell's joyful weekend.

Osella at the second corner and gone into the pits for a new front wing assembly, and Alessandro Nannini had collided with Bernd Schneider's Arrows. Two top men out of the running already.

Scarcely believing what we were seeing, we watched the spectacular Alesi ease away from the opposition at tremendous speed — but looking absolutely safe and steady. The brilliantly driven, light and nimble Tyrrell with its torquey Ford V8 engine was blowing the newer and more powerful V10s and V12s into the weeds. So much so that on lap nine Berger, struggling to keep in touch, slid into the tyre wall and lost time in the pits fitting new tyres and a replacement rear wing. Black mark for Gerhard, and now Senna was second — eight seconds behind Alesi and certainly not gaining. Behind the Brazilian it was a novel sight too — a tightly packed battle for third place between de Cesaris, Piquet, Boutsen and Prost — with the Ferrari now trailing an ominous smokescreen.

On lap 15 Berger emerged from the pits right in the path of the battling quartet as they approached Turn One. Andrea and Nelson made it past the McLaren, but Boutsen and Prost didn't. As they exited the corner, Berger inadvertently baulked a furious, fist-shaking Boutsen, who not only lost his fifth place to Prost but had his visor covered in oil as he chased the smoke-belching Ferrari. Sadly that was almost the end of Alain's first race for the Prancing Horse; hardly had he moved ahead of de Cesaris's Dallara into fourth place, as the Italian's engine started to give up the struggle, than his too expired. It was beginning to look as though Ron Dennis had been right.

Lap 26 out of 72, and Senna was charging — only 1.7 seconds behind Alesi with Piquet a fine third, Boutsen fourth, Martini fifth, Modena sixth and Nakajima in the second Tyrrell seventh ahead of Mansell, who was closing fast in the remaining (smoking) Ferrari. Four

TEAM ANALYSIS

FERRARI

What a let down! After five months of dedicated development and impressive testing times, confident and optimistic Ferrari fail humiliatingly at Phoenix. Four new cars with revised V12 motor and supposedly bullet-proof semi-automatic gearbox. In first GP for Maranello, Prost only seventh on grid with Mansell a depressing 17th after engine and gearbox problems. With heavily smoking exhaust, Alain up to fourth by lap 17 but retires five laps later (engine). Mansell doggedly advances to fifth, lap 45, but spectacularly spins out of race, lap 50, when clutch fails causing 180 mph spin and flash fire. With no points, chastened team returns to Italy to try harder for Brazil.

TYRRELL

Brilliant! New management, new tyres (Pirelli), new sponsors and new driver line-up pay off with team's best race since Detroit 1983. After being sensational fastest on Friday morning, Jean Alesi takes fourth on grid and leaps into lead at race start. At least 50 bhp down, increases advantage over Senna to stunning nine seconds by lap 13 before being passed, lap 34 — but immediately retakes lead. After being retaken, lap 35, maturely drives to superb second place only 8.7 seconds down. Satoru Nakajima equally inspired. Starts praiseworthy 11th in first Tyrrell race and finishes in points, overjoyed sixth despite oil-smeared visor. Justifiably elated Team Tyrrell second in constructors' World Championship.

WILLIAMS

Despite revised aerodynamics and new Renault RS2 V10 engine, Boutsen and Patrese only ninth and 12th on grid. Thierry fifth by lap nine but then hampered by misfire. Nevertheless finishes happy third. Patrese hits Grouillard's Osella at first corner and pits for new nose/wing assembly. Restarts last. Up to eighth by lap 51 but, delayed by sick engine, finishes ninth (one lap down) after being passed by Bernard, lap 67.

BRABHAM

After fraught winter team arrives at Phoenix on Thursday evening having been bought by Japanese Middlebridge organisation and lost designer Sergio Rhinland to Tyrrell. From excellent tenth on grid with Pirelli tyres Stefano Modena puts heart in team by finishing magnificent fifth despite brake problem. Gregor Foitek starts 24th in his first GP. Up to tenth, lap 31, but out after massive lap 40 collision with Grouillard's Osella.

ARROWS

In new Footwork livery Michele Alboreto qualifies 22nd in 1990 A11B and drives steady race to finish tenth (two laps down). Bernd Schneider replaces injured Alex Caffi in second car ('89 A11) and qualifies 21st despite being too big for car. Into pits for new wheel, lap one, after colliding with Nannini but finishes in encouraging 12th (two laps down).

LOTUS

Poor results for enthusiastic, rebuilt team. In virtually untried car Martin Donnelly and Derek Warwick line up 19th and 24th on grid after Lamborghini engine and suspension problems. Donnelly pushed from dummy grid after ignition failure. Warwick retires from 18th place, lap seven, after repeat of practice rear suspension failure. Still clearly much to do.

Doubts about Brabham's future hung over the team until only days before the race. Stefano Modena cheered everyone up by finishing fifth.

OSELLA
Two cars for Grouillard in new Fondmetal livery. Olivier pre-qualifies third and then achieves highest-ever Osella grid position - eighth (on Pirelli tyres). Collides with Patrese at second corner but up to 15th place after two tyre stops. Hit at high speed by Foitek, lap 40, and retires with bent suspension. Nevertheless an encouraging start.

LEYTON HOUSE (ex-MARCH)
The campaign begins as 1989 finished — disastrously. With complaints of "no grip" Gugelmin qualifies 26th and last and Capelli, 27th fastest, fails to do so. Ivan starts race, thanks to Alliot's exclusion, but retires from 17th, lap 21 (electrics). Gugelmin finishes 14th and last, six laps down, after tyre stop and with engine vibration. A truly depressing start to the new season.

BENETTON
Last year's cars for Piquet and Nannini, with 25 more horses and improved aerodynamics and suspension. Nelson an encouraging sixth on the grid. Alessandro a discouraging 23rd (misfire). Piquet excellent third laps 17-27, before fitting new tyres to eliminate understeer. They fail to do so but he finishes full-distance fourth. Nannini pits for new wheel after colliding with Schneider lap one. Pits again lap 41 after running over Foitek debris but finishes 11th (two laps down).

DALLARA
Andrea de Cesaris shows he can do it by qualifying excellent third (on Pirelli) and then racing third before retiring from fifth, lap 26, with sick motor. Gianni Morbidelli, replacing sick (hepatitis) Emanuele Pirro, fails to qualify after destroying car in Friday morning practice.

MINARDI
In unaltered 1989 car on Pirelli tyres, Pier-Luigi Martini superb second on grid in first-ever Minardi front row position. After poor start suffers from lack of downforce and finishes seventh (one lap down). Paolo Barilla starts excellent 14th but, too big for car, has to retire from 13th, lap 55, with numb left arm.

LIGIER
Car as 1989, but some 15 kg lighter, for new drivers Philippe Alliot and Nicola Larini. Alliot qualifies 20th but harshly excluded after mechanics illegally attempt to supervise course removal of his crashed car. Larini starts 13th but retires, lap five, with stuck throttle.

McLAREN
New MP4/5B with revised aerodynamics featuring distinctive five-tunnel diffuser for Senna and Berger. From pole position in first race for McLaren, Berger holds second to brilliant Alesi until sliding into tyre wall on lap nine. Into pits for new tyres and rear wing. Sets record lap (1m 31.050s, 93.311mph) in attempted recovery but retires from last place, lap 45, with broken clutch. With regained motivation Senna drives superbly controlled race to take lead from Alesi on lap 35, win for 21st time by 8.7 seconds and lead the championship. McLaren leads constructors' contest.

Fresh environment, rekindled motivation. After two inauspicious years with Lotus, Nelson Piquet bounced back with a fine fourth on his Benetton debut.

LOLA
Lola return for Japan's Aguri Suzuki and Frenchman Eric Bernard. Impressive race for both. Bernard pre-qualifies second and Suzuki fourth (and for the first time after disastrous 1989 at Zakspeed). Both then qualify — 15th (Bernard) and 18th. Eric up to eighth by lap 31 before spinning down to tenth lap 52. Recovers well to finish eighth (one lap down). Suzuki, having first F1 start since Japan 1988, seventh on lap 53 but, troubled by faulty brakes, fails to rejoin track after entering escape road.

SUBARU-COLONI
Bertrand Gachot fails to pre-qualify porky flat-12 engined car when gear selector rod breaks on first lap.

EUROBRUN
With Judd V8 (not Neotech V12) power, Roberto Moreno pre-qualifies fastest in 30 kg overweight car and then qualifies excellent 16th. Races to delighted, trouble-free 13th place (five laps down). GP newcomer Claudio Langes fails to pre-qualify.

ONYX
Confused team under new ownership, but with previous boss Mike Earle, appears minus "Moneytron" logos. In pressured circumstances Stefan Johansson hits wall, destroys car and then fails to qualify spare. With gearbox locked solid in his car and no spare, JJ Lehto also sadly fails to make the cut.

AGS
Both Gabriele Tarquini and Yannick Dalmas fail to pre-qualify.

LIFE
After a lap five black box failure, Gary Brabham fails to pre-qualify the unique and little-tested W12-engined/1989 Team First-chassised car for its and his first Grand Prix.

19

The first race of the season, and the first of many surprises. Jean Alesi threads his Tyrrell through from the second row to lead the McLarens.

Pirelli men in the top eight!

As Piquet made one of the few tyre stops of the race (in an unsuccessful effort to overcome understeer), Boutsen moved up to third but we had eyes only for the superb battle for the lead. By lap 30 Senna was with Alesi, and on lap 34 he made his move at Turn One, outbraking Jean to pass on the inside. "That's it folks. Race over." Like hell it was! No sooner had Ayrton moved right, to position his McLaren for the left-handed Turn Two, than Alesi was inside him to retake the lead! Fabulous! But he didn't stay there long, for on the next lap Senna repeated the manoeuvre and this time he firmly closed the door at Turn Two and, despite valiant efforts by Jean to fight back, pulled away to consolidate his advantage. And now we had another indication of the Frenchman's maturity

for, realising that Senna was his master, he settled for second by driving well within his limits and more than quickly enough to keep the rest at bay. Which meant that we could now pay attention to what was going on behind him!

At half-distance, with Senna now leading Alesi by two seconds and a record lap for Gerhard Berger (1m 31.050s, 93.311mph) shortly before he retired with a broken clutch, Piquet was chasing Boutsen for third, Modena was up to a superb fifth and Mansell was in the points in sixth. And that's the way it stayed until lap 45, when Nigel took Modena. For just five laps. On lap 51, Ferrari's cup of humiliation ran over when, at 180mph, a cloud of smoke, followed immediately by a giant ball of flame, heralded a violent spin which Nigel deftly

Former McLaren designer Steve Nichols was looking forward to the new challenge presented by Ferrari.

With Alex Caffi injuring himself in a cycling mishap, Bernd Schneider deputised at Footwork Arrows. The German did a fine job to come home 12th in the year-old A11, having outqualified team-mate Michele Alboreto's newer chassis.

overcame before coasting to retirement. Ron had definitely been right. How are the mighty fallen and I'm jolly glad that I didn't have to face the justifiable wrath of Fiat/Ferrari's mega-boss Gianni Agnelli on the team's return to Maranello.

And that effectively ended the Phoenix Grand Prix. Having built a 23-second lead by lap 62, Senna paced himself to win his 21st Grand Prix by 8.7 seconds from the sensation of the race Alesi. In a misfiring Williams-Renault, Boutsen was happy to take four points for third place ahead of Piquet (giving the lie to the people who had said he was past it). Modena was an excellent fifth to raise the morale of the whole Brabham team, who had been so close to not being at Phoenix at all, and Nakajima was an equally magnificent sixth in his first race for Uncle Ken (who thus had both his cars finish in the points). And three of the top six were on Pirelli tyres — a rich and justly deserved reward for the Milan firm's winter endeavours.

The second Phoenix race had again failed to enthuse America about Formula 1 and the event's long-term existence has to be in doubt, which is sad for Grand Prix racing needs a successful presence in the USA to give its World Championship credibility. But for the aficionados it had been great. With the notable exception of Senna's brilliant victory, it had produced a totally unexpected result and, given that variety is the spice of life, that was good. But Phoenix was an atypical circuit. Would it be back to the old routine in two weeks' time at the Brazilian Grand Prix on the sweeping new Interlagos circuit? We hadn't got long to wait to find out!

Despite the uncertain financial climate, time and money was found to restore Interlagos to Grand Prix condition. This was the first F1 visit for nine years.

From the apathy of Phoenix, the Grand Prix scene moved to the boiling passion of Brazil where the inhabitants are turned on by Formula 1 even more than the North Americans are turned off.

But not, this year, to Rio de Janeiro. Instead, after a nine-year gap, a return to the Brazilian race's former home — the sinuous and demanding Interlagos circuit at Sao Paulo — amidst chaos and alarm. Brazil's new-broom President Fernando Collor had resolved, like so many before him, to correct his country's financial plight and raging inflation by, unlike them, implementing a series of draconian measures. A new currency — the Cruzeiro — was introduced. People were denied access to

their savings. The banks were closed. The money supply was shut off. Credit cards were no longer accepted.

Most Grand Prix people were far from enamoured with Rio but, quite apart from the monetary shambles, Sao Paulo was even worse. For where Rio has its glorious beaches, fine restaurants and tourist attractions to distract visitors from the surrounding poverty, muggings and general air of menace, squalor and deprivation, Sao Paulo has a massive and smoggy industrial sprawl. Even Emerson Fittipaldi dislikes it, and it's where he comes from!

So, as practice began, the atmosphere was far from contented. But considerable consolation was the track itself. In its previous form, Interlagos had been over four miles long and acknowledged to be one of the finest Grand Prix venues in the world. But now, after four months of frantically concentrated work and the expenditure of millions of pounds, the elderly and bumpy circuit had been superbly rebuilt and reduced in length to 2.7 miles without losing any of its challenge to the drivers or attraction to the spectators. Everyone thought it was a magnificent effort. Some of the facilities may have been unfinished, but that didn't affect the racing or the effervescent enthusiasm of the Brazilians. Sao Paulo is where Ayrton Senna Lives. Ayrton Senna is their idol. Ayrton Senna was leading the World Championship but, despite six attempts, had yet to win his home race. In their tens of thousands they enthusiastically came to see him prepare to do so in 1990. And Ayrton didn't disappoint them. On Saturday afternoon in the closing minutes of final practice, with yet another of the superlative laps which he seems to be able to produce at will, he took his 43rd pole position ahead of team-mate Gerhard Berger, the two Williams-Renaults of Thierry Boutsen and Riccardo Patrese, the Ferrari teamsters Nigel Mansell and Alain Prost and the top Pirelli driver, Tyrrell's Jean Alesi.

On Sunday, seemingly the whole of Brazil was at Interlagos. The President arrived by helicopter and the State Governor by car — with 30 outriders. No one was going to miss their hero achieving his and their ambition — victory in Brazil. In ideal conditions, Senna took the lead at the start and slowly but surely pulled away from the opposition. At the very first corner there was an incident with Alesi hitting de Cesaris and involving Nannini, who took to the pits for a new nosecone. But as the race progressed things developed behind Senna in

So near, yet ... Ayrton Senna was on course to win his home Grand Prix, until tangling with Nakajima's Tyrrell as he attempted to lap him.

Patrese walks away, a spirited drive terminated by a broken oil cooler.

an unexpected way. For Berger, a disappointment in Phoenix, was passed by a charging Thierry Boutsen on lap eight and by a very smooth and confident looking Alain Prost on lap 17. The McLaren steamroller seemed to be faltering a bit, especially as Nigel Mansell in fifth place was catching Gerhard. With Patrese sixth ahead of Alesi, Martini, Modena and Piquet, things were in an interesting state. On lap 27 we had the first major pit stop, which made things even more so. In shot Mansell — but not just for new Goodyears. Unbeknown to us he had been grappling with the effects of a broken roll bar, which helped his Ferrari's handling not at all. Off came the steering wheel for investigation, but nothing could be done; down to ninth, out went Nigel to start a superb drive against adversity.

But now the man to watch was Alain Prost in the other Ferrari. With five wins in Brazil behind him, no points at Phoenix, a faultless car and tyres which had now settled down nicely he was well and truly fired up. On lap 30 he moved up to second as Boutsen peeled off into the pit lane for new rubber. With failing brakes, Thierry's hopes of six points disappeared as he slammed into one of the new tyre and wheel assemblies that were waiting to be fitted to his Williams. By the time he rejoined the circuit with a new nosecone he was down to 11th — and lapped by Senna. On lap 35, just under half distance, and with all the leaders having changed their tyres, it was Senna leading Prost by ten seconds with Patrese third, Berger fourth, Piquet fifth and Jean Alesi, the leading Pirelli driver, a fine sixth and in the points. And everything looked pretty static.

But in Grand Prix racing you never count your chickens before they're hatched. The unexpected was about to happen. After 1989 you'd have thought that Senna would have been determined to curb his habit of cutting things very fine indeed when passing — but no. As he came up to lap the tenth man, Satoru Nakajima, the McLaren and the Tyrrell made contact. Naka continued unscathed but, just like Japan 1989, Senna was into the pits for a new nosecone. An amazingly short 23 seconds

TEAM ANALYSIS

FERRARI

A real morale builder after Phoenix. Following concentrated post-Phoenix car development Mansell and Prost fifth and sixth on grid despite problems with qualifying tyres. Prost fastest during Sunday warm-up. Then drives magnificent race to take lead on lap 41 and retain it to end. Alain's 40th GP win, his first for Ferrari and his sixth in Brazil. Now second in championship. Mansell severely hampered by broken roll bar and after-effects of heavy cold, but drives equally praiseworthy race to finish fourth after delay in pits investigating problem. Ferrari now second in constructors' championship and confidently looking forward to improved performance from new chassis and engine at San Marino GP.

TYRRELL

Another fine race for Uncle Ken's rejuvenated team. Wonder-boy Jean Alesi starts a stirring seventh (top V8 and Pirelli runner). Collides with de Cesaris approaching first corner, but up to fifth by lap 31. Fourth lap 39 but then, affected by decision to run non-stop, loses grip and finishes seventh (one lap down) as top ''non-works'' driver. Down one place in championship to third. Nakajima has problems learning circuit and starts 19th. In tenth place, lap 40, moves over to let Senna through but hits ''marbles'' and embarrassed to collide with McLaren. Naka continues unaffected to take excellent eighth place only one lap down. Team Tyrrell third in constructors' championship.

Some things never change (1): Andrea de Cesaris abandons his shunted Dallara.

WILLIAMS

Boutsen and Patrese take excellent third and fourth on grid. Thierry fine second laps 8-29 but, with failing brakes, hits replacement tyre/wheel when making tyre stop. With new nosecone restarts 11th. Fights back and finishes fifth (one lap down) thanks to Patrese's retirement. Riccardo up to third laps 35-37 but then spins down to sixth. Recovers to fifth but retires, lap 66, with broken oil cooler.

BRABHAM

Team now owned by Japanese Middlebridge organisation. Stefano Modena starts 12th and races eighth-tenth, battling with Nelson Piquet until lap 40 when spins, stalls and retires. Still raw Gregor Foitek, driving last race for Brabham, crashes in Friday practice but qualifies 22nd. Retires from 19th, lap 15, when misses gearchange and breaks driveline.

ARROWS

Not a distinguished meeting. Alboreto qualifies only 23rd (clutch problem). Collides with Grouillard lap seven. Fourteenth by lap 18. New tyres lap 23 but out lap 25 with massive oversteer caused by duff rear shocker. Alex Caffi returns to team with mended collar bone. In unfit state 25th on grid. Thirteenth by lap 23. After two stops (tyres lap 30 and to remove cockpit padding lap 40), retires exhausted from 14th lap 49.

LOTUS

Team still going through bad patch. After electrical and fuel pressure problems Donnelly and Warwick start 20th and 24th. Derek in for tyres and wing adjustment lap 14 when 17th. Retires from 18th lap 26 (electrical failure). Martin up to strong 11th laps 18-21. Retires from 12th, lap 44 (after tyre stop), when numb braking leg causes spin.

OSELLA

Olivier Grouillard pre-qualifies third and starts 21st. Collides with Alboreto lap seven and retires with steering/suspension malfunctions.

LEYTON HOUSE

Team's ghastly form continues. With total inability to get car to handle neither Gugelmin nor Capelli qualify. ''No excuses,'' says team manager Ian Phillips.'' We'll be testing at Imola for three weeks to get it right.''

AGS

Tarquini again fails to pre-qualify but Yannick Dalmas does so and then takes 26th on grid for first race since Imola '89 , and team's first start since Canada '89. Collides with Suzuki in warm-up and retires from 16th, lap 29, with resultant broken suspension.

BENETTON

Both drivers struggle for grip in practice. Piquet starts 13th, Nannini 15th. On B-compound Goodyears intending to run non-stop, Sandro involved in first corner Alesi/de Cesaris collision. Stops for new nose then drives strongly to finish frustrated tenth (with a puncture) three laps down. Piquet does much better. With two laps to go, after tyre

'Now here's what we do ...' Camel Team Lotus discusses race tactics.

stops on laps 36 and 48, scrambles past gripless non-stop Alesi to finish sixth (one lap down).

DALLARA
De Cesaris qualifies excellent ninth but collides with Alesi before first corner and retires. Gianni Morbidelli qualifies strong 16th for his first GP. Spins with jammed throttle first lap. Loses five laps in pits but finishes 14th (seven laps down). A good effort.

MINARDI
Pier-Luigi Martini starts excellent eighth in spare after destroying race car in practice when wheel comes off. (Brisk interview with mechanic follows.) Races non-stop to meritorious ninth (two laps down) despite brake problems. Paolo Barilla qualifies 17th and progresses to 13th, lap 25, before retiring lap 38 (engine).

LIGIER
Alliot, delighted with improved car balance, qualifies tenth. Down to 21st, lap 20, after spin. Then runs at tail of field benefiting from retirements to finish 12th, three laps down. Troubled practice for Larini who starts 20th. After coping with dodgy clutch runs ahead of Alliot to finish 11th (three laps down) in state of exhaustion.

McLAREN
Senna starts home-town GP in his 43rd pole position after typically stunning last-minute lap. Holds commanding lead for 31 laps before tyre stop. Regains lead lap 35. On lap 41 collides with Nakajima when Satoru slides on "marbles" after moving over. Rejoins third with new nose but, with excessive downforce, is unable to close on race leaders Prost and Berger. Settles for third. Yet to win in Brazil but continues to lead World Championship — now only four points ahead of bitter rival Prost. Berger second laps 1-7, passed by Boutsen lap 8 and Prost lap 17.

Despite cockpit discomfort, understeer, foot pain and "noise from the clutch" finishes second with record lap during late charge (1m 19.989,121.088 mph). McLaren leads constructors' championship, seven points ahead of Ferrari.

LOLA
Bernard and Suzuki sail through pre-qualification first and second (how different for Aguri after his Zakspeed miseries in 1989!) and then qualify 11th and 18th. Sadly both retire from race — Bernard from last but one on lap 14 with gearbox problem, Suzuki from 14th on lap 24 with suspension failure (following warm-up collision with Dalmas).

SUBARU-COLONI
In the "White Whale" pre-qualifying impossible for Bertrand Gachot.

EUROBRUN
With ignition problems in one car and insufficient fuel in the other, Roberto Moreno sadly fails to pre-qualify for his home event. Claudio Langes only has six laps and also misses out.

MONTEVERDI-ONYX
Team now owned by Swiss businessman Peter Monteverdi. Mike Earle and Joe Chamberlain back in charge and further changes certain. With grip, engine, suspension and transmission problems, neither Johansson nor Lehto qualify.

LIFE
In a team which appears to be a complete shambles, poor Gary Brabham fails to complete even one pre-qualifying lap when one of his W12 engine's conrods breaks.

later he was out again and charging hard, but this time to no avail. The replacement nose-wing settings were marginally different and the resultant excess of downforce defeated even him. ''I moved over to let Ayrton through,'' said a highly embarrassed Nakajima, ''but as I did so I got on to the dusty bit off the racing line and just slid into him.'' It's easy to criticise when you're not in the driving seat, but Senna could again be accused of impatience. Now instead of being ten seconds ahead, he was over 30 behind.

Right or wrong, it cost him the home win he so desperately longed for. He could and did close on team-mate Berger, who was second but could do nothing about the man he wanted to beat above all others — Alain Prost. So the brilliant Frenchman won his 40th Grand Prix, his first for Ferrari, and his sixth in Brazil to increase his record total of World Championship points to 601.5. But best of all from his point of view he had beaten his bitter rival Ayrton Senna where it hurt most — in Sao Paulo, Brazil. Alain had tried to make up their 1989 quarrel before the race by offering to shake Senna's hand and heal the rift, but Ayrton would have none of it. ''I'm very, very happy for me — it's maybe the best win in my career. It's the first with Ferrari

Sponsor, what sponsor? Yannick Dalmas qualified the AGS to start his first race in almost a year, although he didn't go the distance.

after only two races and also for the team it's fantastic,'' said Alain. It would be more than unwise to downgrade McLaren though. Senna had been well ahead when he collided with Nakajima, and his failure to win had been nothing to do with his car, which had been the fastest and had run perfectly. Berger's comparatively unimpressive performance (if third place and the fastest lap of the race — lap 55 in 1m 19.899s, 121.087 mph — can be called unimpressive!) was misleading too. Afterwards, he said that he still didn't fit the car properly and had been suffering from a great deal of pain in his braking foot during the race. Nevertheless, with a new Ferrari chassis and engine waiting to be introduced at Imola for the San Marino Grand Prix, it seemed that McLaren really had got a battle for the 1990 honours on their hands. Meantime, the team could console itself with the knowledge that it led the constructors' championship by four points after two races.

But the Brazilian Grand Prix wasn't only noteworthy for the drives of the first three — Prost, Berger and Senna. When Nigel Mansell left the pits in ninth place on lap 28 he had the knowledge that his roll bar was still broken but, being Nigel, he just got his head down and

Some things never change (2): the location may have changed, but some things about Brazil never will ...

Unusual, but unloved. The Life featured an innovative W12 engine (inset), but Gary Brabham became fed up with chronic unreliability after Brazil, preferring a competitive drive in Formula 3000 to a fruitless F1 opportunity.

went for it. On lap 37 he was sixth, on lap 39 fifth, and on lap 40 fourth. He slipped to fifth on lap 42, when he was passed by Riccardo Patrese on new Goodyears and, as ever, driving an excellent race. And there he looked like staying, until on lap 66 the unfortunate Riccardo retired with a broken oil cooler. That was the luck Nigel needed to return him to the fourth place that he held to the end — the last man to complete the full 71-lap distance. Team manager Cesare Fiorio was delighted, and Ferrari really was back in the hunt.

With Thierry Boutsen fighting his way back through the field to finish fifth, another battle that really had the attention of the Brazilian crowd was the one between local hero Nelson Piquet and Jean Alesi for the last points place.

Nelson, on Goodyear tyres, stopped twice in a successful effort to overcome extreme understeer whilst Alesi, on Pirellis, drove through non-stop. With his tyres just about shot, Jean was really struggling for grip in the closing laps and Nelson, who had been 11th on the 49th lap, was taking great chunks out of his lead with a determined charge to close the gap. On lap 69, with one to go, he did it. Past the helpless Alesi into sixth place to finish in the points for the second time in two races. At a rumoured $150,000 per point scored, it was well worth his trouble!

To many people, the Grand Prix season starts at Imola with the San Marino race, but I've never understood their attitude. If Senna had won in Brazil, he would have gone into round three with two victories and 18 points — a daunting advantage over his rivals. As it was, his lead of four points over Prost was far from depressing for the Frenchman, who could be very sure that, at Imola, Ferrari's home ground and the lair of the fanatical *tifosi,* he would lack nothing in mechanical and psychological support!

Winning smile: not only had Prost scored his first victory for Ferrari, and his 40th in all, he'd also beaten arch-rival Senna in the latter's back yard.

The Imola crowd only has eyes for one team. Nigel Mansell was on stupefying form, although his efforts brought little reward, engine problems puttting him out.

When the Formula One transporters rolled from their bases to Imola, near Bologna, for the San Marino Grand Prix, it had been six weeks since the last race. Phoenix and Brazil seemed more a part of the previous season than 1990, and a lot had happened in the interval. The teams had used the welcome time to test new or revised cars they were going to have to use from then on, to comply with stricter FISA safety regulations. At three major sessions at Imola itself, McLaren, Ferrari and Williams had all headed the times. So with a bit of luck things were going to be even more competitive at round three of the championship than they had been at the previous two!

Imola, with its ultra-fast (almost 200 mph) sections, brake-sapping chicanes, gradients and a selection of really daunting corners, is a very demanding circuit. If a car goes well here, it will go well anywhere. It is hard on brakes, demands meticulous setting-up of the suspension and is extremely tough on fuel consumption. So what happened at the San Marino GP was going to be a pointer for the rest of the season. And what a pleasure it was to be there! Phoenix had been a totally unsuitable circuit in characterless and apathetic surroundings. Interlagos had been a super circuit in a depressing and worrying atmosphere. But Imola is a magnificent venue in a vibrant Italian setting, where enthusiasm for Grand Prix racing knows no bounds — especially if Ferrari look as though they are going to do well!

When the *"tifosi"* thronged into Imola in their tens of thousands for Friday's practice, they were full of optimism that their beloved Ferrari would be at the front of the grid. Prost had won in Brazil and the further developed 641/2 (new bodywork, revised chassis and suspension and different engine internals) had gone well in the tests. But they were a bitter disappointment in qualifying, Mansell fifth, Prost sixth and both of them nearly two seconds off the pace. Because once again McLaren-Honda had sprinted away just when it looked as though some of the others had caught up. For the 44th time in his incredible career, it was Ayrton Senna in pole

position, but it hadn't been easy. His team-mate Gerhard Berger, looking far more relaxed and at ease with himself than he had been in America and Brazil, had been convincingly fastest until Ayrton, responding to the challenge, had made one of his typical, carefully planned and meticulously executed attacks to knock a breathtaking half-second off Gerhard's already record-breaking time. It was Senna's sixth successive pole at Imola, and again he looked to be invincible on race day.

But if the Ferraris were disappointing the Williams-Renaults were just the reverse. Riccardo Patrese had been fastest at the second of the Imola tests, and was a superb third on the grid — one place ahead of his team-mate Thierry Boutsen. And seventh behind the Ferraris there was something really new — the amazing looking new Tyrrell 019, with its "Stuka-like" anhedral front wings, driven by the new French superstar Jean Alesi. A magnificent achievement, for not only was Jean the fastest Pirelli and V8 driver, he was ahead of Nelson

Martin Donnelly gave the midfield cause for consternation when he spun in their midst. The Ulsterman recovered to finish eighth.

Fifth and sixth places fell to Piquet and Alesi, although they were both delayed when they collided early in the race.

Piquet and Alessandro Nannini, eighth and ninth in their new and very impressive Benetton-Ford 190s.

In Sunday morning's final half-hour warm-up when, for the first time, all the cars were in race trim, things were really close. Senna, Mansell, Berger, Boutsen, Prost was the order with a mere four-tenths covering the five of them, Patrese only another two-tenths behind and one second covering the top eight. It was going to be a close race — with added unpredictability caused by the fact that the correct tyre choice was going to be critical. Not until the race began was it revealed that the four top teams' Goodyear-shod drivers had opted for a variety of different combinations which were subsequently to affect their final positions — and Alesi's Pirelli race tyre was known to be a very good one.

It was perfect weather for the 61 laps on race day. When starter Roland Bruynseraede pressed the button for green, Berger made such a good start that FISA had to check the video to make sure he hadn't jumped it. Not that it did him much good for he missed a gear and, by Tosa, the first major corner, Senna was ahead. Behind him at the super-fast Tamburello Mansell put two wheels on the grass to cause an impenetrable dust cloud that resulted in Nakajima and Capelli crashing and Moreno retiring. But if people thought they were now going to see the McLarens of Senna and Berger dominating things at the front, they soon changed their minds. At the 155 mph Piratella Boutsen took second from Berger (a McLaren passed fair and square!) with Patrese fourth followed by Alesi, who had forcefully taken both Mansell and Prost. On lap four, with Mansell now ahead of Alesi, there was uproar at Imola. Senna out! With a lead of some 1.5 seconds the Brazilian wobbled into the sand trap at Rivazza! "As I came down the hill I realised I was losing my brakes. The car was all over the place and I was just trying to get out of the way of the others." Which he did — to retire with, of all things, a broken right rear wheel. And with the 1988/89 winner out, the 1990 San Marino Grand Prix was now wide open.

TEAM ANALYSIS

FERRARI

Following impressive Imola test with revised chassis, aerodynamics, engine and suspension, Mansell and Prost qualify disappointing fifth and sixth. After nearly going off at first corner Nigel drives superb race, with suspicious oil smoke from lap four, to run second to Berger by lap 22. In spite of being side-swiped when lapping de Cesaris, Mansell challenges for lead on lap 36 but has 190mph, 360-degree spin on grass verge when Gerhard moves over. Retains second and fights back but retires lap 39 (engine). Prost advances to fourth but stops for softer tyres lap 27 and is passed by Nannini with whom he fights to end of race. Despite second fastest lap fails to pass Alessandro and finishes fourth to close to within one point of Senna in championship. Crestfallen Ferrari now equal second with Williams in constructors' championship.

TYRRELL

Designer Sergio Rhinland returns to Brabham and is replaced by ex-Ferrari man George Ryton. Dramatic new Alesi-driven 019 with unique anhedral front wings fourth fastest in Imola tests and seventh on grid (top V8 and Pirelli user). Nakajima starts 19th and retires at first corner after violent accident which destroys car (driver OK). Underpowered Alesi initially superb fifth in spare car but down to ninth laps 23-26 after collision with Piquet and resultant tyre stop. Recovers brilliantly to finish sixth (one lap down).

WILLIAMS

A magnificent race for Williams who are now right on the pace with excellent chassis and further revised Renault RS2 V10. Boutsen overcomes practice brake problems to start fourth. Leads race laps 4-17 after Senna retirement, but out lap 18 with engine failure caused by missed gear. In fastest car at Imola (191.68 mph during qualifying), Patrese starts third and then drives inspired race. Up to second after Mansell retirement, lap 39. After third fastest lap of race passes Berger to take lead lap 51 and stays there to win his third GP in 195 starts and advance to fourth in championship. A richly deserved victory.

BRABHAM

Gregor Foitek replaced by David Brabham (Sir Jack's third son) and designer Sergio Rhinland returns from Tyrrell. New BT59 with narrow-angle Judd V8. ''But without its awaited transverse gearbox and new rear suspension it is the front of a horse and the back of a camel,'' says Sergio! In first F1 drive Brabham, with virtually no experience of car, does well but fails to qualify by only three-tenths. Modena starts 14th. Retires from same position, lap 32, after spin with jammed brakes.

ARROWS

Amazingly neither Alboreto nor Caffi able to qualify. ''We just weren't fast enough.''

The Larrousse team gave the 1990 Lola its first airing. Both cars breezed through pre-qualifying, but Aguri Suzuki (pictured) retired from the race with clutch failure.

LOTUS

After further personnel changes including departure of chief designer Mike Coughlan, team makes much-needed improvement. Warwick and Donnelly qualify 11th and 12th and both finish for first time in 1990. Derek seventh (one lap down) despite oil-leak problem and Martin, after 360-degree lap one spin, a close eighth (also one lap down) — covered with Derek's oil!

OSELLA

In much-revised car, Olivier Grouillard pre-qualifies third. Retires from 14th and last, lap 53, with broken wheel bearing caused by lap 10 collision with Paolo Barilla.

LEYTON HOUSE

Little improvement to terrible season. Manager Ian Phillips hospitalised with viral meningitis and Ivan Capelli writes off new car at Imola tests. But major aerodynamic problem now identified and remedial action in hand. Best-yet 1990 qualifying sees Gugelmin start 12th and Capelli 18th — but neither finishes race. Ivan rammed by Nakajima at first corner. Mauricio pits twice with misfire before retiring from last, lap 25.

AGS

Team arrives with sophisticated new JH25, but withdraws Dalmas due to hand injury. In untested car, Tarquini fails to pre-qualify.

Gary Brabham may have left Life, but younger brother David stepped in to the F1 arena, replacing Gregor Foitek at Brabham. With the team running the new BT59 chassis for the first time, he sadly failed to qualify.

BENETTON
New B190 a vast improvement on previous car. With revised Ford V8 engine, Piquet and Nannini qualify strongly at eighth and ninth (after Nannini race car destroyed in collision with inevitable Andrea de Cesaris). Alessandro in great race form. Up to third lap 39 following Prost tyre stop and Mansell retirement. After terrific battle with Alain for rest of race, takes third by half a second and sets fastest lap (lap 60: 1m 27.156s, 129.356mph). Piquet down to 11th laps 10-12, following heavy landing after colliding with Alesi, but finishes excellent fifth — the only driver to have scored points in all three opening races. Team improves to encouraging fourth in constructors' championship.

DALLARA
In first 1990 race following illness, Emanuele Pirro qualifies 21st but retires lap one (engine). Andrea de Cesaris follows usual form by colliding with Nannini in practice and Mansell during race. Qualifies 17th but retires from 13th, lap 32 (wheel hub problem).

MINARDI
Spirits high following announcement that team is to have Ferrari engines in 1991. In new 190 Pier-Luigi Martini excellent ninth fastest in Friday qualifying, but crashes at Acque Minerali exit on Saturday and cracks ankle bone so no race. Barilla starts 26th thanks to Martini withdrawal. Drives steady race to finish 11th, two laps down.

LIGIER
Alliot starts 16th, Larini 20th. Both happy to finish — Philippe ninth (one lap down) and Nicola tenth (two laps down).

McLAREN
After dominating Imola post-Brazil tests, Senna takes 44th career pole position (sixth in a row at Imola) and leads race for first three laps. Then sensationally departs track at Rivazza to retire with broken right rear wheel. After Boutsen retirement, Berger leads race laps 18-50 before

being brilliantly passed by Patrese. Finishes second only 1.2 seconds ahead of Nannini. Senna still leads drivers' championship — by one point. Berger equal second with Prost. McLaren leads constructors' contest by comfortable ten points, but the competition is getting stronger....

LOLA
Introduction of new chassis. Bernard and Suzuki easily pre-qualify first and second and then qualify well at 13th and 15th. Bernard 8th-10th for most of race but, delayed by transmission problems, finishes 13th (five laps down). Suzuki drives well to hold station with Bernard before retiring from 11th, lap 18, with broken clutch.

SUBARU-COLONI
Even with revised aerodynamics and 23 kg weight reduction, car not good enough for Bertrand Gachot to pre-qualify.

EUROBRUN
After pre-qualifying fourth fastest, Roberto Moreno destroys car in major crash on Saturday but qualifies 24th with Friday time. In poor physical shape, retires on lap one after throttle jams on dirt from Nakajima crash. Claudio Langes fails to pre-qualify.

MONTEVERDI-ONYX
Yet another management upheaval sees departure of team's founder Mike Earle as well as designer Alan Jenkins and driver Stefan Johansson amid legal action against new owner Peter Monteverdi. Gregor Foitek replaces Johansson and major staff reductions effected. In revised car, Foitek starts 23rd and Lehto 25th. Foitek retires from 14th (out of 16) lap 36 (engine). Lehto encouraging 12th (two laps down) with cracked exhaust in first GP finish.

LIFE
Disillusioned Gary Brabham leaves "totally disorganised and unprofessional" team and is replaced by Bruno Giacomelli, who fails to pre-qualify.

Victory at Imola erased bitter memories of 1983 for Riccardo Patrese. Then, he crashed while leading late in the race. This time, there was to be no such mistake.

For 14 laps Thierry Boutsen, driving beautifully, held the lead from Gerhard Berger with, seemingly, no problems. But he had one — a sticky gear shift which, on lap 18, caused him to select first instead of third and to grenade his Renault RS2 V10. Rotten luck, for Thierry had looked set to score his third victory. So now it was Berger at the front ahead of Patrese, but the fastest man on the track and third in the race was Nigel Mansell — in a Ferrari which was smoking suspiciously just as it had in Phoenix. On lap 22, with a magnificent passing move at Tosa which set the *tifosi*-thronged hillside alight, he sliced inside Patrese to take second place and then, with a succession of fastest laps, he set about catching Berger. By lap 25 Nigel had got the gap down to 3.1 seconds, but then he had the misfortune to try to pass the much reviled Andrea de Cesaris's Dallara. As Mansell moved inside, de Cesaris moved across and contact was inevitable. Nigel was very lucky indeed that the only result was a four-second delay. With Berger now that much further

ahead, and Patrese almost on his gearbox followed by Prost, Nannini and Piquet, Nigel, in his inimitable fashion, put his head down and charged. By lap 36 he was right behind Berger; at the 195 mph Tamburello he pulled out to pass the Austrian on the inside line — which was exactly where Gerhard now was. Immediately Mansell was on to the wide grass verge and, with no grip, into a giant, whirling, 360-degree spin. How he held it and recovered is beyond my understanding, but magnificently he did so and continued his charge. But to no avail. Three laps later his smoking engine gave up and, bitterly disappointed and very angry indeed, he pulled into the pits to retire. Needless to say each of the drivers saw the incident differently. Nigel: ''My friend Gerhard moved over on me.'' Gerhard: ''I saw Nigel out of the corner of my eye just as his spin began. I'm very sorry because I don't like that to happen.'' It was Berger's second major incident at the Tamburello in two years, for it was there that his horrific 1989 Ferrari crash had occurred. Not his

A heavy practice accident put Pier-Luigi Martini out for the rest of the weekend, although the Italian happily escaped serious harm.

favourite corner!

But with Mansell out Gerhard certainly couldn't relax, for now Patrese was attacking. With his Williams in perfect condition, the Italian (who had gone off while in the lead at Imola in 1983, with only five laps to go) was driving a superb race, ahead of an equally inspired Alessandro Nannini, now up to third. Next came Prost, who had made a sensational 6.7s stop on lap 29 to change his B compound Ferrari Goodyears for a set of softer Cs. Ferrari may have cruelly been denied their chance of winning, but all around the circuit the *tifosi* were spellbound by two superb races between Berger and Patrese for victory, and Nannini and Prost for third — followed by Piquet and a lonely Jean Alesi, who had stopped for new Pirellis after a spin.

Riccardo Patrese, Formula One's most experienced driver (San Marino was his 195th Grand Prix), meant to win this one. On lap 40 he was 5.5 seconds behind Berger. ''My car was perfect and the brakes were fantastic so I

started to push very hard.'' On lap 51 that took him into the lead and the thousands who, seven years before, had jeered at him when his Brabham had slid into the bank at the Acque Minerali to let Patrick Tambay's Ferrari through to win, cheered him to a man. Surely nothing could stop him now? Berger was clearly beaten and being caught by the Nannini/Prost battle. And nothing did. Riccardo very deservedly won the San Marino Grand Prix to avenge 1983, and admitted that he had driven his last lap with tears in his eyes as he concentrated on not repeating his mistake.

With a loss of power and the wrong tyre choice, Gerhard Berger finished five seconds behind Patrese, but only 1.1 ahead of Alessandro Nannini and 1.7 ahead of Alain Prost. The battle between the Benetton and the Ferrari had been fierce. Lap after lap Alain sat behind Nannini's gearbox, unable to get by. Such was their pace that on his last lap but one Sandro clocked the fastest lap of the race (1m27.156s, 129.356 mph — marginally slower

As Senna holds sway from Berger, Alesi locks up his brakes further back, and prepares to give the Ferraris a fright ...

than Prost's 1990 McLaren lap record) and Alain was the second fastest man of the day, only eight-thousandths slower. Third fastest was Patrese, which underlined the fact that he was now very much one of the top men.

At Imola, Grand Prix racing had the shot in the arm that it desperately needed to boost public interest. In the year's first three races, three different drivers had won in three different cars with three different engines. Nelson Piquet finished fifth, the only driver to have scored points in each of the three rounds, and in so doing put both Benettons in the top six. With Jean Alesi bringing his Tyrrell home sixth ahead of the Lotuses of Derek Warwick and Martin Donnelly, both of whom finished in a 1990 GP for the first time, the San Marino Grand Prix had hopefully shown that 1990 was going to be different.

And with things now so finely balanced, the next Grand Prix, the world's most famous at Monaco, was something to look forward to!

Popular victory: after 195 Grands Prix, Riccardo Patrese's third success was well-received. Messrs Berger and Nannini don't seem quite so elated to be heading for the lower levels of the victory podium.

And you thought the M25 was busy? At the first start, Berger's ill-advised manoeuvre on Prost at Mirabeau resulted in this roadblock. Only Senna and Alesi escaped delay. The red flag followed within seconds.

It had been an intriguing and very satisfying opening to the season as the Grand Prix teams and their followers settled into every nook and cranny of picture-book Monaco to prepare for the rigours of round four. Three different winners from three different teams in the first three races, and only four points separating the top four in the championship. The Ferraris and the Williams-Renaults showed real signs of being competitive with the McLaren-Hondas, and Jean Alesi had emerged as a new superstar. But Monaco is a very different kettle of fish to Phoenix, Interlagos and Imola.

With its narrow twists and turns, its climbs and descents, its consequent need for fierce acceleration and braking, its physically demanding, concentration-sapping two-hour duration and the near-impossibility of passing, Monaco is unique. It is grossly inconvenient for the teams with its cramped, appallingly overcrowded working conditions, and it is equally unpopular with the media. Wherever you are, you need to be somewhere else. You have to walk there and it's always uphill! But the sponsors love it, and nowhere else do the onlookers get such close proximity to Formula 1 racing in such a glamorous setting, with the buildings cascading down to the harbour, yachts sparkling in the sunshine and jet setters showing themselves off. If Monaco doesn't turn you on, nothing will.

Have boat, will travel.

It certainly turned Ayrton Senna on. When Saturday's qualifying practice session ended, he had taken his 45th pole position with a lap of quite breathtaking brilliance. At 1m 21.314s it was a full second faster than his own 1989 pole time, an awe-inspiring average speed of 91.552 mph around Monaco's 2.068 miles. And if he hadn't been baulked by Gregor Foitek's Onyx in the swimming pool section on an even faster lap, he would almost certainly have been another second quicker. Quite incredible. But so was Alain Prost. The four-times Monaco winner wound himself and his Ferrari up to 1m 21.776s, which put him second on the grid. In Sunday morning's half-hour warm-up he was only one-tenth slower than Senna. But even more impressive was Jean Alesi, third on the grid in his anhedral-winged Tyrrell. The 019 may have been underpowered with "only" some 650 horses from its Ford V8, but power matters less at Monaco than at other circuits. This deficiency was more than compensated by Alesi's on-the-limit driving and his super-sticky Pirelli tyres. With Patrese, Berger, Boutsen, Mansell and Martini

occupying the next five positions on the grid, the place to be on lap one was obviously the first corner — Ste Devote — which traditionally causes a pile-up as everyone tries to get round it in the lead.

Needless to say the man who did so was Senna. Making no mistake he was well ahead up the hill to Massenet and, to everyone's surprise, there was no collision behind him. A trouble-free first lap at Monaco. Amazing! Well, it would have been, but this year's accident was just delayed a bit. As the jostling, writhing snake of thrusting hopefuls dived into the right-hander at Mirabeau, Alesi almost unbelievably slipped inside Prost and up to second before Alain realised he was there. Berger, optimistically trying to follow Alesi through, wasn't so lucky. As Alain turned in he was rammed by the McLaren. In less time than it takes to say it, there was a stationary shambles which stopped the race.

With their cars *hors de combat*, Prost and Berger legged it back to the pits where their teams' spare cars were hurriedly adjusted for their use in the restarted race. Adjusted,

Hot stuff; Prost fends off Alesi and Berger during their second-place dispute.

TEAM ANALYSIS

FERRARI
Dismay and shame at Monaco. After brilliant lap using revised engine, Prost qualifies superb second and is only 0.1s slower than Senna in Sunday warm-up. Rammed by Berger on first lap and has to restart in spare car set up for Mansell. Holds untroubled second place for 30 laps but retires, lap 31, after gearbox electronics fail due to exploded battery. Down to fourth in championship. Mansell damages car in Thursday practice before qualifying lowly seventh (traffic), but strong fourth in Sunday warm-up. In seventh place, lap 20, hits Boutsen and pits for new front wing. Then stages magnificent recovery from 15th, including second fastest lap of race. Up to fourth by lap 55 only to retire, lap 64, with same problem as Prost. Team desperately needs reliability.

TYRRELL
Team's wonderful 1990 continues on very high note. In nimble new 019 with unique front wings, sticky Pirellis and torquey Ford V8, wonderman Jean Alesi dynamic third on grid for first Monaco GP. Flabbergasting move snatches second from Prost at Mirabeau lap one before race is stopped. After restart chases Alain and takes second on lap 31 when Ferrari expires. Then staves off determined efforts of Berger to take second second place of season — and fourth fastest lap of race. Back to third in championship. Magic! Nakajima, unhappy on street circuits, starts 21st and spins out of 10th place to retire on lap 37.

WILLIAMS
After grip and handling problems, Patrese and Boutsen start fourth and sixth. Riccardo up to fourth after Prost retirement lap 31 but out lap 41 with valve gear derangement. Thierry bothered by sticking throttle from

Pre-qualifiers of the world unite. While most of the F1 paddock are still having breakfast, Bertrand Gachot's unwieldy Coloni-Subaru gives way to Roberto Moreno's nimbler Eurobrun. The talented Brazilian survived this part of the weekend, but failed to make the race.

start which necessitates hammering brakes and tyres. Survives being struck by Mansell, lap 21, and is happy to finish fourth (one lap down).

BRABHAM
Transverse gearbox and new rear suspension still not ready. Stefano Modena qualifies 14th and unavoidably hits Piquet's Benetton in first lap Mirabeau accident. Restarts with new nose cone. Retires on second lap with transmission failure. David Brabham starts in first GP after admirable qualifying drive on demanding circuit. (First son of former winner and World Champion to do so.) Races at rear of field until retiring, lap 17, with broken CV joint.

ARROWS
After a multitude of problems, Alboreto again fails to qualify. Alex Caffi starts 22nd for his first race of year. Benefiting from retirements, a steady run nets fifth (two laps down) for team's first 1990 points. Team desperately missing departed designer Ross Brawn, and must be giving concern to 1991 engine supplier — Porsche.

LOTUS
Sadly no Monaco reward for greatly improved team. Martin Donnelly an impressive 11th on the grid for his first Monte'Carlo GP and Derek Warwick 13th (usual traffic). Donnelly starts in spare and frustrated to retire on lap seven after running tenth (gearbox). Derek drives super race. Fifth by lap 41. Down to sixth laps 44-63. Back to fifth laps 64-66 but failing brakes cause spin and retirement after stalling (and nearly collecting Senna!). Still no points for Lotus after four races.

OSELLA
Olivier Grouillard pre-qualifies strong third but fails to qualify after breaking four driveshafts in two Saturday practice sessions.

LEYTON HOUSE
Another grisly meeting. Full of optimism after personnel changes and record-breaking tests at Pembrey. But Monaco very different. Handling/engine problems prevent Gugelmin from qualifying. Heroic last-minute lap gets Capelli on to grid 23rd. Starts race in spare after clutch fire halts car following first start. Works up to 14th by lap 12 but retires lap 14 with failing brakes. Will things never improve?

AGS
Once again Tarquini and Dalmas fail to pre-qualify. It's tough in F1.

BENETTON
With Edsel Ford there to watch, Piquet qualifies 10th and Nannini 16th in spare car after smashing race car on Saturday. Alessandro starts race in spare (set up for Piquet) after engine dies in rebuilt race car on first parade lap. Retires from 10th, lap 21, when oil pressure fails. Piquet hit by Modena lap one Mirabeau multiple collision. Up to seventh in repaired car by lap 21. Collides with Boutsen lap 33. To pits for new front wing, but then black-flagged under new rule for being push-started at Loews Hairpin following Boutsen incident.

A steady run gave Alex Caffi his first points as an Arrows driver.

DALLARA

Excellent ninth-place qualification on Monaco debut for Pirro, followed by disastrous race. No problems at first start but engine refuses to fire at second and disconsolate Emanuele pushed away. De Cesaris, hampered by damaged wrist tendon, starts 12th. Progresses to praiseworthy sixth, lap 31, but retires lap 32 (throttle linkage).

MINARDI

Both Martini (hobbling after Imola crash) and Barilla in new M190 cars. Pier-Luigi starts eighth and Paolo 19th. Martini starts strongly, passing Mansell on lap one, but slows with ignition problem and retires from eighth, lap seven. Barilla, in first Monaco GP, up to eighth (out of 11) laps 48-52 before retiring, lap 53, with broken gearbox.

LIGIER

Same-row starts for Larini and Alliot, 17th and 18th. Nicola runs 14th laps 8-11 before retiring lap 13 (gearbox). Philippe seventh laps 41-47, but also retires with gearbox malady, lap 48.

McLAREN

Another demonstration of consummate artistry and overwhelming dominance by Ayrton Senna, who starts race from his 45th pole position, leads from start to finish, creates new record lap (1m 24.464s, 88.08 mph), and wins masterfully-judged 22nd GP by 1.1s nursing down-on-power engine. Berger less impressive. Starts only fifth ("partly the car, partly the traffic and partly me"). Rams Prost at Mirabeau on first lap and halts race. Restarts in ill-fitting spare set up for Senna. After Prost retirement, vainly chases Alesi with no first gear to finish third 2.1s

behind Senna. McLaren overall dominance now sees Senna and Berger first and second in drivers' championship and team leading constructors' contest by massive 20 points. Here we go again?

LOLA

Now usual easy pre-qualification for both Bernard and Suzuki — first and second. Both then qualify for their first Monaco GP — Suzuki excellent 15th, Bernard 24th (traffic). Aguri retires from strong 11th (in spare car), lap 12 (engine). After steady start, Bernard applies pressure and finishes excellent sixth (two laps down) after stirring battle with Foitek. Team Larrousse's first 1990 point could save it having to pre-qualify after Silverstone.

SUBARU-COLONI

Team now in total disarray. Gachot fails to pre-qualify.

EUROBRUN

With no testing, unfortunate Claudio Langes does not pre-qualify. Similarly handicapped Moreno does so (fourth), but then fails to qualify

MONTEVERDI-ONYX

Amidst unhappy team atmosphere pending move to Switzerland, both Foitek and Lehto qualify. Gregor commendable 20th and JJ 26th. Foitek up to best- ever sixth, laps 67-72, resisting challenge from Bernard which ends with lap 72 collision. Gregor spins, stalls and retires. Lehto grapples with dodgy cogbox until gearless retirement, lap 53.

LIFE

Giacomelli does record eight pre-qualifying laps. Then engine destructs.

because the spare Ferrari had been set up for Nigel Mansell, who had a different gear-change pattern to Prost on his semi-automatic gearbox, and the spare McLaren had been prepared for Senna. Berger had been uncomfortable enough in his own car as it was …

As so often in the past, the story of the race for the lead is easily told. Ayrton Senna, who had won in a Lotus-Renault in 1987 and a McLaren-Honda in 1989 (and thrown away victory in the final stages of 1988), took his third Monaco win in totally commanding style. He led from the green light to the chequered flag with a faultless drive, which included a record 59th lap in 1m 24.468s (88.08 mph), and although he only won by 1.1s he knew exactly what he was doing. ''Half a second would have been enough!'' But it was a very different story for the places.

Ligier's undistinguished season continued. Larini and Alliot (pictured) qualified on row nine, but both retired with gearbox failures.

For the first 30 of the 78 laps, Senna was followed by a three-car battle between Prost, Alesi and Berger, who were in turn closely chased by the two Williams-Renaults of Patrese and Boutsen. Although no changes for nearly half the race may sound pretty dull, it was anything but. All the time you had the feeling that the Prost/Alesi/Berger positions could change if any one of them did something wrong, and the same applied to the Patrese/Boutsen struggle. Behind them it was equally exciting. After a poor start, Nigel Mansell caught and passed Pier-Luigi Martini before the Italian retired, and then closed on Boutsen. Closed so much in fact that, on lap 21, he nudged the rear of the Belgian's car and had to shoot into the pits for a new nose wing. After that, Nigel passed more people in his fight back to the front than the rest of the competitors combined did in the whole race!

On lap 31 the Ferrari rot set in. Into the pits and out of the race went Prost, wiping acid off his hands from an exploded battery that had ceased to power the electronics which control the gear-changing hydraulics. So up to second went the amazing Alesi, driving in his first Monaco Grand Prix. Gerhard Berger, now without first gear, could do nothing about the Frenchman. Patrese, fourth, was the next to go when, on lap 40, his Renault engine's pneumatically-operated valve gear decided that it had had enough. Rotten luck for '82 winner Riccardo who, after his San Marino victory, was hoping for better in his 196th GP. Now Thierry Boutsen was fourth with a sticking throttle, thus having to drive on his brakes. A hard-charging Derek Warwick was up to an excellent fifth in his Lotus-Lamborghini (a desperately needed fillip to the Hethel team's fortunes). Enter Nigel Mansell! Since he had returned to the fray in 15th place out of 16, Nigel had been driving like a man possessed. Past Bernard, Foitek, Nakajima, Caffi, Barilla and Alliot until, on lap 41, he was sixth behind Warwick. Three laps later he was fifth ahead of the Lotus, and on lap 55 he was effortlessly past Boutsen into a superb fourth place.

A lap behind the leading trio after his stop, Nigel had little chance of making up any more places but, with three hard won points

First point: having battled for most of the race with Foitek's Monteverdi-Onyx, Bernard muscled his way through to claim sixth place, to the relief of the Larrousse Lola team, desperately seeking to escape pre-qualifying.

seemingly in the bag, his spellbinding charge was negated on lap 64. Like Prost, he had to retire with an exploded battery. What a bizarre thing to stop two of the finest drives of the race; once again Ferrari went home with egg on its face. And now the first four places were set. Senna led Alesi, Berger and Boutsen and was driving cautiously to finish by dropping his revs whilst richening his Honda engine's mixture to compensate for the fact that he had lost power. Which is why, after 161.3 Monaco miles, he won his 22nd victory by a mere 1.1 seconds, with just 2.1 seconds covering the first three home in one of the closest Grand Prix finishes for years.

In their different ways, all the first three had superb races. Senna because he had driven faultlessly, and had won with a record lap in spite of his engine problem. Alesi because, by finishing second and beating Berger's McLaren-Honda in his first Monaco Grand Prix, he had again underlined the fact that his is a very rare talent. "I am looking forward to working with Alesi next year!" said Honda's top man Osamu Goto after the race. Well he might. And Berger had done very well indeed in a car which didn't really fit him.

But where luck had deserted Senna at Imola, it was certainly with him in Monaco. On lap 67 Derek Warwick, who had been struggling with ever-decreasing brakes for a long time, spun to a standstill exiting the swimming pool complex, coming to rest out of sight. With a marshal giving him a wrong signal, Ayrton missed the Lotus by a hair's breadth. Next time round, Senna shook his fist at the miscreant who responded with a gallic gesture not used in polite company. "Very dangerous" said Ayrton afterwards. "Things like that can destroy your concentration!"

Behind all this, with little Alex Caffi in fifth place earning the Arrows team two much-needed points, its first of 1990, there was a battle royal for sixth between Gregor Foitek's Onyx and Eric Bernard's Lola-Lamborghini. They both deserved that last point, for they'd

There was no doubt that Senna would be favourite at Monaco. Never in the slightest trouble, the Brazilian judged his race to perfection. Note the compact dimensions of the on-board camera, mounted just behind the driver's right ear.

The winner forces a smile, despite the less than appropriate backdrop. Although Prost had proffered a hand at the start of the year, in the wake of the bitter '89 feud, he and Senna were still not on speaking terms.

each driven an excellent race, but it was Bernard who got it as the result of contact which left him in the race and Foitek out of it. That point was not only the very stylish and impressive Eric Bernard's first ever, but the one which could well save his team from having to be involved in the hated pre-qualification sessions after the British Grand Prix. And, as a tailpiece, it's worth recording that a bit of history was made when Nelson Piquet, having worked his Benetton up to seventh position, was black flagged under a new rule, having been push-started after he'd spun to a standstill following contact with Boutsen's Williams at Loews Hairpin. Now Senna led the drivers' championship by six points and McLaren the constructors' by a massive 20. If 1990 wasn't to be another Woking whitewash, the opposition had to get its act together for the Canadian Grand Prix in two weeks' time.

Did he jump? Gerhard Berger's premature getaway earned him a one-minute penalty, but race-winner Senna still beat him in the rush to the first corner.

For round five of the championship, the Grand Prix teams made their second trip of the year across the Atlantic Ocean — but in a very different frame of mind to their first. Whilst they'd got nothing against Phoenix, Arizona as a city, it doesn't exactly make the pulses race. Its interest in Formula 1 is minimal, and its circuit is a mockery of what it ought to be. But although Montreal is on the same land mass, it provides a stimulating contrast in terms of enthusiasm, attractiveness and suitability.

Phoenix is surrounded by arid desert whereas Montreal is on the St Lawrence Seaway, and its Gilles Villeneuve island circuit is surrounded by water. With no disrespect intended, Phoenix is a characterless architectural clone of many other high-rise American cities, whereas Montreal, with its strong French tradition, is an exciting place with a vibrant, cosmopolitan atmosphere. And where America is apathetic about Formula 1, the Canadians are really fired up — especially in Montreal, associated with

the great Gilles Villeneuve. So it is no hardship to be at the Canadian Grand Prix!

The 2.73-mile track around the *Île de Notre Dame* has been aptly described as a street circuit without the houses. It is on the site of Expo 67, weird buildings of which are still there, and it is a circuit that the drivers really like — apart from its bumps, a by-product of Quebec's bitter winters which ravage all roads. With its two hairpin bends, very fast straightish sections and wide variety of corners, it is a real driver's circuit.

One that is hard on brakes and fuel consumption and that calls for good torque and a wide spread of power plus, of course, the right chassis balance.

Something that Montreal did have in common with Phoenix this year was the fact that rain on Saturday wiped out the possibility of improving on the first day's practice times. So Sunday's grid was based on Friday's achievements, with a lot of dashed hopes and expectations as a result. For instance, the view that the Brazil and San Marino results had shown that the opposition could now give McLaren a hard time certainly took a knock, the ''red and whites'' occupying the front row of the grid for the third time in five races. Senna had pole position (his 46th!) with Berger alongside him. Prost's Ferrari was third, less than half a second slower, but half a second becomes 35 seconds at the end of a 70-lap race. Something new was the fact that the Benettons were going better in Montreal than they had all season. Alessandro Nannini was

a strong fourth and his team-mate Nelson Piquet, responding as always to a good car, was fifth. Good news and real encouragement for team boss Flavio Briatore, engineering supremo John Barnard, designer Rory Byrne and all Mike Kranefuss's Ford engine men. And the Benetton's improved form was to be more than underlined in the race. Canada's 1986 winner Nigel Mansell was down in seventh on the grid behind the previous year's victor Thierry Boutsen and just ahead of Jean Alesi — of whom everyone now expected miracles every race. They were to be disappointed this time.

It was wet on Sunday, just as it had been on Saturday, but it was obvious that the circuit was going to dry out as the race progressed. No doubt about the need to start on ''wet'' tyres; the problem was going to be deciding the best time to come in and change to slicks. Too early, you'd be in danger of going off with no tread pattern to cut through the still-slippery surface. Too late, you'd lose time on overheated ''wets''.

Mansell notched up his second points finish of the year, eventually taking third. Here, he leads Patrese and Warwick early on. The latter went on to finish sixth, thereby scoring Lotus's first point of the year.

It takes two to tango: neither Pirro nor Alboreto lasted long.

Gerhard Berger was first away, but sadly for him he fed in the power just before the lights turned to green. Realising his error he backed off immediately — and that is exactly when starter Roland Bruynseraede pushed the "go" button! So Gerhard not only collected a one-minute penalty for jumping the start, but was beaten to the first corner by Ayrton Senna who, as usual, got it exactly right. Past Alain Prost shot Nannini, Alesi and Piquet, and by the end of the first lap Senna led by over 1.5 seconds. On lap four Boutsen passed Prost too, so now the Ferraris were running a lowly sixth and seventh. Were they going to disappoint us all again?

With an ever-widening dry line developing, but with the rest of the track still wet and slippery, there were 23 stops for tyres during laps ten to 17, and they created a multitude of place changes. Nannini actually led on laps 12-14, whilst Senna made and recovered from his stop. But, significantly, it was Berger, who

had switched to slicks as early as lap ten, who not only led on the track but had really got his head down and was pulling away from everyone — including Senna. However, when the flurry of tyre stops had been completed the order was Senna, Prost (driving superbly but in trouble with fading brakes), Boutsen, Piquet, Mansell, Warwick, Patrese and Donnelly. Note that the two Lotus drivers were well up, benefiting from smooth V12 Lamborghini power which was just right for the tricky conditions. But what about the charging Nannini, who had been going so well? Poor Alessandro's fraught season had produced another bitter twist. Rejoining after his lap 15 tyre stop he hit an unfortunate groundhog (yes they really do exist!) and was back into the pits for repairs. Five laps later, passing Nakajima, he put his slick-shod wheels on to a wet patch, lost control and finished what could have been a great race in the armco.

TEAM ANALYSIS

FERRARI

Getting better, but still not good enough. Prost a strong third on grid but Mansell only seventh due to puncture. Poor start for Alain (down to sixth laps 4-9) but up to second by lap 16. With failing brakes, passed by Piquet and Mansell and finally finishes fifth 0.034s behind Berger. Mansell charges to fourth by lap 20. Then passes Prost to finish third. With welcome reliability in Canada, Prost and Mansell advance to third and eighth in drivers' championship and team to second in constructors'.

TYRRELL

For first start in Canada, Jean Alesi eighth on grid. Nakajima 13th. Electrifying start elevates Alesi to fourth by first corner. After lap 13 tyre stop, collides with de Cesaris and stops for new nose. Loses control on wet patch, lap 27, and destroys already-retired Nannini Benetton. Nakajima has straightforward race in spare car to finish 11th (three laps down)

WILLIAMS

Thierry Boutsen, first in 1989, sixth on grid. After lap 13 tyre stop unwisely moves off dry line, lap 20, trying to take second from Prost. Loses control, rams Larini and retires in bad odour with suspension damage. Patrese starts ninth. Makes early tyre stop, lap 10. Fifth by lap 27 but then slides down due to failing brakes which cause lap 45 retirement.

Ayrton Senna and McLaren designer Neil Oatley compare notes prior to another masterful drive by the Brazilian. Canada marked his 23rd GP victory.

BRABHAM

Combination of first Canadian drive and wet Saturday prevent David Brabham from qualifying. Stefano Modena, happy with 10th on grid, has strong drive in "1989" car (still with in-line gearbox) to finish seventh, two laps down.

ARROWS

Much-needed Alan Jenkins (ex-McLaren and Onyx) joins as chief designer. In uplifted atmosphere, both drivers qualify — Alboreto 14th and Caffi 26th. Michele collides with Pirro, lap 12, and retires. In new car but with bad back, Caffi again soldiers on to finish eighth, two laps down.

LOTUS

A point at last! After an encouraging Monaco, Warwick and Donnelly (first time in Canada) qualify 11th and 12th using new undertray. Both then have excellent race, progressing through field together to sixth and seventh by lap 44. Martin then obliged to retire lap 58 (dropped valve). Warwick takes first point of 1990 with sixth place despite brake and loose undertray problems. Things are looking up …

OSELLA

Olivier Grouillard pre-qualifies second and qualifies even better 15th. Then spoils it all in race by becoming mobile chicane on hard Pirelli ''wets'' through refusing to move over on slippery track. Understandable but unpopular! Rear wheel sticks at early tyre stop, lap ten, but finishes 13th five laps down.

LEYTON HOUSE

With unsurprisingly low morale after succession of 1990 reverses and continued absence of popular team manager Ian Phillips, due to severe illness, spirits little improved following failure of Gugelmin to qualify and Capelli starting only 24th. (Main problem is extreme difficulty to set car up efficiently.) But Ivan improves things by driving to tenth, albeit three laps down, the team's second finish of the season.

AGS

Sad to record the Gonfaron team's two capable drivers Tarquini and Dalmas, both of whom have scored World Championship points, fail to get through pre-qualifying with the good-looking JH25.

BENETTON

Team Benetton really come good in Canada. Further work by Ford on V8 engine, allied to an excellent chassis, results in Nannini and Piquet qualifying fourth and fifth — by far the team's best 1990 grid to date. The race even better. Nannini second laps 1-9 and then leads laps 10-11 until tyre stop immediately after which he hits an unfortunate groundhog and pits for repairs. On lap 22, in a passing move, Sandro hits wet patch and goes off into armco to retire. Nelson Piquet shows he can still do it when car is right. Very impressive third between Prost and Mansell laps 20-48. Then cleanly past Prost to second, lap 49, to stay there until chequered flag for best finish since Mexico 1987. Up to fifth in drivers' championship and team up to fourth in constructors'. Great encouragement for the future.

DALLARA

With engine electronics problem that inhibits maximum speed, Pirro qualifies lowly 19th and de Cesaris poor 25th. Emanuele collides with Alboreto when 12th, lap 12

Now almost fully recovered from his Imola accident, Pier-Luigi Martini struggled to qualify 16th, and was punted out by Suzuki's Lola on the very first lap. With Barilla failing to qualify, it was an inauspicious weekend for Minardi.

and retires. Andrea stops twice — for tyres and damage check after Alesi collision. Retires from 14th lap 51 (gearbox).

MINARDI
Team has similar electronics problem to Dallara. Martini, almost fully recovered after San Marino crash but frustrated by slow car, starts 16th. Hit by Suzuki on first lap and spins off. Unable to restart so out. Paolo Barilla fails to qualify for first race in Canada.

LIGIER
Not an auspicious meeting. Alliot qualifies 17th and retires from 15th, lap 35, with debris-affected engine. Larini hurts elbow before qualifying 20th. Blamelessly removed from race, lap 19, when Boutsen rams him in over-ambitious attempt to pass Alain Prost.

McLAREN
Another demonstration of total McLaren superiority marred only by a momentary lapse by Gerhard Berger. Third front-row grid monopoly from five races with Senna's 46th pole (30 out of the last 37!) and Berger second. Gerhard (for whom revised seating position is now "90 per cent right") slightly anticipates start with resultant minute's penalty. Second on track to Senna laps 1-9, but leads on road after tyre stops from lap 15 to end of race. Despite penalty finishes brilliant fourth 0.034s ahead of Prost on time and makes record lap on last circuit (1m 22.077s, 119.645 mph). Senna drives masterfully controlled race to lead on time for all but two laps (tyre stop). Wins his 23rd GP despite having no first gear from lap 12 tyre stop. His "unhurried" race time 45 seconds slower than that of Berger's. "I believe I showed today that Senna can be beaten," said Gerhard. McLaren now 29 points ahead of Ferrari in the constructors' championship.

LARROUSSE-LOLA
Usual pre-qualification success with Suzuki third and

Bernard fourth. Eric qualifies 23rd but destroys race car in Saturday crash. Races spare. Happy to finish ninth (three laps down) in first Canadian GP. Suzuki starts well in 18th after massive Spa sports-prototype race crash previous weekend. Hits Martini lap one and pits for new front wing. Battles on with throttle problem to first 1990 finish - 12th (four laps down).

SUBARU-COLONI
As usual Bertrand Gachot fails to pre-qualify awful car, but hopes for better future as Christian Vanderpleyn (ex-AGS) joins team as designer.

EUROBRUN
With no testing due to under-funding, Roberto Moreno does very well to pre-qualify fastest, but then fails to qualify. Langes fired but recalled. Again fails to pre-qualify.

ONYX
General exodus by mainly British team personnel expected following announcement that Stefan Johansson-motivated injunction, to stop move to Switzerland by new owner Peter Monteverdi, now lifted. However, both drivers again do well to qualify - Foitek 21st and Lehto 22nd. Both then have engine power-loss race problems. Gregor retires from encouraging tenth, lap 54. Lehto out lap 47 when 17th and last.

LIFE
Giacomelli — whose income-per-lap must be astronomical — again fails to pre-qualify when his Life W12 engine dies on his eighth circuit. Majority of team equity sold to Italian consortium rumoured to be trying to buy Lotus team's 1989 Judd engines. They certainly need them.

Boutsen, winner here one year ago, was cast as villain after he speared the innocent Larini in his rash attempt to pass Prost.

And now it was Boutsen's turn. The 1989 winner was third and on the gearbox of Prost's Ferrari when, on lap 20, they came up to lap Nicola Larini. Seeing a chance to box Alain in behind the Ligier, Thierry dived to the left off the dry line, lost adhesion, half-spun, rammed Larini and exited with a deranged front end to find a very grumpy atmosphere when he reported in. What a difference a year can make!

Meanwhile Nelson Piquet, displaying the skill and verve that we'd enjoyed so often in the past but had seen little of in his previous two seasons with Lotus, had been closing up on Prost, whilst Nigel Mansell had similarly been getting closer and closer to Nelson. Now, running together second, third and fourth, they enthralled the crowd and the world's TV millions with a magnificent display of on-the-limit Grand Prix driving at its very best. From lap 20 to lap 48 they were together. The gaps between them varied as they lapped their slower rivals, but together they remained — until lap 49. Coolly, calmly and with professional precision, Nelson sliced past Prost at the far hairpin — up to second! Alain's brakes, already far from good, had really suffered when he had to anchor up violently to avoid hitting Boutsen when the Belgian did his harpoon job on Larini, and now they were shot. So the champion offered no resistance when Mansell passed him at the same place to move up to third a lap later.

But behind this flying trio all was not well. Jean Alesi had started off magnificently, and had been up to second during the tyre stops. Like Nannini, he'd then got it all wrong. Firstly, he tagged Andrea de Cesaris (in the wars again!) after he'd switched to slicks. With a new nosecone, he was out again only to do exactly the same thing as Alessandro at exactly the same place — off the dry, on to the wet and into Sandro's Benetton to complete the destruction the Italian had begun. No points for Jean this time, and a new Benetton needed for Mexico.

So smooth and efficient had Senna's progress been that it was all too easy to overlook him, but he was calmly controlling the race from the front despite the fact that, unknown to his audience, he had lost first gear at his tyre stop. Partly because of this, and partly because his pit-to-car radio was telling him the exact situation, he was dropping further and further behind his team-mate on the track. In fact Berger was now very much the man of the race as, in a car which fitted him much better after a lot of work since Monaco, he carved great lumps off the gap between himself and the Benetton/Ferrari battle ahead. By lap 65, with a record lap in 1m 22.6s, he was fifth on time despite his penalty.

Then another record at 1m 22.222s; as the last lap began with Senna a controlled ten seconds ahead of Piquet, who was three seconds in front of Mansell, it seemed amazingly possible that Berger might just be able to take fourth off the brakeless Prost. Which is exactly what he did! Gerhard's last lap was another new lap record — 1m 22.077s (119.645 mph) — and it made his penalised race time 0.034s faster than Prost's to give him a magnificently deserved fourth place.

''I could have won that race,'' said Gerhard,

Nelson Piquet showed all his old flair to score his best result since 1987, taking his Benetton to second place.

Grouillard tucks his Osella inside Lehto's Monteverdi-Onyx. The Frenchman qualified extremely well, but was criticised for inadequate use of his mirrors. The Finn's turbulent season continued with another retirement.

"and I think I showed today that Ayrton can be beaten." Maybe, but as people knowingly pointed out that Berger's race time minus his penalty was some 45 seconds less than Senna's, they conveniently overlooked the fact that Ayrton hadn't been under presure the way the Austrian had, and could undoubtedly have gone faster — especially if his gearbox hadn't been misbehaving. It had been a super race with spectacle and excitement all the way though. The Ferraris had been reliable. The Benettons had shown that they were increasingly becoming a force to be reckoned with. Derek Warwick's sixth place (and Martin Donnelly's seventh until his retirement on lap 58) had shown that Lotus were slowly but surely getting it all together. Nelson Piquet's second place (his highest since Mexico 1987) had

shown that if the machinery is right, so is he. But no thinking person believed that McLaren was now threatened. In Canada, both their drivers had been on the front row of the grid, Senna had won his 23rd Grand Prix in dominant fashion and Berger had gained sixty seconds on Prost, and almost that on Piquet and Mansell, as well as obliterating the previous lap record by nearly three seconds.

The school report on McLaren's opposition would have read "An improvement. Doing very well, but must try even harder." For now, after only five races, the Woking Wizards led the constructors' championship by a daunting 12 points. Admittedly, not nearly as much as in 1988 and 1989, but quite good enough thank you!

Martin Donnelly sends up the spray during the sodden early going. His Lamborghini V12 eventually suffered a dropped valve.

Riccardo Patrese got the jump on Berger at the start. His advantage was short-lived, and he slipped back to an eventual ninth. Team-mate Thierry Boutsen upheld Williams-Renault honour in fifth.

1990 may well have seen the last Mexican Grand Prix, as its existing contract ended with the fifth running of the event at the Autodromo Hermanos Rodriguez. For the participants, Mexico is a long way from being the most popular race in the World Championship. With other countries eagerly trying to get aboard the Formula 1 gravy train (Austria, Czechoslovakia, Singapore and South Africa to name but four), a move to almost anywhere else seems pretty attractive to most people. With an altitude of some 7,400 feet, Mexico City's thin air makes any exertion a gasping effort and when you make it you fill your lungs with filthy smog. The weather is hot and humid, the traffic is in a state of permanent paralysis, you have to be more than careful about what you eat if you are to avoid the dreaded Mexican trots, the poverty is immensely depressing and the police are intimidating and corrupt. So there wouldn't be too much resistance to a move.

But from the racing point of view, dumping Mexico would be a pity. The 2.75-mile circuit is excellent, with a demanding layout and first-class facilities. It is admittedly very bumpy (with the area's susceptibility to earthquakes, it could hardly be anything else) but the 180-degree, 165 mph Peralta Curve, which leads into the long 200 mph main straight, is generally regarded as the most demanding Grand Prix corner of all. Spectating from there certainly makes you appreciate that Formula 1 drivers are a race apart. Setting up the car to cope with it

Tattered dreams: his right rear tyre in fragments, Senna crawled in to retire, having led for much of the way.

and with the continuous series of eight bends on the far side of the circuit, which are entered at about 65 mph and left at over 160, calls for real skill — and close attention from the drivers! Another of the problems is the fact that the rarefied atmosphere causes a power loss of some 25 per cent and a similar reduction in downforce which, in turn, makes the correct choice of tyres essential in order to minimise loss of grip. So Mexico 1990 had a very special atmosphere, and it led to by far the best race we'd had thus far.

As an indicator of what was to come, the first four on the grid were separated by a mere half-second. In pole position for the second time in six races was Gerhard Berger, and he was over half a second faster than Senna's 1989 pole time. But it wasn't another all-McLaren front row. Alongside the Austrian, just two-tenths slower, it was the evergreen Riccardo Patrese in his Williams-Renault, with Ayrton Senna in an unaccustomed second row slot for his 100th World Championship drive. After a gigantic, ten-tenths effort Nigel Mansell had put his

Ferrari into fourth place on the grid, but his team-mate Alain Prost, totally unable to make his qualifying tyres work, was right down in 13th — his lowest starting position since his first Grand Prix season in 1980. Not good for Alain who, nevertheless, seemed remarkably serene under the circumstances, with the knowledge that he had got an excellent race set-up for his Ferrari. With Boutsen, Alesi, Martini, Piquet, Nakajima, Modena, Warwick and Donnelly in front of him, as well as the McLarens, Patrese and Mansell, he was going to need it!

Tyre choice could well decide the race (it did actually), and as usual there were different opinions about what to use. Soft compound Goodyear Cs for the McLarens, Ferraris and Benettons but harder Bs for the two Williams-Renaults. Warwick and Donnelly had a mixture of both with Bs on the left where there'd be the most wear, whilst the two Tyrrells had medium Pirellis all round. Off like a rocket into the lead went Patrese, but he wasn't there for long. At the end of the lap he dead-heated with Senna, and a lap later he was third behind Berger with

Closing in ... the magnificent Prost's charge from 13th on the grid eventually brought him within striking distance of team-mate Mansell. It was a quite brilliant drive by the Frenchman.

Boutsen fourth, Piquet fifth, Alesi sixth and Mansell down to seventh. With Prost 13th, where he'd started, things didn't look good for Maranello. But they looked good for Benetton! Nelson Piquet, a totally different man to 1989, was third by lap five and Nannini had started what was to be a superb climb up through the field.

Senna, in his usual masterful way, was nearly ten seconds ahead of Berger by lap 12, but next time round Gerhard was into the pits for new rubber. ''After three laps I knew I must stop. I thought if I did it at the beginning I would still have a little bit of time to catch up.'' Right enough, but he'd got a lot of it to do for he was now down in 12th with some very handy runners ahead of him, including Senna, Piquet (now second), Boutsen and Patrese (third and fourth), Mansell (fifth) and Prost (sixth) — having moved up seven places in 12 laps. So, watch the Ferraris (and Sandro Nannini who, by lap 15, had taken Alesi and was running seventh).

Watch the Ferraris indeed! They may not have gone as well as they would have liked in qualifying, but in the race they were terrific. By lap 32, with a succession of fastest laps, Nigel Mansell was third and closing fast on Piquet. Prost too was past both the Williams drivers, up to fourth behind Mansell — and catching him — as Patrese, slowed by what had turned out to be the wrong tyre choice, started to slide down the field behind Nannini, now sixth and in the points. Senna, of course, was in a race of his own, maintaining a comfortable cushion of 18 seconds ahead of the battle for second. At just over half-distance in the 69-lap race, Mansell took Piquet's second-placed Benetton (now beginning to suffer from worn Goodyears) and set about catching the leader whilst Prost closed on Nelson. For now Alain, in a perfectly balanced car as the fuel load went down, was the fastest man in Mexico. Driving as well as he had done in his magnificent career, he demoted the multi-coloured Benetton to third on lap 42 and, like Mansell earlier, put together a string of seemingly effortless fastest laps. For the

TEAM ANALYSIS

FERRARI
Superb result after patchy practice. Mansell starts excellent fourth only 0.5s slower than Berger's pole time, but Prost down at lowest-since-1980 13th ("No grip"). Both drive stunning race. Mansell initially down to sixth but third by lap 25. Passes Piquet for second lap 37, but loses place to Prost lap 55. Spins lap 67 and passed by Berger but breathtakingly regains place at 180-degree, 165 mph Peralta Curve on lap 68 to finish second. Prost sixth by lap 13. With continually improving car balance, steadily gains places. Past Patrese, Boutsen, Piquet and, on lap 55, Mansell to second. Into lead past Senna (right rear puncture), lap 61, to win 41st GP with record lap 58 (1m 17.958s, 126.858 mph). "Maybe my best race ever … "Alain up to second equal in championship and Nigel to equal fourth. Magnificent 99th GP victory and first one-two since Italy 1988 lifts Ferrari to second in constructors' championship amidst disturbing news that designer Enrique Scalabroni and aerodynamicist Henri Durand are leaving team. Are usual Maranello politics now going to mar exciting championship prospects?

TYRRELL
Very heartening qualifying. Alesi starts seventh for first Mexican GP (top V8 and Pirelli), Nakajima excellent ninth. Satoru has lap one spin and then retires after colliding with Suzuki, lap 11. Alesi races in top eight for whole race. In sixth place but slowed by misfire passed by Piquet, lap 64. Finishes seventh (now in top seven for five out of six 1990 races) and still brilliant equal fourth in championship.

WILLIAMS
Riccardo Patrese starts superb second on grid (only 0.2s slower than Berger's pole time) with Boutsen fifth. Both

Poor Roberto Moreno's luck didn't improve. Having done enough to qualify the underfinanced Eurobrun, he was thrown out for receiving a push-start following a practice spin.

decide to race on Goodyear B-compound tyres which turn out to be too hard for conditions. With grip and brake problems, Boutsen finishes fifth only 0.3s ahead of Piquet. Patrese stops for softer C tyres when 11th, lap 43, and recovers to finish ninth (full distance).

BRABHAM
Still with "long" gearbox, Modena qualifies tenth and Brabham confident, best-yet 21st. Stefano races strongly to finish 11th (one lap down). Sadly, David has short and messy race, retiring on lap 12 after repeatedly calling in to pits with electrical problems.

ARROWS
Both drivers adversely affected by severe handling problems. Alboreto starts lowly 17th and Caffi fails to qualify. Michele finishes 17th (three laps down) with gutless engine. Car improvements from newly-appointed designer Alan Jenkins urgently needed.

LOTUS
Closely-matched Derek Warwick and Martin Donnelly qualify 11th and 12th. Run together for most of race with Martin sensibly nursing tyres to finish excellent full-distance eighth in first Mexican GP ahead of Warwick, tenth, who suffered deteriorating grip (one lap down).

OSELLA
Grouillard again pre-qualifies fastest and starts race strong 20th on grid. With no second gear and deteriorating gear selection from lap 25, does well to finish 19th (four laps down).

LEYTON HOUSE
Amidst strong rumours that designer Adrian Newey is leaving, demoralised team unable to make CG901 car go fast enough. Both Mauricio Gugelmin and Ivan Capelli fail to qualify after struggling with appalling handling.

AGS
Unhappy technical director Hugues de Chaunac, disenchanted with lack of progress, leaves AGS prior to both Tarquini and Dalmas failing to pre-qualify once again.

BENETTON
Team's 1990 season continues to encourage. After qualifying problems with tyre choice (Nannini) and fuel pump (Piquet) Nelson starts eighth, Alessandro 14th. Piquet drives super race to advance to second on lap 13 and stay there until lap 37. Down to eighth after lap 45 tyre stop but recovers to finish full-distance sixth only 0.3s behind Thierry Boutsen. Nannini equally impressive. Sixth on lap 32, up to fourth lap 44. Passed by Berger but regains place when Senna retires and finishes fourth to give team second both-in-top six finish of 1990. Team Benetton up a place to equal third in constructors' championship.

DALLARA
Still hindered by Magneti Marelli ignition mapping problem, de Cesaris and Pirro qualify 15th and 18th.

Both Lola drivers had their moments during the course of the weekend. This is Bernard.

Emanuele has throttle stick open on first lap and then retires, lap 11, when engine expires. Andrea has steady race to finish 13th (one lap down).

MINARDI

Like Dallara, Minardi inhibited by Magneti Marelli ignition problem. Despite this, excellent Pirelli qualifiers help Pier-Luigi Martini to be fastest for first 40 minutes on Friday before finally qualifying seventh. With below-par engine finishes 12th (one lap down). Paolo Barilla (first time in Mexico) starts 16th and finishes 14th (two laps down).

LIGIER

Lacklustre no-points season gets no better in Mexico. Nicola Larini recovers from Friday food poisoning to qualify 24th before racing to finish 16th (two laps down). Alliot, like Larini, has major problems setting up car to start 22nd. Has similarly reliable but unimpressive race to finish 18th (three laps down).

McLAREN

Team retains 100 per cent seasonal pole position record with Berger there this time. But Senna "only" third with cautious tyre choice. Ayrton leads by end of lap one, and builds dispiriting 18-second cushion by lap 42. But lead thereafter steadily declines, due to slow puncture and joint Ron Dennis/Senna decision to stay out. Prost and Mansell pass Ayrton to take first and second, laps 61 and 62. Tyre disintegrates and Senna retires from 100th GP lap 64. Berger pits for new tyres from second place lap 13. Rejoins 11th and drives inspired recovery race — just like Canada. Back in points lap 50. Fifth past Boutsen lap 55. Fourth past Nannini lap 61. Third lap 64 (Senna out). Thrustingly (and dangerously) past Mansell to second, lap 67, but brilliantly taken by Nigel lap 68 to finish third

by 0.2s. McLaren men still one-two in drivers' championship and team still lead constructors' contest by diminished but commanding 18 points.

LOLA

Bernard destroys car at daunting Peralta Curve in practice and Suzuki almost does same on pit lane wall (after having had another massive crash at Le Mans the previous weekend). But both qualify (25th and 19th) after pre-qualifying second and fourth. Suzuki out lap 11 after being rammed by countryman Nakajima. Bernard retires from 15th, lap 13 (brakes).

SUBARU-COLONI

Car goes better than usual, but Gachot still fails to pre-qualify.

EUROBRUN

After pre-qualifying third and qualifying an excellent 21st on Friday, the unfortunate Roberto Moreno is disqualified on Saturday for being push-started after spinning. Claudio Langes re-appears but does only minimum three (unsuccessful) pre-qualifying laps to comply with rules.

ONYX

Both Foitek and Lehto qualify and again Gregor, at 23rd, out-performs JJ, who is 27th fastest but gets in when Moreno is disqualified. Foitek drives another good race to finish 15th (two laps down) but Lehto, with a very woolly engine which won't even pull sixth gear, retires lap 27.

LIFE

Usual engine failure (lap one) prevents Giacomelli pre-qualifying.

Together in the race as they had been in qualifying, evenly-matched Lotus twins Donnelly and Warwick came home eighth and tenth.

Kerb-happy: poleman Gerhard Berger was his usual press-on self, perhaps a little too much so for Nigel Mansell's taste. Their battle for second late in the race was memorable.

record, Nannini was now fifth behind Piquet, Boutsen sixth, Alesi an excellent seventh in a Tyrrell handicapped by sheer lack of speed and Berger eighth. Now with Bs on the left and Cs on the right, Gerhard was gaining hand over fist on everyone in front of him. Yes everyone — just as he had done two weeks before in Canada.

It was at this point that we began to wonder whether all was well with Senna. When you

rival Prost who'd do so, for Alain was very clearly catching Nigel. And to add sensation to excitement, Berger was now up to sixth and in the points with fastest lap!

Spellbound, we watched the gaps come down until, on lap 54, Senna's lead was cut to ·9.5 seconds as Prost closed to two seconds behind Mansell. The next lap the Ferrari positions were reversed. Prost second and

Eyes on the future: things continued to look bright for Benetton, Nannini finishing fourth.

watch a motor race you have to watch the gaps and the gap between Senna and Mansell was slowly but surely shrinking. Lap 43: 17.9 seconds. Lap 46: 13.8 seconds (and Piquet down to eighth after a tyre stop with Nannini, Boutsen, Alesi and Berger up to fourth, fifth, sixth and seventh). Lap 52: 10.6 seconds. With 19 laps to go was this another Monaco-style Senna demonstration of how to win by the minimum amount, or was something amiss! As if the intriguing thought of Mansell taking the lead wasn't enough to keep us on our toes, the realisation came that it might be Senna's arch-

Mansell third! Then, relentlessly, Alain reduced the length of the tarmac between himself and Senna until, on lap 61, he sliced past the McLaren — which must have been sweet satisfaction for the Frenchman. To have closed from 13th to first was an incredible achievement and to have caught and passed Senna in the process made it even better for him. But, to be realistic, it wasn't simply a case of Prost's and Ferrari's superiority. Senna had a slow puncture. "I felt the car getting unstable and I thought it was a tyre problem. I called up the pits on the radio and was told to stay out."

'Wanna sip?' Mansell proffers some of his hard-earned Moët & Chandon. For the passing move he pulled on Berger at Peralta, he merited at least a jeroboam or two ...

"I thought third place would be better than bringing him in," said Ron Dennis. "I was wrong." Third place? Yes, because by the time Ron had spoken Mansell was past Ayrton to give Ferrari first and second on the track for the first time since Italy 1988.

But Ayrton wasn't even to finish third. With his right rear wheel rim now striking sparks off the tarmac, his tyre was in shreds. With no hope of getting a single point in the six laps that were left, he limped back to the pits and out of the race. So now Prost, with a new lap record behind him (1m 17.958s, 126.858 mph) was almost home for a famous victory ("Maybe my best race ever ...") with Mansell fighting for second against — Gerhard Berger! For Berger, maintaining his meteoric progress, had closed to within half a second of the Englishman after Nigel had a spin from which, by selecting reverse gear rapidly, he'd immediately recovered. But he'd lost time and on lap 67, with an almost suicidal tyre-smoking manoeuvre, Gerhard thrust his way past the Ferrari into second place which was only his because Mansell had moved over to avoid being rammed. After that you could almost feel Nigel gritting his teeth with determination as he set about recovering his lost place. With one lap to go he did it in a way that no-one would have thought possible. He passed Berger on the outside of the notorious Peralta Curve, where just getting around flat out by yourself is a very considerable achievement! Anyone who saw it will never forget it.

Prost won his 41st Grand Prix brilliantly, his second for Ferrari, by 25.5 seconds. Mansell beat Berger into second place by 0.179s! Nannini was a praiseworthy fourth (from 14th at the start), Boutsen fifth and Piquet fought his way back to sixth after his tyre stop to finish only three-tenths behind Boutsen, 2.1s ahead of Alesi. In the euphoria of the moment, it was easy to overlook the fact that Senna's downfall had been no fault of his or the car's, but the fact remained that Ferrari's magnificent one-two had put new life into the Grand Prix scene.

The French Grand Prix, where Prost had won for McLaren in 1989, was next. A repeat of Mexico, to give Ferrari its 100th Grand Prix win, would do nicely!

There were sparks from both car and driver in France. Ivan Capelli came within three laps of pulling off a sensational victory for the rejuvenated Leyton House team.

Four of 1990's first six Grands Prix had been "long haul" events — Phoenix, Brazil, Canada and Mexico. Now the season entered a more settled phase with the next eight races being held in Europe — to the great relief of the 19 teams contesting the World Championship. For, without the need to travel thousands of miles to the next event almost as soon as they'd got back from the last one, they could get on with some regular testing between races and develop their cars progressively.

At the post-Mexico Silverstone tests Nigel Mansell had been fastest for Ferrari. The Maranello men thus went to the Paul Ricard Circuit, near Marseille, for the French Grand Prix with optimism fortified by the fact that it seemed to be a lucky race for Alain Prost, four times a previous winner. The 2.37-mile Castellet circuit is situated on the top of a rocky plateau, which gets bakingly hot when the weather is good (and it was this year). Its main feature is the long Mistral Straight, leading into one of the most demanding corners in Grand Prix racing — the Courbe de Signes, a sweeping right-hander which the top men take at some 170 miles an hour. That in turn is followed by the "Double Horseshoe", a double right, double left complex, and a series of swooping long bends which lead into the start and finish straight. It is a circuit where the key to success is to get the right chassis balance to keep the tyres in good shape early in the race when the fuel load is heavy — and finding that balance isn't easy.

Everybody likes Le Castellet and the beautiful Provence region in which it is situated, so there was general regret that, just as Mexico had probably seen the last of Formula One, so could Castellet after 1990. Moves (stongly resisted by the teams) were being made to transfer the race to the far less attractive Magny-Cours circuit in 1991.

Le Castellet had been completely resurfaced, so it was obvious that speeds were going to be higher. But few people expected them to be as high as they were. After the five hours of practice, Nigel Mansell was in pole position for the first time since Mexico 1987 (40 races) with a time of 1m 04.402s. That was 2.8s faster than Prost's '89 pole for McLaren, and it was clear that the faster speed, allied to the 30-degree heat, was going to make the correct choice of tyres and the time to change them during the race absolutely critical. It was obvious that Ferrari's advances had been continued since

Mexico. Mansell and Prost had each had two cars during qualifying, and one of each pair had been equipped with a more powerful development of the V12 engine. With Prost fourth on the grid, the two Ferraris sandwiching the McLarens of Berger and Senna (third for the second race in succession), and a mere 0.038s covering the four of them, it looked as though the two teams now had equal equipment. But there were other heartening situations too. Nannini's Benetton, fifth on the grid, was little slower than the four ahead. Patrese and Boutsen's Williams-Renaults were on the pace in sixth and eighth and, most heartening of all, the two British Judd V8-powered Leyton House cars of Capelli and Gugelmin were seventh and tenth. In 1988 the Marches, as they were then known, had been terrific, but their new car introduced in 1989 had been a dismal failure that had continued into 1990. But changes masterminded by designer Adrian Newey before he had left the team (after Mexico) had obviously transformed them. Just how much we

Mansell and Nannini chase the McLarens down the Mistral Straight, at the end of which lies the impressively fast Courbe de Signes.

Martin Donnelly bagged second fastest race lap, just one-hundredth of a second slower than Mansell's new circuit record.

were yet to see in a race that was everything any enthusiast could have hoped for.

Sunday was hotter than ever, and deliberations about which of the various tyre compounds to use and when to come in went on right up to the start of the 80-lap race. Mansell led away, but was immediately passed by Gerhard Berger's McLaren and Prost too was passed by Nannini and Patrese. It wasn't looking good for Ferrari, but appearances can be deceptive! On lap two, Senna moved past Mansell up to second and it seemed like a replay of the old story. "Have McLaren been sandbagging all the time?" I asked on the BBC TV commentary, "concentrating on getting the best set-up for the race and not worrying too much about their grid positions." They had, but it wasn't to be the answer.

From laps two to 26 there were no changes in the first six positions, but it was anything but boring. Berger first with Senna right behind and trying in vain to get by because Gerhard, with

less downforce, was quicker down the straights. Mansell was third with the Brazilian's McLaren in his sights and with Nannini's Benetton almost tucked under his rear wing. Riccardo Patrese, only a few lengths back, was fifth and having to work very hard indeed to stop Alain Prost from passing his Williams-Renault. Two McLarens, two Ferraris, a Williams and a Benetton in the top six, and all very closely matched. Then, on lap 27, Prost made a masterly tactical move. Realising that he was stuck behind Patrese and that an early change of tyres could be a very smart move, he dived into the pits for a new set of Goodyears. After an excellent 7.3s stop he was down to eighth, but his astute decision was to pay big dividends for, as his rivals came in to make their changes, Alain was already out there on fresh rubber making up places.

Berger was the next to stop. It took an over-long 12.7s to get the job done and he was down to 11th with Senna now in the lead. Two laps later, Senna was in; if Berger's stop had

TEAM ANALYSIS

FERRARI
Quite magnificent weekend for Maranello. Nigel Mansell fastest in practice to give Ferrari record 108th GP pole position (his 13th and first since Mexico '87). Down to second lap one and then third laps 2-27, but back into lead laps 30/31 prior to lap 32 tyre stop. Fifth until further stop, lap 61. Fights back from eighth including fastest lap of race (new record, 1m 08.012s, 125.412 mph) but disgruntled to retire from seventh with exploded motor, lap 73. Super confident Prost starts fourth after being fastest in Sunday warm-up. Sixth laps 1-26 trying to get past Patrese. Early tyre stop, lap 27. Down to eighth, but third laps 34-53 battling with Gugelmin. Past Mauricio to second and then past inspired leader Ivan Capelli, lap 78, to win 42nd GP (fifth French) and give Ferrari record 100th victory. Alain, now only three points behind Senna in championship, cheerfully predicts continued Ferrari success following British GP introduction of more powerful engine.

TYRRELL
Jean Alesi surprising fastest on straight at 199.02 mph on Friday, but qualifies only 13th mainly as result of Pirelli tyre unsuitability on fast tracks. Up to seventh laps 21/22, but retires with broken differential following lap 24 tyre stop. Nakajima notable second-best Pirelli grid position in 15th. Races midfield until lap 64 retirement with no gears.

WILLIAMS
Talented Adrian Newey joins team after departure from Leyton House. Both cars practice with new monoshock front suspension, but race usual system. Patrese and Boutsen start sixth and eighth. Thierry hit by Capelli at first corner and retires from seventh, lap nine, when engine blows. Riccardo drives usual strong race and actually leads on lap 32 prior to bad tyre stop which demotes him to tenth. Despite misfire recovers to finish full-distance sixth.

BRABHAM
Team at last successfully tests new transverse gearbox but races usual longitudinal box. Modena and Brabham, hampered by Pirelli tyre unsuitability, start 20th and 25th before having straightforward races. Stefano finishes 13th (two laps down) and David takes first GP finish 15th (three laps down).

ARROWS
Another ho-hum meeting, Alboreto and Caffi start 18th and 22nd. Michele equals previous 1990 best finish (Phoenix), tenth (one lap down). Alex retires from 18th lap 23, with broken left rear suspension.

LOTUS
Team Lotus down in the dumps. With new ''McLaren-type'' five-tunnel rear diffuser both Derek Warwick and Martin Donnelly struggle to get cars balanced in practice. Again closely matched to start 16th (Derek) and 17th. Both then run reliably with two tyre stops to finish 11th (Derek) and 12th separated by only 0.8s after over one and a half hours of racing. Martin Donnelly sets praiseworthy second fastest lap of race, only 0.1s slower than Mansell's record.

OSELLA
For the first time in 1990, Olivier Grouillard fails to pre-qualify.

LEYTON HOUSE
What an astonishing turnaround! After a totally demoralising lack of success in 1989, and repeated failures even to qualify in 1990, two of the team's top men, designer Adrian Newey and Tim Holloway, resign — but not before major aerodynamic and stiffer chassis changes have been implemented. These prove brilliantly successful and result in Capelli qualifying seventh and Gugelmin tenth. Their races turn out to be sensational. With calculated decision to start on soft-compound

Confirming Leyton House's return to form, Mauricio Gugelmin held off Alain Prost for many laps as he ran second to team-mate Capelli. Incredible to think that neither had qualified in Mexico.

Goodyear C tyres and try for non-stop race, Ivan and Mauricio in amazing first and second places laps 33-53. Prost passes Gugelmin, lap 54, before Mauricio retires lap 59 with blown engine. Capelli also passed by Prost, lap 78, but finishes superb second (three seconds ahead of Senna after two laps with failing fuel pressure) to astound establishment and ensure that Leyton House will not have to pre-qualify after British GP. A brilliant achievement by the team and its Judd engine, but bitter gall for Newey and Holloway.

AGS
For the first time (and on their home circuit) both Tarquini and Dalmas pre-qualify. Only Dalmas qualifies , and is classified 18th in race (five laps down). Some encouragement for the Gonfaron team.

BENETTON
Nannini qualifies as top V8, fifth, on his 31st birthday, with Piquet ninth. Alessandro harries Mansell for third place laps 2-27. Then attacks Prost for second and makes fourth fastest lap of race after tyre stop, laps 58-75. Sadly retires after sterling drive (lap 76, electrics). Nelson makes early tyre stop from seventh, lap 20. Down to 15th, but fifth by lap 61. Profits from Nannini retirement to finish fourth, one second ahead of Berger, for sixth points race of 1990.

DALLARA
Facing danger of having to pre-qualify after British GP, de Cesaris starts down in 21st and Pirro 24th (Pirelli problem). Emanuele retires from 22nd lap eight (brake disc). De Cesaris finishes 15th (five laps down) but disqualified for being underweight.

MINARDI
With "unsuitable Pirellis", Martini qualifies only 23rd and retires from lowly 16th, lap 41 (electrics). Barilla fails to make race.

LIGIER
With no points to avoid dreaded pre-qualification after British GP, rumours abound that team has been bought by Renault. Major qualifying effort gets Alliot in 12th, Larini 19th. Reliable but unimpressive races for both to finish ninth (Alliot, one lap down) and 14th (Larini, two laps down with brake problem).

McLAREN
Are there cracks appearing in the seemingly impregnable McLaren facade? With "low friction" revised Honda engine and new dashboard to comply with FISA "get-out-quick" ruling, Berger ("This place doesn't suit me") nevertheless qualifies close second to Mansell. Senna, yet to win in France, starts third for second successive race after unusually sliding off course twice. "Pole position is not so important here and I concentrated on setting up the car for what is going to be a very difficult and demanding race." He wasn't kidding. Berger/Senna first and second laps 2-27. Gerhard pits for tyres lap 28. Senna in to lead. A 12.7s stop drops Berger to 11th, now with inoperative first gear. Ayrton in for appalling 16.6s tyre stop lap 30, and down to eighth. Neither recovers as much as expected but, profiting from retirements, finish third

(Senna) and fifth. "Third place could decide the championship later," says Ayrton.

LOLA
After opening of very impressive new Signes factory, Eric Bernard qualifies encouraging 11th and Suzuki 14th after pre-qualifying now-unusual first and second. Excellent race follows with both finishing in top ten for first time — Suzuki best-yet seventh (one lap down) and Bernard eighth (also one lap down), despite loss of clutch on lap 43.

SUBARU-COLONI
Another pre-qualification failure for Bertrand Gachot.

EUROBRUN
Roberto Moreno does not pre-qualify, and neither does Claudio Langes.

MONTEVERDI-ONYX
With pressure from the unwanted move (by the team's mainly British personnel) to Switzerland now adversely affecting morale and effort, "we just couldn't get going" says engineer Ken Anderson. Neither Gregor Foitek nor JJ Lehto qualifies.

LIFE
Usual token appearance and usual failure to pre-qualify by Bruno Giacomelli.

No more "horns"! The Williams FW13 practised with a new Benetton-style nose housing an experimental single shock-absorber front suspension system.

A home hero bows out: Alesi's hopes of repeating his '89 Ricard result were scuppered by differential failure.

been bad, Ayrton's was a disaster. It took 16.6 seconds, so on the tyre stop he had lost over nine seconds to his arch-rival Alain Prost, who was now fifth — three places ahead of Ayrton. And still they came! Mansell in from the lead he had held for two laps on lap 32. He rejoined sixth after a reasonable 9.8s stop. Then the race's fourth leader in 32 laps, Riccardo Patrese — but a tardy 12.7s at rest dropped him right down to tenth. It wasn't until lap 34 that things settled down, and when they did it was a sensational situation.

First and second were the two Leyton House-Judds of Capelli and Gugelmin, yet to come in (we thought), followed by Prost — no doubt congratulating himself on his early stop — Alessandro Nannini, Nigel Mansell, Senna, Piquet and Berger. "Really nice to see the Leyton House chaps up front after all their hard times," we said, "but they won't be there for long. They'll have to come in soon, but even if they don't the Professor will have them for lunch." For 20 glorious laps, hardly able to believe our eyes, we watched the distinctively liveried Miami Blue cars stay ahead. Time after time, Prost tried to get past Gugelmin at the daunting Signes Corner. Time after time, Mauricio coolly resisted him. We hadn't seen anything like this for far too long and it was great!

But Prost wasn't to be denied. His Ferrari was perfect except for a slighty slow gearchange from his semi-automatic box. On lap 54, with the thrusting Nannini right behind him, he sold Gugelmin a dummy on the left at Signes and dived past on the right — up to second with Capelli some eight seconds ahead, and 26 laps to go. Four laps later Nannini too had taken Gugelmin and next time round, lap 59, Senna was fourth because Mauricio was out. After a quite magnificent drive, which had more than earned him the second place he had worthily held for so long, his engine cried enough and gave up right at the entrance to the pit lane, giving poor Mauricio the shortest possible unwanted walk back. So now it was Capelli, Prost, Nannini, Senna, Mansell, Piquet, Berger and Patrese; but just to show who was really in

Taking the strain: Capelli feels the effects of his afternoon's endeavours.

The master at work. Unable to crack the Leyton House twins, Prost had to leave it late before registering his 42nd Grand Prix victory.

charge, Ivan Capelli set a cracking new lap record in 1m 08.373s (124.8 mph) to draw away from the charging Prost. So much for any theories about his tyres starting to fail!

But it didn't last long. Mansell, down to fifth after a second stop for new tyres, had really got the hammer down in an effort to get back into the points, and his 64th lap was the fastest of the day in 1m 08.012s (125.412 mph). He never got back into a scoring place though, for on lap 73, with only seven to go, we saw a tell-tale plume of blue smoke coming from the back of the Ferrari to signal that his race was run. A thoroughly fed up Nigel, despondently realising that his chances of finishing the year as champion were heavily reduced, finally had his day made when he returned to his pit and was required to take a drug test! Nigel's race may have been over, but our excited enjoyment of it certainly wasn't. For suddenly Ayrton Senna was third. Alessandro Nannini, seemingly secure in the place and really deserving it after a hard and determined drive, suffered a total electrical failure in his Benetton's Ford V8 engine and was out.

Capelli was still very much in though — with Prost trying as hard to get by him and into the lead as he had with Ivan's team-mate 24 laps earlier. On lap 77, with only three to go, the brilliant Frenchman succeeded. 'It wasn't easy though,'' he said later. ''I had a hole in my left rear tyre and it was giving me a big vibration.'' But pass he did to win his fifth, and third successive, French Grand Prix, his 42nd in total. In doing so he gave Ferrari a record 100th Grand Prix victory to add to the record 108th pole position and the record lap that had been achieved by Nigel Mansell. What a wonderful day for Maranello! And what a wonderful day too for Leyton House. In Mexico, neither Capelli nor Gugelmin had even qualified . In France they had run first and second for 20 memorable laps and were now not only safe from having to pre-qualify in the second half of the season, but potential winners before it was over. A magnificent achievement.

''I'm really looking forward to Silverstone,'' said a very happy Prost. ''Nigel and I will have the new engine. I know from the tests that the Ferrari will go well there, and I know from previous experience that it's a circuit where McLaren are not at their best.'' So were we going to see Ferrari turn the double into a hat-trick? It was an intriguing prospect!

You could be forgiven for thinking you were in Italy. Support for Mansell reached fever-pitch at Silverstone, hence the proliferation of Ferrari banners.

They might just as well call it the Nigel Mansell Grand Prix. In Brazil they idolise Ayrton Senna, in France Alain Prost. But compared to Mansell's fervent followers, the French and Brazilian enthusiasts are a bunch of wimps. Nigel's fans adore him because he's a gutsy charger who doesn't know the meaning of the word defeat, because he's fiercely patriotic, because he's a natural showman and because he has had some of his finest and most spectacular drives on his home ground. He won his first Grand Prix — the European — at Brands Hatch in 1985 and he won the British Grand Prix at the same venue in 1986. In 1987 he did it again at Silverstone, audaciously passing his Williams team-mate Nelson Piquet with only two laps to go. In 1988 he drove his underpowered Williams-Judd brilliantly in the wet, to finish second to Senna's turbocharged McLaren-Honda, and in 1989 he was a fighting second again, this time in a Ferrari to Alain Prost's McLaren. At Silverstone during the Grand Prix meeting Nigel lives with his family in a motorhome on the infield. He signs autographs by the thousand and he is as one with his passionate army of devotees. They love him and he loves them. It's a mutual admiration society.

Silverstone may, to some, be "just a jumped-up airfield" but, with its 180 mph corners and 200 mph straights, it is also the world's fastest Grand Prix circuit whose owners, the super-enthusiastic British Racing Drivers' Club, plough back every penny of profit into a ceaseless programme of improvements. The facilities, organisation, administration and presentation are superb, the relaxed and friendly atmosphere is equalled only by Australia and the racing is almost invariably close and exciting. In fact, the British Grand Prix is one of the very best. 1990 was to be the last time it was held at Silverstone in its existing form though, for after the Grand Prix the contractors were moving in to rip up part of the 2.9-mile lap before reshaping it with extra corners and welcome gradients.

The British Grand Prix was the halfway point of the 1990 World Championship, round eight of 16, and its prospects were truly exciting. After two successive defeats by Ferrari in Mexico and France, it really did look as though the McLaren team's long-standing dominance had been broken. Silverstone is a circuit where the Woking cars have not been at their best in recent years, and they were up against it — especially as the Ferraris had been improving race by race, the Williams team's Renault engines now nearly equalled McLaren's Honda V10s, Benetton were to use a revised, faster-revving, more powerful Ford V8 and the Leyton House team was clearly now an extra challenge to be taken very seriously. At the

other end of the spectrum, the lesser teams were fighting to avoid having to pre-qualify in the second half of the season. Everyone had something very important to go for!

In near 30-degree heat, and watched by massive crowds totalling over 80,000, the two days' practice were enthralling. With the sort of inspired lap that we were used to seeing from Senna ("one of the best of my career"), Nigel Mansell took his 14th ever, and second

Get those flags waving. Mansell leads from Berger, Boutsen and Prost early on. He continued to dispute the lead in the face of gearbox trouble until his Ferrari finally ground to a halt on lap 55. Shortly afterwards, he announced his intention to retire from the sport.

As in France, Capelli drove a storming race. He had just passed Berger for third when a cracked fuel rail put him out. The following Boutsen benefited from the misfortunes of Ivan and others to take a steady second.

Bad bet? So confident was Nelson Piquet after trying the latest Ford engine that he backed himself to win the race, staking £400 at 40/1. To the bookies' relief, he stalled at the start. As he then tore through from dead last to fifth, that was probably just as well from their point of view.

successive, pole position at a searing 158.6 mph, a commanding 0.6s faster than Senna, who was followed by Berger, Boutsen, Prost and the amazing Jean Alesi in his Tyrrell-Ford DFR. "Obviously they forgot to tell him that Silverstone is a power circuit!" said one wag. Just 0.3s covered Senna to Alesi, Patrese was seventh for the start of his record 200th Grand Prix, the Lola-Lamborghinis were eighth and ninth and Capelli was tenth in his Leyton House. This was going to be a good one!

With all the cars in race trim for the first time, Nigel was fastest again in the Sunday morning warm-up. Nelson Piquet, using the new Ford motor for the first time, was a very significant second, Prost third in the second Ferrari, Berger fourth and Senna fifth — a full second slower than Nigel. The Mansell/Ferrari fans glowed with anticipation! But to start with they were disappointed. Using his superior Honda grunt to the full, Senna took the lead at the first corner and, very closely followed by Mansell and

Berger, held it for 11 laps with Gerhard hotly pursued by Boutsen, Prost and Alesi. Ayrton never looked in command, though, for Mansell was harrying him every inch of the way. On lap nine Nigel got by at the new Bridge Corner, only to run wide and be repassed immediately. But on lap 12, to the accompaniment of a crowd roar that could be heard above the wailing Ferrari, Nigel got the job done. Cleanly past Senna into the lead. Berger was still there behind Ayrton with Boutsen and a cautious Alain Prost "taking it easy at the beginning to preserve my tyres" fourth and fifth. And sixth was the evergreen Riccardo Patrese, driving as well as always.

In 1989 Senna had spun out of the lead and the race. In 1990 he spun out of second place at Copse on lap 14, and was lucky to be able to rejoin in fifth place. A "flawed genius", as James Hunt described him? Whatever, he was soon in even deeper trouble — down in tenth place on lap 17 after stopping to replace his

TEAM ANALYSIS

FERRARI
The Ferrari revival continues — with a vengeance. Nigel Mansell takes his 14th (and second successive) pole position with breathtaking lap at 154.6 mph — "Possibly my best ever." Prost starts from fifth. Mansell runs close second to Senna for 11 laps before taking lead. Passed by Berger lap 22, but back in front laps 28-42 — in spite of malfunctioning semi-automatic gearbox. Loses lead to Prost lap 43 but makes fastest lap of race (1m 11.291s, 149.977 mph) in spite of dangerously unpredictable gearchange. Angrily retires from second, lap 55 (fifth car failure in eight races), when gearbox expires. Prost second by lap 31 and "content to stay behind Nigel" but passes when Mansell slowed by gearchange problem. Stays in front to win 43rd GP (and first-ever hat-trick), take Ferrari into second century of victories and take championship lead from Senna. Mansell sensationally announces retirement from racing at end of season. "Not an emotional decision. I will do my best to help Alain win championship." Grand Prix racing would be the poorer without Nigel ...

TYRRELL
A disappointing British Grand Prix. Alesi outstanding sixth on grid (top V8 and Pirelli runner). Nakajima worthy 12th. Naka retires from 13th, lap 21 (electrics). Jean runs excellent sixth until lap seven, but going too hard for Pirellis. After second tyre stop finishes eighth (one lap down).

WILLIAMS
Bad luck for Riccardo Patrese in his record 200th GP. Starts seventh. Sixth laps 8-15. Tyre stop lap 16 after being hit by Nannini. Down to 20th. Climbs to 15th but retires, lap 26, with shattered undertray from collision. Better for Boutsen though. From excellent fourth on grid, races consistently at front. Third after Senna's spin. Passed by Prost lap 16. Down to fifth after tyre stop but profits from Capelli, Mansell and Berger retirements to finish second. Advances two places to fifth in championship.

BRABHAM
Both race cars fitted with transverse gearbox and new rear suspension for first time. David Brabham fails to qualify after Saturday spin. Modena crashes at Stowe Saturday morning and has to use "long gearbox" spare car to qualify 20th. Excellent 11th by lap 19. Finishes ninth (two laps down), happy with car and Judd engine after problem-free race.

ARROWS
Caffi starts 17th and Alboreto undistinguished 25th. Michele gambles on soft Goodyear Cs. Runs 14th laps 22-34 before lap 35 tyre stop. Retires lap 37 when engine cuts out. On Bs, Alex steadily advances as tyres improve to finish happy seventh.

LOTUS
Another dismal race. With high-speed corner handling problems, Donnelly and Warwick start only 14th and 16th for home Grand Prix. Urgently needing good result, but they don't get one. Martin drives strong race to advance to ninth, lap 17. Retires from tenth, lap 49, immediately after making his fastest lap, when Lamborghini engine suddenly lets go. Fed up and bitterly disappointed Derek Warwick retires from 14th, lap 47, for same reason. "We need to make major changes to the car..."

OSELLA
Grouillard pre-qualifies fourth (only Pirelli driver), but fails to qualify (27th fastest). Team must continue to pre-qualify in second half of season.

LEYTON HOUSE
Leyton House are definitely and hearteningly back (at smooth circuits anyway). With both drivers now in stiffer cars with revised aerodynamics, Capelli starts tenth and Gugelmin 15th. Mauricio sadly fails to start when fuel pump defects on dummy grid. Ivan drives another inspired race. Fourth by lap 33, despite being delayed by lap 16 Patrese/Nannini collision. Fastest man on track laps 20 and 35, and past Berger to magnificent third lap 44. But retires lap 49 with cracked fuel rail. He deserved much better.

Gabriele Tarquini's first race of the year concluded with a blown engine.

Both Lolas finished in the top six. Aguri Suzuki (pictured) scored his first championship point, taking sixth spot, two places behind team-mate Eric Bernard.

AGS
Dalmas does not pre-qualify but Tarquini, benefiting from Goodyear rubber, does (third). Gabriele then qualifies 26th for his first 1990 race in which he retires from 19th and last, lap 42 (engine). Team must continue to try to pre-qualify after Silverstone. Designer Michel Costa resigns.

BENETTON
Great expectations from faster-revving, more powerful Ford V8 engine. Only two exist, so both drivers qualify with "old" motor — Piquet 11th and Nannini 13th. But Nelson second fastest on Sunday morning with new race engine! Then ruins prospects by stalling on grid and starting from back. Kerbs wing endplate lap one and generates unwanted understeer, but up to terrific sixth by lap 31. Fifth laps 49-54, now hampered by loose rear bodywork. Spins and is passed by Senna. Still takes fifth for seventh 1990 points finish thanks to Berger retirement. Nannini encouraging seventh by lap ten but rams Patrese, lap 16, stalls and is obliged to retire.

DALLARA
Pirro starts 19th, de Cesaris 23rd. Hampered by lack of power and speed Emanuele takes 11th place (two laps down) for first 1990 finish. Andrea retires from 19th, lap 11 (gearbox). Team just avoids dreaded pre-qualification from Germany onwards.

MINARDI
Another team having grisly 1990 — no points scored. Martini and Barilla start 18th and 24th. Pier-Luigi retires from 20th, lap three (alternator). Paolo finishes his first Silverstone GP in 12th place (two laps down).

LIGIER
A very sad Silverstone for the once-great French team. Larini and Alliot start 21st and 22nd and race to finish 10th (Nicola, two laps down) and 13th (Philippe, three laps down). Team's inadequate record means it must now pre-qualify for German and subsequent Grands Prix.

McLAREN
At Silverstone, McLaren loses lead in drivers' championship for first time since 1987. Senna second on grid, Berger third. Ayrton leads thrusting Mansell for 11 laps before spinning (!) out of second, lap 12. Down to fifth and then tenth, laps 18-28, after tyre stop. In points sixth, lap 49. To fifth lap 55, when Piquet spins. Fourth after Mansell retirement. Finishes lucky third thanks to Berger stopping, and drops to second in drivers' championship. Gerhard drives storming race. Forces past Mansell to lead laps 22-27. Down to second after Nigel fights back. Then passed by Prost lap 31. Back to second laps 56-60 (Mansell out), but retires lap 61 when throttle system breaks. Now beaten by Ferrari in three successive races. "We'll just have to work harder before Hockenheim," says Ron Dennis.

LOLA
Larrousse Lola-Lamborghini's best race yet. Bernard and Suzuki pre-qualify first and second. Then qualify eighth (Eric) and ninth (Aguri). Both drive terrific races. Bernard up to sixth on lap 56. Fifth when Berger out and takes fourth from Piquet at last corner. Suzuki similarly inspired. In or just out of points laps 16-60, despite lap 58 stop to replace punctured tyre. Takes first World Championship point for sixth place. Both cars thus finish in points for first time and team easily avoids having to pre-qualify after Silverstone. An excellent and well-deserved achievement.

COLONI
Gachot again fails to pre-qualify. Subaru and Coloni part company. Team to use Ford-DFR engine from Germany onwards.

EUROBRUN
Moreno and Langes fail to pre-qualify, despite revised car for Roberto.

MONTEVERDI-ONYX
Once impressive team disintegrating. Foitek and Lehto do not qualify.

LIFE
Sadly, to no one's surprise, another pre-qualifying failure for Giacomelli.

flat-spotted Goodyears, with Mansell leading Berger by three seconds, Prost up to third ahead of Boutsen, Suzuki a superb fifth in the Lola-Lamborghini (his first time ever in the points) and Capelli a charging sixth. But just as noteworthy was the fact that ahead of Senna, in eighth place, was Nelson Piquet, who had started last from the back of the grid after stalling at the start of the parade lap. Some 18 places gained in 50 miles!

Around the circuit, Nigel's fans were getting worried. His Ferrari was making some very strange noises with its engine note suddenly screaming upwards in places where it shouldn't. On laps 21 and 22, their worry turned to dismay as his three-second lead disappeared and he was passed by Gerhard Berger. And no wonder! Unbeknown to us, the Ferrari gearbox gremlins were at it again, changing gears themselves without any help from Nigel. Amazingly, despite the fraught situation he was in, Mansell not only kept going but held his second place ahead of Prost, who was now clear of Boutsen. Capelli was past Suzuki and up to a brilliant fifth in a repeat of his French GP charge — and Piquet lay seventh.

On lap 28 of 64, with Mansell seemingly having mastered his gearbox, he retook the lead from Berger, who was having McLaren handling problems (just as Senna had earlier). Gerhard's difficulties gave the ever-present Prost his opportunity. At just under half-distance, lap 31, Alain passed the Austrian. Ferrari first, Ferrari second, McLaren third, McLaren ninth (for Senna had succeeded only in passing Martin Donnelly's Lotus). How times change!

Last chance: the Ligiers needed points at Silverstone to avoid having to get up early on Fridays for pre-qualifying. Larini is tailed by Barilla, Tarquini, Alliot and Alboreto on his way to 10th. Alarm clocks out lads …

Riccardo Patrese reached a new landmark at Silverstone, becoming the first man to start 200 Grands Prix. The celebratory cake left a better aftertaste than the race itself, the Italian retiring with accident damage.

Alain was ''Happy to stay second behind Nigel. There was no way I was going to be able to pass him at Silverstone and six points would do.'' But the 1990 GP wasn't all Ferrari. There was a lot more going on. The rejuvenated Capelli/Leyton House combination, now fastest at Silverstone just as they had been in France, was up to fourth past Boutsen's Williams and Piquet was sixth — having grittily gained 20 places since the start.

But, sadly, Mansell's third British Grand Prix victory was not to be. As his unpredictable gearbox increasingly took over, he unavoidably slowed and on lap 43 he lost the lead to his team-mate. After 12 more laps he retired gearless, and angry over the fact that, of the two Ferraris, it had again been his that had expired (for the fifth time in eight races). But, considerate as ever with the crowd, he threw his gloves and his balaclava to them as he walked back to the pits, in what later turned out to have been a symbolic gesture of departure. Some consolation to him must have been the fact that his pole position time and his record lap (1m 11.291s, 149.977 mph during a gearbox remission which was allowing him to catch Prost) would be all-time records at the ''old'' Silverstone. Much of the crowd may have felt the race was over, but it certainly wasn't. For now Capelli, superb in his vastly improved

Leyton House, was third and catching Berger! Until lap 49, when he too retired after a race in which he had shown that his team's outstanding form in France had been no flash in the pan. As things were to turn out, Ivan would again have been second if it had not been for a cracked fuel rail. But "if" is a big word in motor racing!

Lap 56. Eight to go. Prost in a secure lead paced himself home to his third successive victory and his fourth in Britain. Berger was second, Boutsen up to third and Senna to fourth — past the redoubtable Piquet who had just spun down to fifth due to loose rear bodywork. And Eric Bernard was sixth. But now McLaren's depression over Senna's race was about to be compounded as Gerhard Berger stopped and retired from second place on lap 61 with a broken throttle. So master tactician Alain Prost won and moved past Senna to head the World Championship ("It feels strange not to be there for the first time since 1987" said Ron Dennis), with a steady, fast and reliable run giving Thierry Boutsen second place ahead of a lucky Senna, profiting from Berger's retirement. But a fine fourth was Bernard, who scrambled past Piquet at the very last corner. With Suzuki sixth to put both the Lola-Lamborghinis in the points for the first time, spirits were high in Gérard Larrousse's efficient and enthusiastic team!

They weren't so high amongst Nigel Mansell's army of fans though. "I've made the decision to retire at the end of the season," said the hero. "It's nothing to do with today — I've been thinking about it for months and I've decided to spend some more time with my family and develop my other interests — especially golf! I shall now do everything I can to help Alain win the championship and, hopefully, win a few races myself." So Adelaide 1990, the World Championship's 500th race, would be Nigel's last Grand Prix. He'd be very sadly missed but, not to worry, we'd still got eight more Grands Prix to thrill to his talent before that happened! At least that's what we thought at the time. Rumours that he'd changed his mind were never far away in the weeks ahead.

'Haven't I been here before?' Prost's unruffled performance netted him his 43rd Grand Prix victory.

Ferrari spent all weekend doing the chasing, although Prost eventually salvaged fourth.

As everyone got ready to go to the German Grand Prix (the third World Championship race in four weeks), they did so with high expectations. 1990 was turning out to be one of the best seasons for a very long time and things were getting better by the race. Three wins so far for the awesome Ayrton Senna, but four for his arch-rival Alain Prost, who now led the World Championship by a slender two points. Patrese had won for Williams at Imola. Neither Gerhard Berger nor Nigel Mansell yet had a victory. The Benetton team was getting stronger and the political "who goes where in 1991?" speculation was well and truly on the boil. So when the teams and their associates assembled at Hockenheim, there was plenty to think and talk about.

Hockenheim is not one of the most exciting circuits in the Grand Prix calendar, but it has got a lot going for it. Its 4.22-mile lap is exceeded in length only by Spa in Belgium, and most of it consists of two long 200 mph arcs through dense and gloomy forest, joined at the top by a sweeping bend known as the Ostkurve. Three chicanes slow things down a bit and the bottom of this lozenge shape is connected by the stadium section — a five-bend complex surrounded by vast concrete grandstands which can hold some 100,000 spectators. It's a bit clinical, but spectacularly fast and very efficiently run. When the day is done, there is beautiful Heidelberg just down the road to delight the eye, with its profusion of excellent restaurants to delight the palate. This year, some off-circuit relaxation was very welcome for the area was sweltering in one of the hottest and most humid periods it had ever known. It was over 38 degrees on Friday and Saturday, with an atmosphere that felt like lead. Exhausting for everyone.

On the two practice days, getting things right for Sunday was critical. Hockenheim is very much a power circuit, so you need low drag for the flat-out forest bits. But the stadium section calls for high downforce to maximise grip around the bends. These two needs are incompatible, so the trick is to find the best compromise. McLaren in particular, stung by three successive defeats, spent most of the practice time optimising their settings, but this didn't stop them from returning to their pole-setting ways. They'd been there with either Senna or Berger for six of the eight races so far, but Nigel Mansell had been top man in both France and Britain. Not in Germany though. On

Friday afternoon Ayrton Senna only did two laps, but they were enough. One to get up to speed, the other to circulate in a fastest-ever 1m 40.198s (151.744 mph) which was breathtaking to watch. With Berger second on the grid only 0.2s slower, and with both of them over 1.5 seconds faster than the Ferraris of Prost and Mansell, it was all too clear that both McLaren and Honda had been hard at work since Silverstone. "Honda have made some improvements and we've done a lot with the car," said Ron Dennis. Quite.

It was a very symmetrical grid. The two McLarens and the two Ferraris were followed by the two Williams-Renaults of Patrese and Boutsen. Alesi spoilt the run by inserting his Tyrrell-Ford between the Benettons of Piquet and Nannini but Capelli, tenth, was followed by the two Lolas of Suzuki and Bernard. "Tyre stops aren't likely," said Goodyear's Lee Gaug. "Nearly all our teams are taking our advice to use Cs (the softest race compound), but the

Alessandro Nannini was in gladiatorial mood. Opting to run without a tyre stop, the Italian led for 16 laps, keeping Senna at bay until his fading tyres finally subdued his defences.

Roll on next season. Minardi will use Ferrari V12s in 1991. After another indifferent weekend, Pier-Luigi Martini could hardly wait ...

Benettons are going to run on the harder Bs.'' Lee was to prove surprisingly wrong, and Benetton's decision nearly won the day for them.

When the race began and Senna ripped off into the lead ahead of Berger, Prost, Mansell, Patrese, Boutsen, Piquet and Nannini, the enormous crowd in the grandstand had a worrying sight to occupy them until the leaders re-appeared. As he shot off from row 12 in his Dallara, Emanuele Pirro clipped David Brabham's front wheel when David jinked to avoid a slow-starting Stefano Modena ahead of him. Pirro slammed backwards into the armco and lay still in the car with a badly wrenched neck. He was still there being worked on by the medics when Senna and the rest came storming round but, happily, was safely removed and taken for a hospital check (which showed him to be OK). For 14 laps, the top five remained the same. Senna, Berger, Prost, Mansell (trying hard to get by his team-mate) and Patrese were followed first by Boutsen and then Piquet and

Nannini as the Benettons got by the Williams. But though the McLarens were in command, they certainly weren't having things their own way. Alain and Nigel may not have been able quite to close, let alone pass, but they were right there and making Senna and Berger go faster than they wanted to in order to protect their tyres. A hard-charging Piquet, chasing Patrese for fifth, overdid it at one of the chicanes on lap 11, overshot and was passed by Sandro Nannini in the other Benetton. Then, on lap 14, Nigel Mansell's race was run. "I ran over something on the approach to the chicane before the Ostkurve, damaged the front wing and then ran over the kerb because of the resultant understeer. After that my car was simply undriveable and all I could do was cruise back to the pits and retire." For the sixth time in nine races, Nigel's season was turning out to be frustratingly unsuccessful.

By now Senna, driving at ten-tenths to break the opposition, had eased away from Berger. Eased away, but certainly not cleared off. And

TEAM ANALYSIS

FERRARI
A setback after three successive victories. Prost and Mansell start third and fourth and run in grid order behind McLarens until lap 16; Mansell trying to pass. Nigel then "ran over something" which damages front wing causing understeer over kerb at Ostkurve. Resultant underbody damage causes sixth retirement (lap 16) in nine races. "Short" seventh gear causes Prost to keep hitting rev-limiter and overheat. Settles for fourth place and three points, but drops to second in championship. Ferrari now 20 points behind McLaren in constructors' contest.

TYRRELL
Unsettled atmosphere in team with talk of Alesi, Postlethwaite (designer), Migeot (aerodynamicist) and Villadelprat (team manager) leaving at end of season. Hampered by comparative lack of power, Alesi and Nakajima start as top two Pirelli users in excellent eighth and 13th. Alesi classified 11th (five laps down), despite retiring lap 41 with broken CV joint. Nakajima retires from 14th, lap 25, after stopping for work on misfire.

WILLIAMS
Boutsen fifth on grid. Patrese sixth. Thierry drops to eighth laps 5-14 but fourth by lap 24. Down to ninth after long (29.5s) tyre stop due to sticking wheel nut, but recovers to finish sixth with first ever fastest lap and lap record (1m 45.602s, 143.961 mph). Riccardo drives reliable race to finish fifth.

BRABHAM
Both Modena and Brabham have problems wih new transverse gearbox before qualifying 17th and 21st. Stefano hastily switches to "long" gearbox spare car after transverse gearbox problem on warm-up lap. Then breaks clutch at start and retires lap one. Brabham hit by Pirro whilst avoiding Modena at start and retires lap 12 with failing engine.

ARROWS
Cars quicker than in previous testing but still only 18th (Caffi) and 19th (Alboreto) on grid. Michele retires from 19th, lap 10 (power loss). Caffi happy to finish ninth (one lap down) in reliable but underpowered car.

LOTUS
Team's future unsure with rumour that sale under way to consortium headed by ex-team manager Peter Collins. After problems making qualifying tyres last a lap, Warwick and Donnelly start lowly 16th and 20th. Frustrated Martin retires lap two (broken clutch). With blistering tyres and "car jumping around so much that I was getting double vision" Derek happy to finish eighth (one lap down). But to dismay of sponsor, Camel team still only has one point after nine races ...

As the McLarens swept cleanly into the first turn, there was pandemonium at the back of the field. Emanuele Pirro's Dallara was pitched into the pit wall after hitting David Brabham's Brabham, and it took the medical crews four laps to release the unfortunate Italian. Happily, his injuries amounted to no more than whiplash.

OSELLA
Olivier Grouillard pre-qualifies third but fails to qualify.

LEYTON HOUSE
Mauricio Gugelmin plagued by repeated fuel pump breakages during practice but qualifies 14th. Capelli starts tenth. Both drivers opt to start on harder Goodyear B compound tyres and go for non-stop race. Gugelmin picks up dust at start which jams throttle. Manages to clear it but retires from 19th with dropped valve lap 13. Ivan Capelli drives usual storming race despite reduced power due to valve spring problem. Loses fourth gear lap 29 but still finishes seventh — having run sixth laps 30-37.

AGS
Gabriele Tarquini does not pre-qualify. Dalmas does so (fourth) but, 29th fastest, fails to qualify for race.

BENETTON
Now with six new Series Four HB Ford V8 engines, team

in great shape at Hockenheim. Despite gigantic 125 mph off which destroys car during Friday qualifying session, Nannini starts ninth behind Piquet, who is strong seventh on grid. New tub flown out from Witney and built up for Nannini to race. Both drivers decide to use Goodyear B compound tyres and run non-stop. Piquet/Nannini up to sixth/seventh laps 3-10. Nelson overshoots chicane lap 15 and switches places with Sandro. Both improve to third (Sandro) and fourth lap 16. Nannini to second past Patrese lap 17 and then, sensationally, into lead lap 18 when Senna stops for tyres. Piquet third laps 19-23 but retires lap 24 when engine blows. Nannini valiantly holds off Senna until lap 34, when tyre deterioration forces him to give way. Finishes superb second with fourth fastest lap of race and moves up to equal sixth in championship. Team now totally competitive with McLaren, Ferrari and Williams and move up to third in constructors' championship.

DALLARA
A very poor meeting for the team. De Cesaris fails to qualify. Pirro starts 23rd but hits Brabham's front wheel, slams into armco and badly wrenches neck. Race continues while he is removed from car (lap four) prior to hospital check which happily proves to be satisfactory.

MINARDI
Barilla qualifies 27th and therefore fails to get into race. Martini starts 15th, but makes no upward progress before retiring lap 21 (engine).

LIGIER
At Hockenheim the fallen team has to pre-qualify for the first time. Alliot and Larini do so easily, first and second. Both then get in race but not impressively — Larini 22nd and Alliot 24th after ''trying too hard and having huge spin.'' In avoiding Pirro accident, Alliot stalls and is push-started by marshals. After stopping to have seat belts done up is informed on lap 12 that, to his intense dismay and frustration, he is disqualified for having been push-started. Larini finishes tenth (two laps down) having stopped twice for tyres.

McLAREN
Glorious revenge for Mexico, France and Britain! With a further revised and more powerful Honda RA 100E V10 engine, Senna and Berger dominate qualifying first and second on Friday (1.5 seconds faster than the Ferraris) and then concentrate on their race set-ups. From his 47th pole position Ayrton takes lead from start but is pushed very hard indeed by Berger, Prost and Mansell. Decides to make early tyre stop (lap 17) and rejoins second just behind Nannini. Held off by Sandro for 16 magnificent laps, but retakes lead lap 34 when the Benetton's B compound tyres (non-stop run) start to deteriorate. Wins 24th GP (third successive German) and regains championship lead, four points ahead of Prost. Berger second laps 1-15. Down to fifth laps 16-18 (tyre stop). Back to third lap 24 and stays there to finish 2.1s behind Nannini. One more lap and he might have been second. ''My engine was not strong,'' said a gloomy Gerhard. McLaren's 84th GP win puts them 20 points ahead of

Ferrari in constructors' championship. ''We will now work on the response characteristics of the latest engine,'' said Honda's Osamu Goto!

LOLA
Relieved of the dreaded need to pre-qualify, Suzuki and Bernard celebrate with excellent 11th and 12th places on the grid. Eric drives to preserve tyres. Up to eighth lap 30, but retires lap 36 with lack of fuel pressure. Suzuki, strong 10th in warm-up, suffers from race understeer caused by tyre wear. Fine seventh laps 30-32, before lap 34 retirement (broken clutch).

Learning the trade. David Brabham takes a leaf out of the Gerhard Berger Racing Manual. The Australian qualified 21st, but got involved in Pirro's startline shunt and eventually went out when his Judd V8 lost power.

COLONI
Gachot drives Ford DFR-powered Coloni for first time but, with no pre-race testing, is not able to pre-qualify after spinning and damaging car.

EUROBRUN
As usual Langes does not pre-qualify and nor, this time, does Moreno.

MONTEVERDI
''Onyx'' dropped from name and team now based at Binningen, Switzerland. Lehto goes much better than last three races, the team having found his differential was fitted back to front! JJ qualifies 25th and Foitek 26th. Gregor, last but one, spins out of contention lap 20. Lehto slowed by misfire. Hits kerb and damages steering arm. Carries on to finish unclassified 16th, six laps down, with flapping engine cover.

LIFE
Usual failure to pre-qualify by Giacomelli.

Brilliant in qualifying, Senna drove a copybook race to snatch back the championship lead Prost had pinched at Silverstone.

then came the excitement. On lap 16 Gerhard came in for tyres (what was that you said, Lee?) and was down to fifth behind Nannini and

'No, Jean, they go in your ears ...' It was a busy weekend for Alesi. Rumoured to have signed contracts with about half the paddock for 1991, he called a press conference to try and quell media speculation about his future.

Piquet when he rejoined. Prost came in at the same time, but had an awful stop with a sticking left rear and slipped to seventh place. So now it was Patrese second ahead of Piquet and Nannini, but only for one lap as the Benettons, with their latest specification Ford V8 engines, were going like smoke. Riccardo had to give way to Sandro. And so, amazingly, did Senna. Ayrton too decided that a new set of Goodyear boots were needed, and on lap 18 he came in to get them. It was a superb stop, for the McLaren men, who had been practising hard after their problems in France, got Ayrton's wheels back on the ground only 6.2 seconds after he had stopped. As Senna joined the track, Nannini passed him to take the lead. At the end of the lap we saw the thrilling sight of the first five cars — Nannini, Senna, Patrese, Piquet and Berger — ear-splitting past the grandstands separated by only 4.5 seconds. Great stuff!

And then for 16 marvellous laps we sat

spellbound as Senna tried unsuccessfully to catch and pass Nannini. Almost unbelievably, he couldn't — any more than Berger could Piquet until Nelson retired on lap 24 with a blown engine. When Ayrton had said that McLaren no longer had the power advantage over the opposition that they'd formerly enjoyed, we'd thought it was part of his psychological campaign to improve his terms for 1991, but it was clearly true. In fact Nannini was, if anything, getting away from Senna. "I lost power slightly and backed off," said Ayrton. "That was due to the high ambient temperatures," said Honda race boss Osamu

Amid persistent rumours of management takeovers and sponsorship withdrawals, Lotus had another torrid weekend. In the circumstances, Derek Warwick was happy to finish eighth.

Goto. Maybe, but it was the same temperature for Sandro's Ford!

With Piquet out, Berger up to third and Patrese down to sixth after a tyre stop, Prost was now harrying Boutsen for fourth, and on lap 25 he got there. But no further. Amazingly, after two and a half days of practising with alternative set-ups, Ferrari had given Alain too short a top gear with the result that he was constantly hitting the rev limiter in seventh and overheating. "Three points for fourth was better than retiring with a blown engine so I settled for that." Patrese passed Boutsen for fifth, and when Thierry went in for a tyre stop (that took nearly 30 seconds because of a sticking wheel nut) he dropped down to ninth, with Ivan Capelli up into the points in sixth ahead of the two Lolas of Suzuki and Bernard. In fighting his way back to an eventual sixth place, Boutsen took his first fastest lap in a Grand Prix (1m 45.602s, 143.961 mph — a record) to show that the Renault engine, like the Ford, was now right up with the Honda.

But Senna was not to be denied. On lap 18 he had been 1.7s behind Nannini. By lap 21 he had cut the gap to half a second. A spurt by Sandro increased it to 1.5 seconds and then 1.8s on lap 27. Back came Ayrton. "I realised he was running non-stop without a tyre change and as his grip gradually deteriorated I got closer and picked up a very good tow which helped me get by." Which he did on lap 34. "He slipstreamed me on the run down to the third chicane, and by that stage my tyres were not as good as his. In the last few laps I had a little problem with the engine oil temperature going up so I took it easy with the throttle and everything was OK," said Nannini — but it nearly wasn't. Berger was on a charge and on the last lap he reduced Sandro's lead over him from 4.9s to 2.1. Another lap and he would have made it McLaren's first one-two of 1990, but there wasn't one so he didn't.

So at the end of the German Grand Prix, Ayrton Senna had added his 24th win to his 47th pole position with an absolutely immaculate drive. He made the right decision to change tyres when he did, and then took his time to make his successful challenge to Nannini. His car worked perfectly and so did

he. But Berger wasn't too happy. "I didn't have the best engine and it didn't feel very strong."

"That, too, was the high ambient temperature plus the fact that Gerhard spent a long time running close behind other cars," said Osamu Goto. Undeniable, but another demonstration that Honda's previous dominance was greatly reduced. "We will now work on improving the response characteristics of the latest engine," was Goto's reaction.

Senna first, Nannini second, Berger third, Prost fourth, Patrese and Boutsen fifth and sixth, and Capelli seventh for Leyton House. Boutsen fastest and Senna back at the top of the drivers' championship. If Nigel Mansell and Nelson Piquet had been able to keep going, the German Grand Prix would have been even

'It's great to be back.' After three races without a win, Ayrton Senna was relieved to be back on top of the victory podium. But Nannini hadn't made it easy for him.

better, but no one was complaining. It may not have been as exciting as Mexico, France and Britain but, with seven races to go, the championship was still wide open. McLaren might well have a reduced power advantage but Hungary, where this would be less important, was next, and Nigel Mansell had won there brilliantly in 1989 ...

Boutsen leads away on lap one. For the rest of the race, the Belgian's mirrors were continually filled by a random mixture of McLarens, Ferraris and Benettons. Despite the pressure, and the fact that he didn't pit for fresh tyres, Thierry held on to score his third GP win, and his first in dry conditions.

Two weeks after the German Grand Prix, we went to beautiful Budapest with the knowledge that 1990 was the last year of the contract for Formula One races at the superb Hungaroring. But any worries that we wouldn't be returning were dissolved when Bernie Ecclestone announced a new five-year deal.

That was a relief, because the Hungarian event has established itself as one of the best. Budapest is a magnificent city with its striking streets and boulevards, Austro-Hungarian Empire buildings and the River Danube to delight the eye. It desperately needs a coat of paint, but this year there were signs that this is slowly happening and, thanks to Hungary's newly elected democratic government, there was certainly a discernible improvement in the atmosphere with a sprinkling of new western

cars added to the hideous smoke-belching Trabants and even bananas on sale! The Hungaroring itself, specially built in 1986, is right up to date though, with a superb location and the very best of facilities. At 2.46 miles long, it runs around the edge of a large depression in countryside about 20 minutes outside the city. It not only has straights, corners and curves, but that rare commodity at modern GP circuits — gradients. All of which makes for an excellent track marred only by one thing —

extreme difficulty in passing. There is only one place where it can safely be done — the end of the start and finish straight before the 180-degree Turn One — and this was to lead to some very hard feelings after the race.

Because of the passing problem, a good grid position is even more important than it is at most other circuits. The Hungaroring is slow (if you call a lap at almost 110 mph slow!), bumpy and lacks grip. You need a lot of downforce, a good front end for rapid changes of direction and a fit driver, for the race lasts nearly two hours. McLaren, with its 1990 chassis problem, was expected to struggle, and by that team's exalted standards it did.

Both Senna and Berger went off on Saturday and on Sunday, for the first time in 1990, there was no McLaren on the front row of the grid. For the first time since Spain 1987, 46 races ago, it was occupied by two Williams drivers, Thierry Boutsen in his first-ever pole position and Riccardo Patrese. The Williams obviously suits

the Hungaroring. Patrese had been on pole in 1987, and had led the race for 52 of its 77 laps. This year's car was even better thanks to aerodynamic improvements and engine tweaks from Renault. Jean Alesi's Tyrrell had been expected to be well up on the grid too, because of its superlative handling and the fact that at the Hungaroring absolute power is less important. It was, but even Jean's spectacular driving could only get it to sixth with the two McLarens (Berger third, Senna fourth — his lowest position of the season so far) and two Williams ahead of him and Nigel Mansell alongside. Alain Prost was down in eighth between the Benettons of Nannini and Piquet, but seemingly not too bothered despite the passing problems he would have if he was to advance. He was fastest in Sunday's half-hour warm-up and we were mindful of the fact that, in 1989, Mansell had brilliantly won from 12th on the grid. Hungary 1990 looked like being a bit special.

'Which way to Wimbledon Stadium?' Berger contemplates the rash manoeuvre which put paid to both him and Mansell. The tactics of both McLaren drivers attracted widespread criticism after the race.

'Which channel's the snooker on?' Throttle problems prevented Piquet from matching team-mate Nannini, but the spate of late retirements gave him an unexpected third. Further good news for Benetton came in the form of confirmation that Camel would support the team in 1991, and that both drivers would be staying put.

The weather on Sunday was superb. Sunny, bright and hot — but not too hot. Ideal for the usual massive crowd of Hungarians, East and West Germans, Czechoslovakians and the enormous contingent of Gerhard Berger fans from Austria. Once again, it was going to be a race where tyre wear would be a critical factor; once again, there was the usual agonising about who would use which compound. As the cars assembled on the start line, the pro-Ferrari crowd was delighted to see Senna having to transfer to his spare car because of a radiator leak. When the race began, they were even more pleased when he dropped from fourth to sixth after the first corner! But Boutsen got it absolutely right with a magnificent start which took him into the lead ahead of a thrusting Gerhard Berger, who took Patrese as Mansell and Alesi took Senna behind him. Those exciting moves began one of the finest and most closely contested Grands Prix we'd seen for ages. It was indeed turning out to be a vintage year.

Thierry Boutsen had always been regarded as a "grade two" driver. Very good, smooth, fast and steady, but certainly not in the superstar bracket. His two wet-weather 1989 wins in Canada and Australia had been inherited, and he was thought lucky to have had them. But in Hungary he changed a lot of perceptions. In a quite superb race, resisting extreme pressure from five of the world's finest, and most experienced, drivers every inch of the way, he achieved his third victory from the front without ever putting a wheel wrong and nobody could have done it better. For 47 of the 77 laps, he led a tightly packed foursome comprising himself, Berger, Patrese and Mansell followed — and very closely — by Alesi (until lap 37), Senna, Nannini and Piquet. Alain Prost, of whom so much had been expected, was never really in it. Down to tenth on the first lap, he climbed to seventh by lap 34 only to retire three laps later when his gearbox locked up. For lap after lap, three seconds or less covered the first four with Berger doing everything he knew to get past the

TEAM ANALYSIS

FERRARI

Disaster! Both drivers use new 037 engine in practice and race — but to no avail. Neither Mansell nor Prost qualifies well — Nigel fifth and Alain eighth. Prost fastest in Sunday warm-up, but makes no real progress in race, spinning out of seventh, lap 37, when transmission locks up. Alain now ten points behind Senna in championship. Mansell drives usual gutsy race. Fourth in enthralling Boutsen/Berger/Patrese/Mansell battle for lead for 47 laps. To third lap 48 (Berger tyre change). Passed by Nannini and Senna lap 53. Fourth laps 56-63 (Patrese tyre stop). Third laps 64-71 after Senna rams Nannini but controversially nerfed into retirement by charging Berger, lap 71 (Nigel's seventh failure to finish in ten races). With no points Ferrari now dismally 26 points behind McLaren in constructors' championship.

TYRRELL

Tyrrell/Alesi/Pirelli combination seems tailor-made for Hungaroring but nothing achieved. Jean a creditable sixth on grid after being fastest for much of Friday. Goes off twice (race and spare cars) in Sunday warm-up. Fifth for first 20 laps. Down to seventh and then eighth, laps 34-36, stuck behind Martini. Rams Pier-Luigi trying to pass and retires, lap 37. Nakajima starts 15th and retires, lap 10, when failing brakes cause corner overshoot and rear wing damage.

WILLIAMS

Making the most of aerodynamic and Renault engine improvements, Thierry Boutsen takes first-ever pole position with Patrese second on grid (first all-Williams front row since Spain 1987). Thierry then drives superb non-stop race to lead whole way, resisting continuous pressure from successively second-placed Berger, Patrese, Nannini and Senna. Beats Ayrton by 0.29s to win his third and best GP (his 1989 Canadian and Australian wins were inherited, Hungary was not). Patrese third in four-car battle for lead for 47 laps, Second from lap 48 until lap 56 tyre stop. Third laps 64-71 but finishes fourth despite stop delay with fastest lap of race (record 1m 22.058s, 108.16 mph). Team Williams up to third in constructors' championship and very optimistic about the future.

BRABHAM

Team arrives in Hungary after being locked out of factory for alleged rent arrears. David Brabham fails to qualify for his first Hungarian GP. Modena starts 20th but retires from same position, lap 36, with engine failure.

ARROWS

From 22nd and 26th on the grid, Michele Alboreto and Alex Caffi finish 12th (two laps down) and ninth (one lap down), Alboreto after stopping for tyres lap 44 and Caffi after being slowed by faulty rev-limiter.

LOTUS

Following depressing announcement that team to lose substantial Camel sponsorship to Benetton and Williams in 1991, spirits raised by their best 1990 result. Derek Warwick, much happier with car, starts 11th and races well to finish best-of-year fifth despite second-half brake problems. Donnelly starts 18th and spends 16 laps trying to pass Pirro. Just fails to score first point by finishing seventh, but makes excellent fourth-fastest lap of race (lap 58) only 0.5s off Patrese's record.

OSELLA

Grouillard fifth fastest pre-qualifier, so fails to make the cut.

LEYTON HOUSE

Popular team manager Ian Phillips back in charge after long absence through meningitis. Both cars now on Brembo brakes. Capelli and Gugelmin qualify disappointing 16th and 17th. Mauricio's decision to gamble on non-stop run using soft-compound Goodyear Ds succeeds with eighth place finish (one lap down) despite brake pedal position problem. Ivan up to tenth by lap 37 but retires, lap 58, when gearbox fails.

AGS

Both drivers pre-qualify for the first time. Dalmas just fails to qualify. Tarquini starts 24th and finishes 13th (three laps down), but very unpopular through blocking battling leaders in closing stages of race.

BENETTON

Team's Hungarian weekend starts well with announcement that it is to be heavily sponsored by Camel in 1991. Piquet and Nannini re-sign for '91. Sandro qualifies seventh, Nelson ninth. Nannini drives magnificent race. Seventh laps 2-21. Fifth laps 24-47. Past Mansell to third lap 53. Second lap 56 (Patrese tyre stop). Then harries Boutsen for lead for eight laps closely challenged by Senna recovering from tyre stop. Punted off course and out of race by contentiously aggressive Senna passing move on lap 64. Justifiably very sick about losing real chance of victory. Piquet complains of "very boring race" with "on/off" throttle due to electronics glitch. Finishes contented third after jerky progress through field.

DALLARA

Still no World Championship points. De Cesaris starts elated tenth but retires lap 23 (engine). Pirro unpopular with several drivers for not moving over after starting from 13th. Finishes tenth (one lap down).

MINARDI

Like Dallara still no championship points (for the team which is to have Ferrari engines in 1991). Pier-Luigi Martini qualifies 14th. Down to 21st lap 21 and rammed into retirement by impatient and frustrated Jean Alesi lap 36. Paolo Barilla starts 23rd and drives steady race to finish 15th out of 18 classified (three laps down).

LIGIER

Another reliable but unimpressive meeting. After pre-

The crowd showed rather greater affection for Mansell than Nigel did for Gerhard Berger after the race. As his career drew closer to its expected conclusion, there was still no upswing in the Englishman's fortunes.

qualifying first and second, Larini and Alliot start 25th and 21st. Both then race steadily to finish 11th (Larini) and 14th, Nicola one lap down and Philippe minus three after lap one spin which necessitates front wing change.

McLAREN

For first time in 1990, no McLaren on front row. Berger starts third and Senna fourth after both go off trying to beat Williams' times. Berger straight up to second at start and stays there for 47 laps, vainly trying to get past Boutsen. Down to sixth after lap 48 tyre stop. Up to fifth after Patrese tyre stop and then fourth after Senna punts Nannini off the track. Catches Mansell's Ferrari and then, on lap 71, apes Senna by ramming Nigel. Retires lap 73 with resultant suspension damage. Senna (after changing to spare car on grid due to water leak) down to sixth laps 1-20 and to tenth lap 23 after tyre stop (puncture). Then makes typically forceful recovery. Sixth by lap 37. Third lap 56 and second lap 64 after removing Nannini. Catches Boutsen but fails to pass. Finishes second to increase championship lead to comfortable ten points. McLaren now leads Ferrari by 26 points in constructors' championship, but its drivers' stock car tactics at Hungaroring leave very sour taste in most people's mouths.

LOLA

Bernard and Suzuki 12th and 19th on grid. Bernard finishes praiseworthy sixth (in points for third time), despite almost total brake failure at half distance. Suzuki retires from 17th, lap 38, with engine failure.

COLONI

In second drive in new and vastly superior Coloni-Ford, Gachot fails to pre-qualify by only 0.2s.

EUROBRUN

Moreno and Langes again fail to pre-qualify.

MONTEVERDI

Disorganised team suffering from under-funding. Foitek does not qualify and, disillusioned by "off" caused by broken wishbone (allegedly old stock), quits team. Almost unbelievably, Lehto's differential again fitted back to front and he too fails to qualify.

LIFE

After the usual five laps before his W12 engine expires, Bruno Giacomelli again fails to pre-qualify.

Out of the points since Phoenix, things got no better for Stefano Modena in Hungary. Engine failure put him out at mid-distance.

Williams — but failing. He was quicker in some places, but Boutsen was quicker in others. On the straight past the grandstand, the Williams-Renault was always able to pull away from the McLaren-Honda — as was Patrese from Mansell's Ferrari. The Renault engine men at Viry-Chatillon had indeed done their job well.

Everyone was watching their tyres carefully, preserving them to avoid a stop but, on lap 23, having scrambled past Alesi (and scrambled is the word), Senna surprisingly pulled in (9.9s) for new Goodyears. He had a puncture for the same bizarre reason as at Imola — a trapped stone had machined away the wheel rim. He rejoined tenth to start a brilliant recovery drive that enthralled us — when we could find time to look at it! Because up front the battle for the lead raged unabated. With Nannini now sixth behind Alesi and Piquet seventh, Sandro was charging and catching the tightly-packed leaders as Mansell pushed very hard indeed to get by Patrese. On lap 37 Senna was in the points. Prost had retired ahead of him, Alesi had

collided with Martini whilst trying to lap the Italian and Ayrton had got past Derek Warwick's Lotus and Piquet's Benetton. Not only that but, on new tyres, he was lapping two seconds faster than the leaders. On lap 40, Boutsen had a mere 0.6s over Berger who was 3.5s in front of the Patrese/Mansell duo, which was being rapidly caught by Nannini and Senna. Eight laps later, Gerhard had had enough of trying to pass Boutsen. Feeling he would do better if he changed his tyres with 29 laps still to go, he came in (8.7s) and rejoined sixth. The race order was now Boutsen, Patrese, Mansell, Nannini, Senna and Berger.

It was now that the admirable Patrese, on tyres that were well past their best and despite wanting to come in, demonstrated that not all Grand Prix drivers are single-mindedly selfish. Realising that Boutsen too might be in need of fresh rubber (and he was), Riccardo deliberately stayed out to delay his pursuers and give his team-mate a chance to increase his lead. Which Thierry did, building a cushion of

If only ... For the second consecutive race, Nannini looked a candidate for victory. He was undone again by Senna, though not quite so subtly as had been the case at Hockenheim ...

some seven seconds over the nose-to-tail snake behind him — Patrese, Mansell, Nannini, Senna and Berger. Behind Thierry the action was riveting. On lap 53, for the umpteenth time, Mansell tried unsuccessfully to get past Riccardo, got it wrong, lost momentum and was immediately passed by Nannini and Senna. Down to fifth in a few yards, with Berger snapping at his gearbox. On lap 56, Patrese's selfless action cost him his place as Sandro and Ayrton passed him to second and third and started to close on Boutsen. His fine job done, Riccardo pitted for tyres and rejoined eighth as Boutsen, tyres rapidly losing grip, fought for victory.

Shades of the 1981 Spanish Grand Prix! Then it was Villeneuve, Laffite, Watson, Reutemann and de Angelis nose to tail. Now it was Boutsen, Nannini, Senna, Mansell and Berger, and it looked like anbody's race — if only it wasn't so difficult to pass. Berger got by Mansell only to be repassed in a breathtaking move — on the outside — exiting the daunting

Turn One. And the evergreen Patrese, driving in his 202nd Grand Prix, was catching them all. On his new tyres he made the fastest lap of the race (1m 22.058s, 108.16 mph), but with the prospect of a nail-biting battle for victory right down to the chequered flag two very controversial moves took the gloss off things. On lap 64 Senna, in a typically aggressive move, rammed and damaged Nannini's Benetton to force Sandro's retirement whilst the Brazilian motored on unscathed. And on lap 72 Berger, frustrated by repeatedly failing to get past Mansell, who certainly wasn't about to move over, did exactly the same thing to the Ferrari in exactly the same place. The only difference in this case was that Berger too had to retire. As usual, who was at fault depended on who you were talking to. It is only fair to remember that, with an enormous amount at stake and the adrenalin flowing, drivers will take chances which detached observers may think were foolhardy, not to say plain dangerous. Whatever, the fact was that a wonderful race

Both Dallaras qualified well, de Cesaris 10th and Pirro (pictured) 13th. Only the latter went the distance, finishing a lapped 10th.

Close rivals on the track, close friends off it. Senna was genuinely pleased for Boutsen. It made quite a change to see camaraderie on an F1 podium …

Both Footwork Arrows proved reliable, if a trifle tardy. Alboreto came in 12th, with partner Caffi (pictured) ninth. Better things are expected with the advent of Porsche power to replace the trusty Cosworth V8s.

had been spoiled by what many people regarded as rock-ape tactics and which generated heated discussion (but no protests) afterwards.

But Senna's charge failed to gain him his 25th Grand Prix win. Thierry Boutsen resisted Ayrton's pressure to the end to win by a razor-thin 0.29s, with Piquet profiting from Nannini, Mansell and Berger's departures to finish third ahead of Patrese, Warwick and Bernard — all of whom went the full distance. "My tyres were finished. I couldn't have done one more lap ahead of Ayrton," said Boutsen. It was justice that he didn't have to, for he had driven a magnificent race and, in any case, his great friend Senna was well pleased. "I'm very happy. I expected the Ferraris to be very strong here and second place is perfect for the World Championship." Unless Maranello could pull their socks up for the remaining six races, it looked as though he was right. But we were unlikely to see a better race than Hungary 1990.

'What? Again?' Jean Alesi eases off as the race is halted for a second time, Paolo Barilla having left the road at Raidillon.

The 1990 Belgian Grand Prix revolved around three things: Ayrton Senna, the magnificent Spa-Francorchamps circuit and tyres. If that seems a strange combination, read on!

Senna's contract with McLaren ran out at the end of 1990; such was the demand for his services that a lot of other top potential moves were in abeyance until he had made his mind up about where he was going in 1991. As a result of that, the paddock was a buzzing hive of speculation. Would he go to Williams, who had been having secret talks with the Brazilian? And if he did would Mansell reverse his decision to retire and drive for McLaren? In which case, how would Nigel's fractious contractual talks with Ferrari work out? Would Alesi go to Williams or stay at Tyrrell — or go to Ferrari to join Prost who had re-signed for '91? Or would

Maranello's number two be Ivan Capelli (or even Alex Caffi)? What about Boutsen to Arrows? And lots of other intriguing alternatives? On Saturday morning, though, Ayrton's future was made known with the news that his protracted negotiations with McLaren's Ron Dennis had been successfully completed. He had re-signed for McLaren with a further year's option — reputedly for a handy £8 million. Ron and Ayrton are both very tough dealers, but each professed to be happy. And now that was out of the way, the others could proceed. Was Ayrton worth the money? Obviously, the people who were paying it thought so; their belief must have been considerably strengthened on Sunday evening, for Senna went on to dominate Belgium 1990 with a performance as commanding as any of his considerable past achievements.

He already had three victories at Spa, and ranked them amongst his finest. Small wonder. At 4.3 miles, Spa is not only the longest of today's Grand Prix circuits, but also the most natural and demanding. Unlike the majority of artificial, specially constructed Grand Prix tracks, Spa consists entirely of public roads which are closed for the race, and they make a wonderful venue for those roads are in the beautiful hills and forests of the Ardennes, which are famous for their unpredictable weather. Almost immediately after the start (much too soon, actually), the famous La Source hairpin leads to the breathtaking plunge down to the superfast Eau Rouge which precedes the long, 195 mph climb to the right/left at Les Combes. Then it's down into the valley for a series of swooping bends, on to the daunting 180 mph left-handed sweep at Blanchimont and back to the start by way of the aptly named "Bus Stop" chicane. With a lap speed of over 130 mph, it's a tremendously spectacular setting for the world's finest to show their skills and a setting where, as ever, the right tyres are needed to get the best grid position and to decide the race. It

is all too easy to make them lose grip on a hot qualifying lap, and just as easy to do the same thing during the event — as we were to see..

But first came the qualifying sessions. Berger was fastest on Friday followed by Prost, Senna and Mansell. Senna went quicker in the vital Saturday hour for his 48th pole position, and was the only one to beat his own 1989 pole time. It certainly looked as though the much-discussed McLaren handling problem had been overcome, especially as Berger completed the front row ahead of Prost, Boutsen, Mansell and Nannini. So in excellent weather on race day (unlike 1989, when it was appallingly wet) Senna was where he needed to be at Spa — on the front row. All too often in the past, the closeness of La Source hairpin to the grid had prompted a pile-up within seconds of the green light; it saw one this year too! In the frantic charge away from the line, Piquet's Benetton nerfed Mansell's Ferrari into the armco and triggered several other incidents involving Aguri Suzuki, Derek Warwick, Martin Donnelly, Satoru Nakajima, Stefano Modena and Andrea de Cesaris. Not many others left! Senna led at Les Combes from Berger, Prost,

It was unusually quiet through Eau Rouge on the first lap (facing page). As Senna heads a few stragglers, over half the field are picking their way through the debris back at La Source (inset) ...

Progress at last! Having ditched Subaru in favour of a trusty Cosworth V8, the refettled Coloni pre-qualified for the first time. Bertrand Gachot couldn't get it into the race, but it was a step in the right direction.

TEAM ANALYSIS

A true road circuit in the heart of the Ardennes, Spa is a real challenge to a driver's skill, even on those rare days when it stays dry.

FERRARI

With two previous winners (Prost '83/'87 and Mansell '86), a new engine and a superb chassis, Ferrari was rightly optimistic. But, after re-signing for '91, Prost third on grid behind McLarens and Mansell only fifth. Nigel thumped into armco by Piquet at first start. Takes two subsequent starts in spare car set up for Prost with which very unhappy. Down to ninth lap two. Stops for tyres lap 11 (wanting to retire because of "impossible handling"). Rejoins 16th. Retires from 14th lap 20 complaining of dangerous oversteer. Already poor relationship with Ferrari deteriorates further. Prost fastest in Sunday warm-up. Third laps 1-13. Past Berger to second lap 14. Loses second to Nannini laps 23-26 after tyre stop, but regains it lap 27. Finishes second with record lap (1m 55.087s, 134.895 mph). Now 13 points behind Senna in championship, but not unhappy.

TYRRELL

Alesi and Nakajima justifiably well pleased with ninth and tenth on grid at power circuit. Satoru into spare car after colliding with Modena at first start. Stops lap one to investigate power loss. Rejoins but retires from last place after four laps. Alesi drives usual forceful race to finish eighth in first Belgian GP (one lap down), with heavily blistered second set of tyres.

WILLIAMS

Great disappointment after Hungary. Both Boutsen and Patrese say car "hard to drive" at Spa. Using new "Evolution Two" Renault engine Thierry qualifies fourth, Riccardo seventh. Boutsen up to superb second behind Senna at second start but fourth at third getaway. Third laps 18-21 after Berger tyre stop, but retires lap 22 (broken CV joint). Patrese races fifth until lap 15, when passed by Nannini. Retires from seventh lap 19 with broken gearbox. Spirits low as both drivers uncertain about future with team.

BRABHAM

After starting 13th (Modena) and 24th (Brabham), both drivers get through first two starts unscathed. Stefano advances to tenth laps 22-28. Retires from 11th lap 40 (engine). David Brabham retires from 15th, lap 36, in first Belgian GP when damaged rear light shorts engine electrics.

ARROWS

Both drivers use new cooling system for 1991 Porsche-engined car and Alboreto uses new floor which improves aerodynamics. Michele just qualifies in 26th ("traffic") but excellent ninth in Sunday warm-up. Alex Caffi starts 19th. Alboreto up to 11th laps 29-35 (during which his blocking of Prost denies Alain chance of victory), but loses power and finishes 13th (one lap down). Caffi contented with tenth place (one lap down).

LOTUS

Acute understeer in practice results in Warwick qualifying 18th and Donnelly 22nd (after losing wheel on Friday due to faulty nut). Donnelly hits Warwick during first start shambles and misses second start. Derek races spare and Martin takes third start in repaired Warwick race car. Understeer persists in both cars. Misfiring Derek finishes 11th, 0.3s ahead of Martin 12th. Both one lap down. Disillusioned Warwick announces his intention to leave Lotus at end of season.

OSELLA

Car balance much improved at Monza tests. Grouillard pre-qualifies fastest and qualifies 23rd. Runs last laps 14-42 to finish 16th (two laps down). Contented in circumstances where '' to finish is the best we can hope for.''

LEYTON HOUSE

After qualifying 12th (Capelli) and 14th (Gugelmin), both drivers avoid trouble in first two starts. Ivan, running ninth on lap 17, unselfishly lets Mauricio through ("My tyres had gone off") but finishes seventh (non-stop, one lap down) despite broken exhaust pipe. Gugelmin delighted to go full distance non-stop and finish sixth to take his first point of 1990. First '90 race where both cars finish and confirmation that a long, awful period of misery and setbacks is on the way out.

For the first time since Brazil 1989, Mauricio Gugelmin bagged a point, taking his Leyton House to sixth.

AGS
Both drivers again pre-qualify (Dalmas second, Tarquini fourth) but sadly neither qualifies.

BENETTON
After qualifying sixth (Nannini) and eighth (Piquet), both drivers plan to race non-stop on Goodyear Bs. Sandro second fastest in Sunday warm-up and drives another superb race. Third laps 18-21 and then second, laps 23-26, sandwiched between Senna and Prost after their tyre stops. Passed by Prost and then, with failing tyres, caught by Berger. Fights hard but down to fourth two laps from end after heart-stopping slide whilst lapping Caffi at 180 mph Raidillon bend. Finishes fourth and up to sixth in championship. Piquet starts in spare after ramming Mansell at first start. Has unintended tyre stop and loses clutch, but races fifth from lap 29 to end. His ninth points finish in 11 races.

DALLARA
Pirro starts 17th from pit lane due to broken water pipe. Switches to spare for second start and then back to repaired race car for third start. Leak returns to force lap six retirement. De Cesaris 20th on grid ("car too slow and poor on fast corners"). Collides with Martini at second start. Retires from 17th out of 19, lap 27 (power loss and oil leak).

MINARDI
New, stiffer floor improves handling but car still too slow. Martini qualifies 16th, takes off de Cesaris after second start and then runs with bad understeer to finish 15th (two laps down). Barilla departs circuit at Raidillon after second start, destroys car, causes race to be stopped and is very luck to survive unhurt.

LIGIER
Alliot fails to qualify after Friday time disallowed (excessive rear wing overhang). Larini starts 21st and immediately breaks differential. Then uses spare. Stops lap eight for new tyres because of "enormous vibration." Stops again for tyres lap 16, but finishes 14th (two laps down).

McLAREN
Senna re-signs for 1991 (with further one-year option) and then takes 48th pole position with Berger second on grid for team's fifth one-two of 1990. Ayrton leads from all three starts and takes masterly 25th GP win (fourth at Spa and third successive Belgian) to equal Jim Clark and Lauda totals. After his Hungarian attack on Mansell Berger fails to win friends at Spa by chopping Prost at second start. Second laps 1-13. Passed by Prost lap 14. Sixth laps 19-21 after tyre stop. Fourth laps 23-41, catching Nannini. Takes Sandro lap 42 to finish third. Both drivers use modified Series Five Honda V10 (more top end power).

LOLA
Suzuki 11th on grid ("It's like Suzuka here — I like it!") and Bernard 15th. Aguri damages car in race warm-up and starts in spare. Collides with Piquet after first start and, with no car left, takes no further part. Bernard has three good starts (!) and is tenth by lap 11. Finishes contented ninth (one lap down), despite long tyre stop (stuck rear wheel) and only having sixth gear for last two laps.

COLONI
Bertrand Gachot's first pre-qualification in Coloni but blows engine. With only one tired replacement, sadly fails to qualify for home GP.

EUROBRUN
Moreno and Langes pre-qualify fifth and sixth and therefore go no further.

MONTEVERDI
The shambolic and under-funded Swiss team announces its withdrawal from the 1990 Grand Prix series — leaving the blameless JJ Lehto and Gregor Foitek without drives. "But we'll be back next year," says Peter Monteverdi.

LIFE
Yet again only five laps; no pre-qualification for Bruno Giacomelli.

Boutsen, Nannini and Piquet, but it was of academic interest. The race was stopped to clear the wrecks and debris. Some 26 minutes later it was restarted. Again Senna led the way, but this time it was a rocket-starting Thierry Boutsen behind him, with Berger leading Nannini, Prost and Mansell. But not for long. At Raidillon, the fearsome flat-out climbing exit from Eau Rouge, Paolo Barilla lost his Minardi, completely destroyed it and was very lucky indeed to escape unhurt.

Out came the red flags again. For the first time since Austria 1987, a Grand Prix was going to be started for a third time. Almost an hour after the first departure, the race got away successfully; in the lead for the third time was ... Ayrton Senna. He, like everyone else, had been worried about the ability of his car's transmission to stand three 650 horsepower racing starts. But it did and, as for start one, it was Berger behind him at Les Combes followed by Prost, Boutsen, Nannini, Patrese and Mansell. Senna never lost his lead, and for 13 laps the top eight remained the same, Senna, Berger, Prost, Boutsen, Patrese, Nannini, Piquet and Alesi. So where was Mansell? Answer: way behind and very unhappy. After his initial, assisted trip into the armco, Nigel had to drive the spare Ferrari. This was set up for Alain Prost, who was much smaller than him and who liked his car to oversteer — which Nigel didn't. On lap 11 he stopped for new tyres, hoping they'd cure his handling problem. He felt so strongly about it that he even discussed retiring. He didn't though, soldiering on until lap 20 when, down to 14th, he pulled out of the race, angry and demoralised. After his withdrawal from the German Grand Prix (with a car that the Ferrari team said was perfectly driveable), his decision to retire from racing and the resultant contractual arguments, Nigel was in bad odour at Maranello.

Meanwhile, on lap 14, the charging Prost had got past Berger to second and had started to close on Senna, cutting what had been a five-second gap to three and a half. Because of the three starts and the resultant extra laps, tyres were getting worn and on lap 18 Berger was the first of the leaders to stop for replacements. Two laps later, with Patrese out

Absolutely nothing went right for Nigel Mansell at Spa. As a result of his remarks after the race, his relationship with Ferrari took another step backwards.

of the race (gearbox) and Prost now less than three seconds behind Senna, it was Boutsen in third place, Nannini fourth and intending to run non-stop, Piquet fifth and Berger sixth — on new Goodyears. It is easier to pass at Spa than at many circuits ... but not when mobile road block Olivier Grouillard, who learned his trade from arch-blocker René Arnoux, is in front of you. As Ayrton Senna discovered. At half-distance, lap 22, Prost closed right up on the leading McLaren as he and Senna came in for a tyre stop that decided the race. As they did so, the unfortunate Thierry Boutsen retired opposite the pits with a broken CV joint instead of taking the lead, doubtless a casualty of the mechanical stress of those three starts.

Senna and Prost may have come in virtually together, but it was Ayrton who left first after a stop that was a full four seconds faster than Alain's. Four seconds which made all the

Nannini holds Prost at bay during their battle for second place. On fresh tyres, the Frenchman eventually squeezed ahead, but by then Senna was too far up the road. Alessandro finished fourth after another classy performance.

difference, for Senna exited the pit lane a whisker ahead of Nannini; by making his McLaren very wide indeed, he managed to stop the Italian from getting his Benetton past him and into the lead. So Ayrton was able to pull away whilst Prost struggled to catch and then pass Sandro. Which he did on lap 27, but by then Senna was nearly eight seconds ahead. With Berger now fourth on his new rubber and Piquet down to sixth, behind Gugelmin's Leyton House after a tyre stop, it was a fascinating race. Whilst Senna carved his usual intimidatory way past the midfield men, Prost fought back brilliantly. With four successive record laps he reduced Ayrton's lead to six and a half seconds on lap 31; with 13 to go, anything could happen.

Unfortunately for Alain, it did. He caught the obstinate Michele Alboreto, who blocked him. By the time he got past the Arrows he had lost four more seconds and was now over ten behind Senna. Nothing daunted, he started all over again and slowly closed the gap, including the fastest lap of the race (1m 55. 087s, 134.891 mph). Prost's charge wasn't enough though, for Senna won his 25th Grand Prix to equal the great Jim Clark and Niki Lauda. Only Prost (43) and Stewart (27) had now won more. But with the race for third very much on, the excitement was far from over. On his new tyres, Berger had been carving great lumps off Sandro Nannini's lead since he'd passed Piquet on lap 23. On lap 37, Gerhard was right with Nannini as the Italian came up behind Alex Caffi at Raidillon. Indeed he was alongside and then past the Benetton as they approached Les Combes. With adrenalin flowing by the bucketful, and probably mindful of the last contest in Hungary, when he had been punted off the circuit, Nannini retook the McLaren, banging wheels all through the two corners. How Sandro, with his tyres now looking very dodgy, kept ahead of Berger for another five laps is beyond me. But he did until, with only

Thierry Boutsen used all the road and more in a bid to please his home crowd. Sadly for the Belgian, a broken CV joint put him out when well-placed.

There was plenty for Ayrton Senna to smile about in Belgium. A new McLaren contract for 1991, a faultless race and an increased lead in the points table.

two laps left, he had a massive slide at the dreaded Raidillon and lost momentum, letting Gerhard by into the third place which he kept to the end.

Finishing between the McLarens of Senna and Berger, in a race he'd very much hoped to win, Alain Prost might have been expected to be downhearted, but he wasn't. ''The car is getting better and better and we've still got five races to go. A 13-point gap isn't all that much, and it is still possible.'' Possible maybe, but not very probable, especially with the ultra-fast Italian GP at Monza coming next — a circuit which would suit McLaren's Honda horsepower very nicely. The Benettons would be a menace too because, with Nannini fourth and Piquet fifth, Spa had shown that they were almost there. Both Senna and Berger had been more than impressed with their speed on the straight. How nice it was too to see Mauricio Gugelmin and Ivan Capelli in sixth and seventh places. It was the first time they'd both finished in a 1990 race, and it was the amiable Brazilian's first point of the year. But more and more it looked as though number one in 1991 was going to be Ayrton Senna's McLaren-Honda.

From amidst the cloud of dust and wreckage, Derek Warwick is already returning to the pits to collect his spare car for the restart!

Every Grand Prix circuit has a unique image and personality. Think of Monaco, Spa, Suzuka or Adelaide and you'll see what I mean. But when it comes to sheer motor racing charisma, Monza has them all beaten. It is the only current venue with a continuous history since the early 1920s. Although it has been modified and updated from time to time, you can still sense the spirit of the legends who have raced and won there. Ascari, Nuvolari, Farina, Clark, Caracciola, Fangio, Varzi, Moss, Rosemeyer, Stewart, Lauda, Piquet and Prost are just some of them. That's a roll call of Grand Prix greats rivalled only by Monaco; it creates a very special Monza atmosphere, heightened by the Latin passion of the *tifosi* — the knowledgeable, pro-Ferrari, flag-carrying, banner-waving, chanting, whistling enthusiasts who pack the circuit.

It's flat and it's very quick. Peter Gethin's 1971 win for BRM at 150.75 mph is still the fastest World Championship race of all time (and yes, I do know that the chicanes weren't there then!). But, despite Monza's appeal, it had been in danger of losing its Grand Prix because of old-fashioned facilities. So an absolutely massive programme of expensive improvements was implemented to overcome the many criticisms. When we got there this year, we found the finest garages, press centre and hospitality units in the world of Formula 1. More guardrails, more run-off areas, a bigger paddock, seven enormous TV screens facing the main grandstands and special booths for the marshals too. With its heady atmosphere, famous shops, restaurants and museum, it is now a magnificent complex which, in 1990, was to see a Grand Prix that would be memorable for the performances of three men — Ayrton Senna, Alain Prost and Derek Warwick.

As usual, Monza was seething with speculation about what was going to be happening next year. Equally interesting was the prospect of a battle between the McLarens and the Ferraris. Test sessions at the circuit since the Belgian GP had enabled McLaren to overcome its high-speed handling problem and Ferrari had further improved its V12 641. Senna was fastest in both the Friday sessions, but was unhappy with his Honda engine so the Japanese technicians changed it. Then on Saturday morning, after only one lap, he was in with a misfire which led to another engine change. In the afternoon, he had to abort his first two attempts to gain his 49th pole position. By the time he got out for his third try, Prost was

firmly at the top of the qualifiers with Gerhard Berger second. With only seconds to go before the end of the hour-long session, Senna catapulted out of the pits, in a car which wasn't properly set up and on tyres which were only good for one lap, to take that 49th pole position with a time that was 0.4s faster than Prost's. It was one of his most inspired achievements: ''Yes, there is a lot of emotion for me in it after all the problems.'' With Berger only 0.001s slower than Prost (who was ''very 'appy'' with his lap and the set-up of his car), Mansell fourth just 0.2s slower than Berger, the amazing Jean Alesi fifth in his underpowered Tyrrell, followed by the Williams of Boutsen and Patrese and the Benettons of Nannini and Piquet, it looked as though Sunday was going to be special.

As if to confirm as much, Prost was fastest in the morning warm-up. However, when the race began, not only did Senna blast off into an immediate lead followed by Berger but, at the second chicane, the impudent Alesi, already

Long jump: Aguri Suzuki lost it under braking for the first chicane during practice, bouncing both high and far. Bob Beamon would have been proud ... The marshals were soon on hand (inset).

First at last. After several near-misses, this was Senna's first win at Monza. Berger and Prost gave chase in the early stages, before the Frenchman moved up to take second.

past Mansell, muscled his way past Prost as well! So, in a race that was vital to his championship prospects, Alain was down from second to fourth. But it didn't go on much longer. Coming out of the 180-degree Parabolica at over 150 miles per hour, Derek Warwick, tight up behind Mauricio Gugelmin's Leyton House, lost downforce and went out of control, spearing into the armco. With wheels, suspension and bodywork flying off the disintegrating Lotus in horrifying fashion, he bounced off the metal barrier into the path of the following cars, all of which mercifully missed him. ''I was conscious all the time. As soon as the car started to slide upside down, I started to organise mentally because I was afraid of fire. As soon as the car stopped I thought of getting out, but I was scared that someone might hit me. My first reaction after that was 'I'm OK' and my second was 'spare car'!'' Almost unbelievably, Derek calmly walked to the side of the track and then broke into a vigorous run back to his pit —

to tumultuous applause from a crowd that knew a real hero and an iron man when they saw one. After a mandatory check by FISA's doctor, Professor Syd Watkins, a laughing Derek, sporting a new helmet to replace the one that had been dragged along the tarmac, was in the spare Lotus making his way round to the grid to take the second start. Because, of course, with a fragmented car in the middle of the track the race had been stopped.

The second start was an action replay of the first. Senna led away, Berger got ahead of Prost and so, to everyone's amazement, did Alesi — again! And the blue and white Tyrrell was right behind the two McLarens when they wailed across the line at the end of the lap. Indeed, not only did it stay there but Alesi's second lap was faster than anyone else's. But the effort to stay with the McLarens was too much for Jean. At the first chicane on lap five the back of the Tyrrell gracefully slid round into the barrier and he was out. ''I was right on the limit and pushing very

TEAM ANALYSIS

FERRARI
Comparative failure at team's most important GP, despite maximum effort with four cars and revised "supermotore". Prost loses pole to Senna at last moment but fastest in Sunday warm-up. Runs third to Berger for 20 laps but gets by to close within five seconds of Senna, lap 43. Despite three record laps is delayed by traffic and vibration from blistered tyres, so settles for second. Mansell starts fourth and has lonely race in fourth place, unable to challenge due to sticking throttle. Is happy to finish for only fourth time in 12 races. Amidst great applause, Prost publicly terminates 18-month feud with Senna after race.

TYRRELL
Designer Harvey Postlethwaite joins Tyrrell board. Alesi brilliant in practice. An outstanding fifth fastest on straight at 197 mph, he qualifies fifth — only beaten by McLarens and Ferraris. Charges into inspired third on both opening laps and holds place until lap five when, trying too hard, spins out of race. Excellent Nakajima drive from 14th on grid. In "perfectly balanced car" moves up through field, benefiting from retirements and tyre stops to finish sixth for second time in 1990.

WILLIAMS
Adrian Newey aerodynamic tweaks and Renault "Evolution Two" engines, but a poor result. Boutsen/Patrese sixth/seventh on grid. Thierry races seventh until lap 19 retirement with broken suspension. Patrese misses first chicane after first start, but after racing with Boutsen/Nannini for opening 18 laps finishes fifth, delayed by lack of grip and brake problems.

BRABHAM
An unhappy meeting for the financially troubled team. With misfire and handling problems, David Brabham fails to qualify for fifth time in ten outings. Stefano Modena starts 17th, but immediately drops to last due to slipping clutch. Up to 15th lap 20 but retires lap 22 (engine).

ARROWS
New floor effects aerodynamic improvement. Caffi 21st on grid and Alboreto 22nd. Alex races spare after damaging race car in morning warm-up. Finishes ninth (two laps down) with misfire and locking brakes. Alboreto also goes off in warm-up. On worn soft B compound tyres slides off on last lap trying to pass de Cesaris, but finishes 12th (three laps down).

LOTUS
Both drivers happier with much improved car after Monza tests. But whole team disheartened by news that Lamborghini engines going elsewhere in 1990. Warwick announces departure at end of season. After best qualifying results since Mexico, Donnelly starts 11th and Warwick 12th (with 0.1s between them to continue their 1990 "togetherness"). Both improve in Sunday warm-

up to ninth (Donnelly) and 12th. Derek has horrific 150 mph crash exiting the Parabolica on lap one, but is miraculously unhurt. Amazingly runs back to garage for spare car and courageously takes restart after being checked by Professor Watkins. Then retires from 13th, lap 16, with broken clutch. In his first Italian GP, Donnelly retires from promising tenth on lap 14 (spectacular engine blow-up).

OSELLA
Revised aerodynamics prove effective at Monza tests. Grouillard pre-qualifies fastest and then qualifies 23rd despite two suspension failures. Up to 16th by lap 15. With engine losing power, stops with deflating left rear tyre lap 26. Retires lap 28 (left rear wheel bearing failure).

LEYTON HOUSE
Car much improved at Monza tests. Mauricio Gugelmin equals best-yet 1990 qualifying position — tenth in France. Capelli, plagued with understeer, starts 16th. Ivan races spare car after warm-up period and climbs to praiseworthy sixth by lap 31. Then retires, lap 37, when engine dies. Gugelmin races behind Piquet and is eighth laps 19-24 before retiring, lap 25, when engine tightens.

AGS
Both drivers again pre-qualify — encouraging the hard-trying French team. Tarquini fails to qualify but Dalmas gets in 24th (and is 16th in Sunday warm-up). Into pits, lap six, with wonky gear selector. After losing five laps and then fourth gear, runs last to finish 14th but unclassified.

BENETTON
Team fails to live up to high pre-race expectations. Nannini and Piquet start eighth and ninth separated by only 0.1s. Sandro (now rumoured to be joining Ferrari in 1990, despite Benetton contract!) passes Boutsen and Patrese to sixth by lap four. Fifth after Alesi retirement and stays there laps 5-30 chasing Mansell. Stops for tyres, lap 31, and resumes eighth after long stop due to clutch problem. With car jumping out of gear under braking, caught and passed by Piquet, lap 43, and finishes eighth (one lap down). Nelson, planning non-stop run on Goodyear Bs, seventh laps 19-30 but then has left rear puncture and stops at same time as Nannini. Consternation in pits! After long (80-second) stop resumes tenth but climbs to seventh past Sandro, lap 43, and stays there to end (one lap down).

DALLARA
Pirro starts 19th and de Cesaris 25th — both on Pirelli CD96 hard compound. Emanuele races with Suzuki for 14 laps before retiring from 14th, lap 15, when missed gear causes terminal spin. De Cesaris steadily moves up field, passing Alboreto on last lap to finish tenth (two laps down) and outrageously blocking hard-charging, Senna-chasing Prost in process.

Driver of the day. Unperturbed by the enormity of his shunt, Derek Warwick gave his all after the restart. A broken clutch was poor reward. News that the team would be losing Lamborghini engines in 1991 didn't help much either ...

MINARDI

Only 28th, Barilla does not qualify. Martini does so (15th), but retires from 16th, lap eight, after spinning and breaking right rear suspension.

LIGIER

After grotty season, team encouraged by news that it is to have Lamborghini V12 engines in 1990 — thanks to heavy government support. All three cars fitted with new transverse gearbox, which gives better balance and tyre wear. But Alliot only qualifies 20th and Larini lucky to get in 26th. Both then drive reliable but slow races with Larini finishing 11th (two laps down) and Alliot 13th (minus three laps) with broken exhaust.

McLAREN

Three long pre-race test sessions at Monza eradicate previous high-speed handling problem. At Honda's 150th GP, using revised version five V10 engine, Senna takes sensational 49th pole position in final minute of Saturday qualifying, after being 28th in morning session with misfire and having only one lap to set time. His 1m 22.533s (157.201 mph) an all-time Monza record. Makes correct decision to race on softer Goodyear B compound and drives to dominant lights-to-flag first Italian GP win (his 26th in all) with record lap of 1m 26.254s (150.419 mph). Increases championship lead to commanding 16 points. Tops meeting by ending

18-month old feud with Prost with emotional handshake and embrace during post-race press conference. Berger starts third (0.001s slower than Prost). Second laps 1-20. With need to pump brakes, passed by Alain lap 21 and unable to respond due to sliding on harder A compound tyres. Finishes third, 1.4s behind Prost.

LOLA

Meeting starts with bad news that capable and well-funded team not to have Lamborghini engine in 1991, having been outbid by Ligier and new Modena team. Bernard starts 13th and Suzuki 18th — after damaging two cars in Friday and Saturday course departures. Neither finishes. Eric out lap 11 (clutch), Aguri lap 37 (electrics).

COLONI

Bertrand Gachot again does well to pre-qualify second but fails to qualify, 30th fastest.

EUROBRUN

Moreno, fifth, and Langes, sixth, fail to pre-qualify.

LIFE

After only three laps before engine blows, poor Bruno Giacomelli fails to pre-qualify for tenth time. Team talks of junking underdeveloped and brittle Life W12 motor and replacing it with Judd V8. Not before time!

Jean Alesi harried the leading McLarens for five laps before spinning off. Steady team-mate Satoru Nakajima (pictured) went the distance, however, claiming a point for sixth place.

hard, but I braked too late and that was it.'' So now Prost was third ahead of Mansell, with Nannini (up from eighth on the grid) fifth leading Patrese, Boutsen and Piquet.

And that's the way it stayed until lap 18, when Boutsen retired with broken rear suspension and Piquet moved up to seventh. Dull? Not at all, because with only 1.5 seconds covering the first three and Senna using softer Goodyear B compound tyres than Berger and Prost (who were both on the harder As), it was clear that somebody's choice was going to be wrong. Were Gerhard and Alain going to be able to push Ayrton hard enough to make him come in for new rubber? Or had Senna got it right — in which case the other two would have less grip and could have their tyres blister. Nigel Mansell, driving in his last scheduled Italian GP, was well behind in fourth place, and no threat — his throttle was sticking and he was having to lift the accelerator pedal with the sole of his racing boot!

With a crushing succession of fastest laps, Senna increased his lead on his softer tyres with Prost pushing hard but stuck behind Berger. Gerhard had a problem too, though. He was having to pump his brakes, and on lap 21 he got it wrong at the second chicane. Zap! Alain was past and now only his championship rival was ahead of him. And the other Ferrari was catching the second McLaren in spite of Mansell's throttle problem. Next came Nannini, Patrese, Piquet and Capelli (Leyton House). Lap 31 brought about the downfall of the two Benettons. Running fifth and seventh, both Nannini and Piquet intended to go through non-stop on their Goodyear Bs, but neither could. Piquet had a puncture and headed for the pits, preceded by Nannini, also on his way

Bottleneck. The first left-hander at Monza is notoriously tight. As Senna leads the rush, those in the midfield are already locking up wheels to avoid the slowing traffic ahead (facing page).

for new rubber. The result was two Benettons in àt the same time and general chaos! Sandro lost a lot of time getting out again because of a faulty clutch and Nelson was stationary for some 80 seconds, losing a lap in the process. There would be no points for either of them at Monza.

On lap 36, Senna broke his own all-time lap record (set with the turbocharged Lotus in 1987) to lead Prost by eight seconds and, with 17 of

He's there somewhere. As Senna and Berger celebrate first and third places on the rostrum, the object of the crowd's affection is obscured by banners.

the 53 laps to go, showed no sign of the tyre wear that the Ferrari pit was hoping for. But Prost wasn't giving up. ''I needed to win to improve my championship chances, but I had made the wrong tyre choice and my As were blistering and creating a big vibration whenever I speeded up.'' That didn't stop him from doing so, though; on laps 37-46 he and Senna swapped record times. Lap 37: Prost. Lap 39: Senna. Lap 41: Prost (1m 26.466s, 150.050

mph, Monza's first 150 mph race lap in its current form). Lap 42: Prost again. Lap 46: Senna, 1m 26.254 — the fastest lap of the race at 150.419 mph. On lap 43, Prost had the gap down to 5.1 seconds, but from then on it extended as the leaders hit traffic. As he always does, Ayrton dealt with it better than Alain. When Prost was outrageously blocked by the inevitable Andrea de Cesaris, who in turn was trying to pass an unhelpful Michele Alboreto, it went up to eight seconds again. In fact, with three laps to go, Senna led by 11 seconds with Prost 1.5 ahead of Berger, who led Mansell by 38 seconds. Patrese lay fifth, the only other driver on the same lap. A worthy sixth was Satoru Nakajima in the second Tyrrell, making up for team-mate Alesi's departure. And that's the way it ended. A first Italian Grand Prix win for Ayrton Senna, his 26th in all and a richly deserved reward for a brilliant drive from pole position. A win, moreover, which increased his World Championship lead over Prost to 16 points — a margin which, taking the 'best 11 scores from 16 races' rule into account, made Prost's target very hard indeed to hit. But for everyone at Monza, the best was yet to come.

Since Imola 1989, there had been a bitter feud between Senna and Prost. This had come to a head at the Japanese GP when Prost collided with his rival, leading to the Brazilian's exclusion and subsequent heavy penalisation by FISA. It seemed as though their mutual hate was to be a permanent part of the Grand Prix scene, but at the post-Monza press conference, to universal acclaim, they made it up, shook hands and briefly embraced. ''We're both professionals with the same passions,'' said Alain, ''but now we're rivals in separate teams having a fair fight for the championship. That is good for the sport and what is in the past should stay there.'' Their reconciliation was a very happy end to a memorable day.

Memorable, but a bit flat. McLaren's sixth win from 12 races gave them a massive 37-point constructors' championship lead over Ferrari. No one begrudged them that (except the *tifosi*!), because they deserved it for being the best. All the same, some variety at the front in the four remaining Grands Prix would be very welcome — and that was up to the opposition.

It looks like the start of most other Grands Prix of the past few seasons. You would never know that Mansell (third) and Prost (fifth) had started from the front row, only for Nigel's fluffed start to let the McLarens through.

"A fantastic day and, I think, a fantastic race for everybody. It's been an incredibly important day for me because I've equalled Stirling Moss's 16 Grand Prix wins." And, in the process, an ebullient Nigel Mansell had driven a brilliant race to end his run of 1990 misfortunes which, until Portugal, had brought him eight retirements from 12 races and not a single victory. But Nigel's great win in a thrilling race dominated by the "Big Four" — Prost, Mansell, Senna and Berger — wasn't the only way he gripped the public's imagination at Estoril. For the paddock was bubbling with speculation that he was going to reverse his decision to retire at the end of the season, and that he would be returning to Williams in 1991. With his followers hoping that it was true, everyone gossiped about the news that Sandro Nannini had rejected an offer to drive for Ferrari and that Nigel's place with the Prancing Horse was to be taken by the spectacular Jean Alesi — after only one full season in Formula One.

The bumpy, mountain-girdled Estoril circuit lies in the Sintra hills near Lisbon, just a few miles from the Atlantic coast and the most westerly point in Europe, the Cabo da Roca. The drivers like its 2.7 miles, featuring gradients and 11 corners of varying speed and severity, the last of which is a long, 180-degree right-hander taken at over 150 mph in fifth gear. It imposes a 4g loading on the drivers for over four seconds! With the need for grip in the turns and speed on the straight, finding the best compromise between high and low downforce is a major problem for drivers and race engineers. Selection of the right tyre compound is equally difficult.

Since there are only two places where it is possible to pass, a good grid position is vital. In the not unreasonable expectation of taking his 50th pole position (he'd been there for 33 of the last 44 races), Ayrton Senna asked for it to be repositioned on the left of the grid, where the tarmac is cleaner and the grip is better. His request was granted, but Senna wasn't the man who sat there on race day. It was Nigel Mansell, with his third pole of 1990 after a scintillating fastest-ever lap of Estoril at 132.24 mph. His team had confidently said that the circuit suited their car (Gerhard Berger had won for them in 1989). To prove they were right, Alain Prost was alongside Mansell on the grid

to make it the first all-Ferrari front row since the 1988 British Grand Prix — 37 races ago. Senna and Berger were third and fourth ahead of Patrese and Piquet, but with Satoru Nakajima withdrawing from the race due to a heavy dose of flu there'd be one less than usual facing the lights. (Only in the case of a disqualification can the 27th fastest qualifier make the grid up to the permitted 26 starters.)

In perfect weather before 80,000 spectators, and with 0.04s covering the first three, a good start for the 71-lap race was going to be as important as ever. However, from his hard-won pole position, Nigel Mansell blew it. ''I gave it full throttle, virtually spun and almost went sailing through the pit wall — and in doing so squeezed Alain out. I freely admit that and have said to Alain I'm sorry. It was the worst start of my career.'' Hardly able to believe their luck, in a situation where getting to Turn One ahead of the rest was so important, Senna and Berger rocketed to the front followed by Mansell, an

With Portugal having no F1 driver of its own as yet, though there are several young hopefuls heading in the right direction, the Estoril crowd tends to favour the Brazilians, who at least share the same language.

Pier-Luigi Martini and Derek Warwick prepare to take evasive action as Stefano Modena spins his Brabham before them.

opportunistic Piquet and a fuming Prost. ''The start decided the race. We'd done a lot of work at Fiorano to improve our starts and my car was the best today.'' (A debatable statement, since Mansell had been commandingly fastest in the morning half-hour warm-up.) But, sadly for Alain, with four cars ahead of him even *he* wasn't going to be able to win the race that was so important to his fourth World Championship chances.

For 12 laps, the first seven remained the same — Senna, Berger, Mansell, Piquet, Prost, Patrese and Boutsen. ''It was a hard race at the beginning,'' said Senna. ''Nigel was pushing Gerhard and Gerhard was pushing me. But because of the circuit they couldn't overtake, so I was able to maintain the pace I wanted to avoid compromising my tyres.'' With Ayrton controlling things from the front, Prost was recovering from his baulked start. After passing Piquet to take fourth on lap 13, he put in a series of fastest laps which took him up to the leading

train on lap 25 — ready for the tyre stops that were clearly going to be crucial. Before they began, Prost was up to third when Mansell slid wide exiting a bend and Alain shot through. And then came those vital tyre stops. Mansell was first on lap 28, in fourth and out fifth. Then Senna on lap 29. ''I waited for the right moment and stopped with traffic ahead of me. When I got back I had a clear circuit.'' His tactically perfect stop took only 6.46 seconds, and he rejoined third behind Berger and Prost. Then it was Alain's turn on lap 31. In from second place for an overlong 8.8 seconds (sticking left rear wheel), and he'd timed it wrong too. When he exited the pit lane, he was down to fifth behind Berger, Senna, Mansell and Nannini. Down to where he'd been on lap one, with it all to do again. Which he never did.

When Berger rejoined after his lap 32 tyre stop, he was third behind Senna and Mansell and chased by Prost, Nannini and Piquet as Nigel began to harry Ayrton. A new lap record

TEAM ANALYSIS

FERRARI
Excellent result from superb race. Using "best ever" qualifying engine, Mansell takes his third 1990 pole position with Prost second to give Ferrari first front row monopoly since 1988 British Grand Prix. Mansell fastest in Sunday warm-up but makes "worst start of my career." Baulks Prost and lets both Senna and Berger through. Races third until lap 27. Down to fifth after lap 28 tyre stop. Second laps 32-49 after leaders' tyre stops. Passes Senna to first, lap 50, but nearly taken out when lapping Alliot at 160mph, lap 53. Proudly wins 16th Grand Prix by 2.8 seconds to equal Stirling Moss and move up to sixth in championship. Prost down to fifth laps 1-12. Passes Piquet to fourth laps 13-26. Second to Berger laps 29-30 but leaves lap 31 tyre stop (8.8s, sticking left rear wheel) too late and rejoins fifth behind Nannini. Fights back with succession of lap records. Fourth laps 33-58. Passes Berger lap 59 but, with no fifth gear, finishes dispirited third and verbally "concedes" championship to Senna. Angry that team manager fails to order Mansell to let him pass. Strong belief that Mansell to reverse retirement decision and rejoin Williams in 1991.

TYRRELL
Alesi qualifies eighth. Flu-stricken Nakajima 20th. Still unwell, Satoru goes off in Sunday warm-up and, on Professor Watkins's advice, decides not to race. Alesi (having signed for Ferrari in 1991) also spins off on Sunday morning, but races reliably to finish eighth (one lap down). Stefano Modena to lead Tyrrell in 1991.

WILLIAMS
Amidst frenzied speculation that Nigel Mansell is to rejoin team in 1991, Patrese qualifies fifth and Boutsen seventh. Thierry races seventh behind Riccardo from lap three until lap 25 tyre stop. Retires from seventh, lap 30 (gearbox). Patrese overshoots pit and lap 27 tyre stop takes 20 seconds. Stops again for tyres, lap 52. Finishes seventh (one lap down), but makes fastest lap of race in record 1m 18.306s, 124.264 mph.

BRABHAM
Modena qualifies 24th and Brabham 26th (for first Portuguese GP). Both retire with transverse gearbox problems — Stefano from 20th, lap 23 and David from 17th, lap 40. Modena to switch to Tyrrell in 1991.

ARROWS
With all development now concentrated on '91 Porsche-powered car, Caffi 17th on grid and Alboreto 19th. Michele has reliable race with planned tyre stop to finish ninth (one lap down). Caffi, in ninth place and intending to go through non-stop on soft Goodyear C tyres, collides with Suzuki, lap 59, and is trapped in car. Race stopped to extricate him. Taken to Lisbon Hospital, where mercifully found to have no serious injuries. Classified 13th (three laps down).

LOTUS
Plagued by persistent understeer, Martin Donnelly qualifies 15th for first Portuguese GP. Dejected Derek Warwick 22nd (fully fit after massive Italian GP crash two weeks earlier). Both greatly improve in Sunday warm-up (Martin a fine sixth, Derek 11th), but both retire early. Warwick out from 17th after five laps (jammed throttle). Donnelly into pits and out of race when 11th, lap 12 (broken alternator).

OSELLA
Grouillard again pre-qualifies fastest but, only 27th, fails to qualify by 0.06s. Team owner Gabriele Rumi angrily blames Pirelli for "having failed to supply us with their new and more competitive tyre."

LEYTON HOUSE
Ivan Capelli qualifies 12th and unwell Gugelmin (virus infection) 14th. Weakened Mauricio drives uneventful race to finish 12th (two laps down) in "badly handling" car. Capelli ninth, laps 39-51, behind Patrese and Caffi. Retires lap 52 (engine).

AGS
Dalmas and Tarquini pre-qualify second and fourth. Yannick qualifies 25th but Gabriele (29th) fails to make the cut. Dalmas retires lap four (driveshaft).

BENETTON
Piquet qualifies well in sixth, Nannini ninth (after having turned down 1991 Ferrari drive). Nelson past Prost and Patrese to fourth at start. Sixth behind Nannini after lap 27 tyre stop. Finishes fifth, in points for tenth time in 13 races. Nannini fourth laps 29-32, then fifth behind Prost. Finishes sixth only 0.8s behind Piquet on new tyres. Makes second fastest lap of race after unplanned lap 53 stop. Both Benettons in points for fourth time. Reliable, but still not quite quick enough over a full race.

DALLARA
Another unimpressive meeting. Pirro 13th on grid. De Cesaris 18th. Emanuele finishes 15th (three laps down). Andrea spins out of race at first corner and sticks in gravel pit.

MINARDI
Pier-Luigi Martini re-signs for 1991 and then qualifies 16th. Races to uneventful 11th (two laps down). Barilla fails to qualify.

LIGIER
Guy Ligier achieves coup by negotiating Renault V10 engines for 1992-94 (after '91 season with the V12 Lamborghini power that his great rival Gérard Larrousse had desperately sought for his Lola team). Reliable, but slow, JS33 qualifies 21st with Alliot and 23rd with Larini. Alliot spins off car in Saturday collision with guilty De Cesaris. On Sunday, turns into race leader Nigel Mansell whilst being lapped at 160 mph (lap 52). Unsurprisingly retires in badly damaged car (Mansell and his Ferrari amazingly unscathed). Larini finishes tenth for fourth time (two laps down).

Ferrari's 1991 line-up was now public knowledge. Frenchmen Jean Alesi (left) and Alain Prost, both fluent Italian speakers, would spearhead the Maranello challenge.

McLAREN
A step nearer both drivers' and constructors' championships (again). For only second time in '90, no McLaren on front row of grid as Senna/Berger start third/fourth at circuit which "is not good for us." Mansell's bodged start enables both to pass Nigel and Prost before first corner. Senna narrowly leads pursuing Berger/Mansell/Prost until perfectly timed and brilliantly executed 6.4s tyre stop (lap 29). Back in lead lap 32 until lets Mansell through, lap 50. Happy not to fight in view of the fact that he was ahead of Prost. Finishes second to increase championship lead to seemingly unbeatable 18 points. Berger second laps 1-28 before leading laps 29-31 (Senna tyre stop). Down to third after lap 32 tyre stop. Passed by Prost lap 59. Finishes fourth 1.7s behind Alain. McLaren now lead Ferrari by 33 points in constructors' championship.

LOLA
Excellent qualifying. Bernard 10th, Suzuki 11th. Bernard retires from 14th, lap 24 (gearbox). Suzuki advances to fine seventh, laps 31-36. In for tyres, then down to 11th with brake problem. Collides with Caffi when 12th, lap 59. Trapped Caffi causes race stoppage. Aguri classified 14th (three laps down).

COLONI
Hard-trying Bertrand Gachot pre-qualifies third, but with tired engine cannot qualify.

EUROBRUN
Reluctantly driving underdeveloped and untested cars to avoid heavy fines for non-appearance, totally dispirited Moreno and Langes yet again fail to pre-qualify.

LIFE
Team dramatically fires up newly-fitted Judd V8 engine 20 minutes before end of pre-qualifying session. Long suffering Bruno Giacomelli, who deserves better, sets off but fails to re-appear.

Rivals on the track, Ayrton Senna and Nigel Mansell ...

...are apparently now quite friendly off it. Overjoyed at having equalled Stirling Moss's 16 wins (a record for an English driver), Nigel congratulates Ayrton on his second place during the rostrum celebrations.

on lap 33 took him almost up to the McLaren's gearbox and on lap 41 he was there. Lapping as one, it was a vivid reminder that their collision the year before had led to their retirement and Nigel's exclusion from the following Spanish GP. They scythed their way past backmarkers until, on lap 50, the pressured Senna moved over to let Mansell through. "Nigel was coming up fast behind me like last year. I didn't have to win and it wasn't worth compromising the championship. So I made a sign where to pass." And Nigel passed! Up to first with a two-second lead, he came alongside 15th-placed Philippe Alliot on lap 53 "flat in sixth in the right-handed Turn Two at 160mph." Alliot was "fighting with Martini and I never saw Nigel coming." The blue Ligier and the scarlet Ferrari collided and Philippe speared into the armco, his car shedding wheels; amazingly, he emerged unscathed. Miraculously, Mansell

raced on. However, the incident had enabled Senna, Berger and Prost (right with the Austrian after a series of record laps) to close up on Nigel, followed by Piquet and Nannini, now fifth and sixth after tyre stops (Sandro's unplanned as he had intended to go through non-stop on Goodyear's harder B compound).

We anticipated another 18 thrilling laps of wheel-to-wheel fighting for supremacy between the world's four top drivers, imagining a scenario whereby Prost, now the quickest man on the track, would somehow get past Berger and Senna to be waved through on the last corner by a generous Mansell, selflessly forfeiting his first 1990 victory to maximise Alain's championship chances!

For lap after lap, the Famous Four thrilled us by circulating, nose-to-tail (even though, we subsequently discovered, Prost had lost his fifth gear). Then, on lap 59, Alain scrambled past

Weekend to forget. Philippe Alliot had his Ligier written off for him by an inattentive de Cesaris on Saturday. In the race, he came together with Mansell at 160 mph and crashed again ...

The flu-stricken Satoru Nakajima damaged his Tyrrell in Sunday's warm-up. Heeding medical advice, he withdrew from the race.

Berger to third. One down. Two to go! He had 12 laps to get by Senna and then gratefully take the lead from his sacrificial team-mate! But it wasn't to be. For, on their 59th lap, Caffi and Suzuki, battling for ninth, collided and spun off — Alex careering heavily into the armco. With Caffi trapped in his Arrows and receiving medical assistance, the race was stopped with ten laps still to go. A wise and correct decision, but one which denied us what would undoubtedly have been a nail-biting finish.

So, from pole position, Mansell brilliantly won his 16th Grand Prix in spite of that bodged start, thus equalling Stirling Moss's achievement that rightly meant so much to him. Senna was second, Prost third, Berger fourth and a mere 5.9 seconds covered the four of them. Piquet was fifth, only 0.8s ahead of his rapidly closing team-mate Nannini, and Riccardo Patrese seventh with a record lap 56 (1m 18.306s, 124.264 mph) on a third fresh set of tyres.

A great race for Mansell, Ferrari, the spectators, TV viewers and a contented Senna, who had finished ahead of Prost to increase his already substantial championship lead by another two points. Not so for a dispirited, depressed Alain, who felt that Ferrari should have ordered Mansell to let him through (and, therefore, Senna too!). If it had happened, Prost could have been worse off, with a winning Senna increasing his lead by three points. ''I'm very disappointed and don't want to think any more about the championship. We've done a lot of work and nothing is going right.'' In fact, mathematically he could still retain his number one for 1991, but in order to do so he'd have to win every one of the remaining three races. Against a very hungry, utterly dedicated Senna backed by the in-depth strength of the highly organised, devastatingly efficient McLaren-Honda team, that seemed more than unlikely. Stranger things *had* happened, but not too often.

We'd see in Spain, one weekend later!

Exit stage left. Having been nudged by Berger, Alesi's punctured Tyrrell heads for an early gravel bath.

At 13.51 on Friday, September 28, a concerted gasp of horror stilled the clamour and hubbub in the press room at Jerez. The television monitors showed the motionless, hideously contorted body of a driver lying on the track, still belted into his seat. The distinctive orange and blue helmet design instantly identified him as Martin Donnelly. As he lay there, it seemed inconceivable that he could still be alive. In 12th place on the timing screens, with only nine minutes of the session to go, Martin had been trying to improve his grid position when something broke in his Lotus-Lamborghini's front suspension. He cannoned off the track and into the armco at the kink just before the 150 mph Ferrari Curve. As it was designed to, the front of the car exploded into fragments of carbon fibre to absorb much of the force of the impact. However, it was the skill and leadership of FISA's Grand Prix doctor, Professor Syd Watkins, backed up by the circuit hospital and the helicopter which lifted Martin's broken body to advanced medical facilities in Seville, that saved the popular Ulsterman.

Immensely relieved by the news that his life was not in danger, his shaken rivals returned to the track to complete the session. Callous and uncaring? I don't think so. Of course they cared that a friend and fellow racer had been seriously injured, but their staying in the pits wouldn't have made things any better for Martin. Motor racing is dangerous and, although progress is constantly being made to minimise the risks, it always will be. Nobody who competes can be unaware, deep down, that they are vulnerable. Two people at Jerez were particularly conscious of that — Donnelly's team-mate Derek Warwick and the intensely religious Ayrton Senna. Both of them went to the circuit hospital to be with Martin and Senna spent a long time at the scene of the accident. Later, alone, he contemplated its significance. Having done so, he got into his McLaren and, with another of his awe-inspiring laps, took the provisional pole position for the 1990 Spanish Grand Prix. On Saturday afternoon, he went even quicker with the

Martin Donnelly and fiancée Diane McWhirter are one of the most popular couples in the Grand Prix paddock. The Ulsterman's fearsome qualifying accident came as a tremendous shock to everyone.

fastest-ever lap of Jerez to claim his 50th pole position. It was a great achievement, but it was naturally overshadowed by the gravity of Donnelly's accident, about which Senna spoke most movingly at the pole position conference. In a way, Warwick's achievement was even greater. For on Saturday afternoon, not really knowing what had caused his friend's accident and having agonised about whether to drive at all, he went out in his Lotus, now fitted with strengthened versions of the suspect components, to go faster than before and to take an outstanding tenth place on the grid. Grand Prix drivers are truly a very special breed.

Spain marked the last European Grand Prix of the year, and it looked as though it was going to be the race which gave Ayrton Senna his second World Championship. Alain Prost, depressed at having had his strong possibility of victory in Portugal destroyed by Nigel Mansell's appalling start, had been very angry with Ferrari. He saw it as a lack of managerial competence and strategic planning (for which read "I don't think Cesare Fiorio is up to the job"), and had more or less conceded the title. But after long talks with Fiat's top brass, Alain had regained his resolve at Jerez. He showed it by taking second place on the grid, well knowing that, on a circuit where passing is well nigh impossible, he had to be at the front. Nigel Mansell was third and happy to be there so that "Alain can make his own start this time." Jean Alesi was a brilliant fourth ahead of Berger, Patrese, Boutsen, Piquet and Nannini, but made a prophetic statement before the race. "My big worry tomorrow is not to hit another car at the start."

Which is exactly what he did — although it wasn't his fault. In the high-speed jostling up to the first corner, Berger side-swiped Alesi, who slewed into a fast-starting Patrese. Riccardo's Williams was damaged, but he sped on. A crestfallen Jean, stuck in the gravel trap, had to make his fuming way back to the pit lane to report to a doubtless unimpressed Ken Tyrrell.

Jerez, in the sun-baked hills of Andalusia and ringed by the Sierra Morena mountains, is generally acknowledged to be the most tiring and demanding circuit of them all. It is invariably

Derek Warwick did a heroic job for Lotus in the wake of Donnelly's accident. Having qualified 10th, he ran as high as sixth before his gearbox packed up.

very hot (some 34 degrees on race day 1990), very hard indeed on both car and driver and provides nowhere to relax. Brakes on. Brakes off. Constant acceleration and deceleration, very wearing on the tyres. It was where the 1990 world title would be decided if Prost did not win. The chips were down.

Leaving the first corner fracas behind them, the two championship leaders blasted round the opening lap absolutely together. Nigel Mansell lay just behind, hotly pursued by the 21 survivors (for the second Grand Prix in succession, only 25 drivers had set off due to Donnelly's absence). For 18 laps, there were no changes among the first 14 places. Senna led with Prost snapping at his gearbox, but the Brazilian was relaxed. Knowing that the colossal grunt of his Honda V10 would keep him ahead on acceleration out of the vital hairpin, and that there was nowhere else that Alain would be able to get by, he raced at a pace which suited his tyres. Mansell was about two seconds behind Prost, followed by Berger, Boutsen, Patrese (hampered by a damaged front left wing skirt), Piquet, Nannini and Warwick (well done Derek!). "This time we

planned a strategy," said Alain. "I always intended to try to pass Ayrton in the pits." By which he meant that tyre stops were again going to be critical, with two stops a possibility in order to minimise race time. Mansell came in first, from third place, on lap 20 of 73. It took 8.6 seconds, and he dropped to seventh. And when he got going he found that, as at Monza, he had a sticking throttle. "Just like a turbo. It wanted to go on when I lifted off." Just the job at Jerez! Then it was Berger's turn on lap 21; in third, out sixth. But with Senna and Prost still together, first and second, who was going to take the initiative? Prost was! With no way to get past Ayrton on the track, he came in on lap 25. This time, unlike Portugal, the Ferrari mechanics got it absolutely right — 6.17 seconds. Excellent! And it only lost Alain two places. He rejoined fourth behind Senna, Piquet and Mansell. Hold your breath — here comes Senna! Lap 27, but he was slightly delayed by Yannick Dalmas's AGS as he approached the pit lane entrance. It was a great stop though — 5.71 seconds.

As Ayrton rocketed out of the pits, Mansell was there, moving over to let Prost through

TEAM ANALYSIS

FERRARI
Brilliant championship-saving repeat of Mexico one-two. After bitterly criticising "lack of Ferrari management and strategy" following his Portuguese setback (and hinting at 1991 team change or retirement), Prost placated by top Fiat management and regains resolve to fight for championship. Determined second on grid and impressively fastest in Sunday warm-up. Second, harrying Senna, laps 1-24. Down to fourth after lap 25 tyre stop but up to second behind Piquet, laps 27-28, thanks to team-mate Mansell's co-operation as Senna exits pits after tyre stop. Passes Nelson to lead, lap 29. In car that suits Jerez, draws away to fifth GP win of 1990, having made second precautionary tyre stop, lap 51. Closes to within nine points of Senna in championship. Mansell starts third and races with Senna/Prost until lap 20 tyre stop. Down to seventh. Selflessly lets Alain through, lap 29, as Senna exits pits. Third laps 42-51. Despite sticking throttle, finishes second to Prost after Senna's retirement (lap 52). Up to fourth in championship. Ferrari now within 18 points of McLaren in constructors' contest. On Monday after race, Nigel announces much-welcomed intention to race for Williams in 1991.

TYRRELL
Alesi superb in practice. Fastest on Saturday morning and qualifies fourth. Collides with Berger and Patrese on approach to first corner ("Gerhard pushed me off") and immediately retires with broken left rear wheel. Nakajima starts 14th and spins out of race, lap 14.

WILLIAMS
Patrese qualifies sixth and Boutsen (who will drive for Ligier in 1991) seventh. Thierry up to third, laps 21-24. Seventh after lap 25 tyre stop. Collides with Berger when fourth, lap 57, but survives to finish fourth on completely worn tyres. Patrese barged over kerb by Alesi on run up to first corner after start. Resultant damage causes two tyre stops (laps 20 and 49), but still finishes fifth and sets fastest lap (record) on new tyres, lap 53 (1m 24.513s, 111.644 mph). Re-signs for 1991 as team-mate to Nigel Mansell.

BRABHAM
Brabham 27th fastest in practice. Team requests permission for him to race, after Donnelly accident causes Martin's withdrawal. This refused. Modena drives spare car after qualifying 24th. Retires from 21st after being harpooned by Dalmas.

ARROWS
Bernd Schneider substitutes for Caffi as Alex not fit after Portugal crash. Fails to qualify and incurs Prost's wrath by baulking Alain during his hot qualifying lap. Alboreto starts 25th ("no grip") and finishes steady tenth (two laps down).

LOTUS
Whole Spanish GP meeting marred by appalling accident to Martin Donnelly, who smashes into armco at some 150 mph when "something in the front suspension" breaks. Gravely injured, but miraculously alive, Martin helicoptered to Seville hospital with multiple leg injuries and other breakages, but pronounced to be out of danger. Thank God for Professor Syd Watkins, who dominates medical proceedings. Derek Warwick agonises about whether to start and courageously decides to do so after suspect suspension elements beefed up. Then qualifies superb tenth. Even better eighth fastest in Sunday warm-up. Gritty sixth when makes lap 23 tyre stop. Eighth at second tyre stop, lap 52, but has to retire with broken gearbox, lap 64. Unfortunate Lotus team's cup of misery flowing over.

OSELLA
Grouillard sails through pre-qualification (third) and qualifies 21st. Retires from 14th, lap 46, with broken rear wheel bearing (again).

LEYTON HOUSE
Both Ivan Capelli and Mauricio Gugelmin re-sign for

The Williams team fettles Riccardo Patrese's FW13B during qualifying. The Italian survived a startline skirmish to finish fifth.

1991. Mauricio qualifies 12th despite heavy virus infection and ill-handling car. Advances to praiseworthy sixth, lap 57, but slides down to finish eighth (one lap down) with broken clutch. Capelli starts 19th and fights up to eighth before having to retire from ninth, lap 61, with acute leg cramp (a by-product of the Leyton House's confined cockpit?).

Jerez marked another milestone in the remarkable career of Ayrton Senna, the Brazilian chalking up his 50th pole position.

AGS
Tarquini and Dalmas *both* pre-qualify and qualify (22nd and 23rd) for the first time in 1990. Gabriele has wheel come loose on parade lap and runs in for spare. Retires on lap six (electrics). Yannick collides with Modena on lap seven but soldiers on for highest 1990 finish to date (ninth, one lap down).

BENETTON
So near and yet so far. Designer Rory Byrne's last race with team before joining fledgling Reynard Formula One organisation. Piquet qualifies eighth (0.1s faster would have been fourth!) and intends to race non-stop on Goodyear Bs. Progresses to second, laps 25/26, and then leads a GP for the first time since Italy '87 (Williams), laps 27/28. Slides wide at bend and lets Prost and Senna through. Long stop from third, lap 42 (battery problem). Rejoins before retiring with return of misfire, lap 48, but makes second fastest lap of race, lap 44 (1m 25.095s).

Nannini starts from ninth on Cs. New tyres when sixth, lap 20. Rejoins 11th and advances to third, lap 52. Stays there to end of race for third 1990 podium finish.

DALLARA
Pirro qualifies 16th and de Cesaris 17th. Emanuele slides out of contention lap one (sand-blocked throttle slides). De Cesaris starts 17th. Into pits from 14th, lap 26, with brake problem. Rejoins last to continue until lap 47 retirement (dropped valve).

MINARDI
Martini 11th and happy on grid. Ninth at lap 21 tyre stop. Resumes 14th. Tenth laps 32-40 but retires lap 41 (wheel nut failure). Paolo Barilla fails to qualify and likely to be dropped for last two races.

LIGIER
Thierry Boutsen signed for 1991/92. Alliot qualifies happy 13th and Larini 20th. Philippe spins into sand trap when well-placed eighth, lap 23, and cannot get out. Nicola has best ever finish (seventh, one lap down) after two tyre stops.

McLAREN
Team uses revised front suspension, new floorpan, rear wing and diffuser after post-Italy tests at Hungaroring. Senna takes emotional 50th pole position. In situation where seventh 1990 victory would clinch championship, narrowly leads Prost laps 1-26. Rejoins third after lap 27 tyre stop and is second behind Prost, laps 29-51. Into pits, lap 52, with suspected puncture. Transpires to be water on right rear tyre from perforated radiator. Rejoins sixth but retires, lap 54. No points and lead over Prost now down to nine. "This is the worst possible situation for the championship." Berger fifth on grid (using B tyres) and side-swipes Alesi on run up to first corner. Third at lap 21 tyre stop. Down to sixth and then fifth, laps 25-41. Second tyre stop from fourth, lap 44. Collides with Boutsen when trying optimistic passing move for fourth, lap 57, and out of race. McLaren constructors' championship lead over Ferrari down to 18 points.

LOLA
Suzuki and Bernard start 15th and 18th. Aguri drives excellent race to take second sixth place of the season with no problems. Eric races with Suzuki until lap 21, when gearbox breaks up to cause retirement.

COLONI
Another good effort by Bertrand Gachot to pre-qualify fourth, but again fails to get into race by qualifying 29th.

EUROBRUN
Another sad failure to pre-qualify by both Moreno and Langes. Moreno tipped for well-deserved drive with Brabham in 1991.

LIFE
After yet another all-nighter, the totally disorganised team fails to give Giacomelli the chance to pre-qualify. Only two laps this time ...

Prost harried Senna for all he was worth in the opening stages, without ever being able to pass. The Frenchman gambled on getting ahead during the first round of tyre stops. His strategy worked to perfection, and his championship chances were rekindled when Senna retired with a holed radiator.

Thierry Boutsen's rear-view mirrors were largely filled with red and white as the race drew to its close. Eventually, the Belgian survived a savaging from the impetuous Gerhard Berger to take fourth.

("with my throttle problem I wanted him to get by me before the twisty bits"). As he did so Senna, on his pre-warmed tyres, jinked through from left to right and somehow got by the Ferrari before the corner (Mansell: "It was very close indeed, but we both made it and I definitely held him up a bit!"). So now it was Nelson Piquet in the lead for the first time since Italy '87 (Williams-Honda), ahead of Prost, Senna,

Mansell, Berger and Nannini. Benetton, Ferrari, McLaren, Ferrari, McLaren, Benetton — with Boutsen and Capelli seventh and eighth.

On lap 29, Nelson blew it. Racing on Goodyear Bs in an effort to go through non-stop, he slid wide on a corner and let Prost and Senna through. So now the two championship contenders were first and second again — but in reverse order to the first 24 laps. Which made

Jerez is smack in the heart of Spain's sherry-producing region. The locals do their best to draw your attention to that fact during the GP weekend; pity there's never much of a crowd to take notice.

After Prost's post-Portugal disgruntlement, it was all smiles again in Spain as he and Mansell chalked up a Ferrari 1-2.

all the difference. Prost's Ferrari was the better car at Jerez, and he strode away from Senna's McLaren to build a lead of over 20 seconds by lap 40. But Senna wasn't too unhappy. Of course, he desperately wanted to win to clinch the championship, but second place would increase the total of his best 11 scores by another two points. He'd settle for that in a situation where he clearly couldn't catch Prost. It didn't work out like that though. Piquet and Mansell were too close for comfort. Although Nelson sadly went into the pits on lap 42, with a battery problem which subsequently caused his retirement, Nigel was still there to keep up the pressure. And on lap 52 he was second! From the commentary box, we'd seen what looked like oil smoke from Senna's car. But it wasn't, it was steam. A wing stay from Dalmas's AGS had penetrated the McLaren radiator.

Ayrton thought his handling problem was a puncture, and so it was, but not a punctured tyre. The punctured radiator was spurting water on to his right rear tyre. In he came for new boots, but three laps later he retired with his engine temperature off the clock.

So Alain Prost won his second Spanish Grand Prix with supportive team-mate Nigel Mansell second to give Ferrari their second one-two of 1990. And, far more importantly for Alain, nine points for victory brought him to within nine of Senna's total, keeping his World Championship hopes alive. At minimum, he'd have to win one of the two remaining races and finish at least second ahead of Senna in the other, but it was possible!

Spain certainly wasn't McLaren's day. With Senna out, Berger was fifth on lap 56 after a second tyre stop — and going for fourth. As he and Boutsen took the final hairpin, he dived inside the Williams in a way that Thierry described as "a bit optimistic." It certainly was, for as the Belgian turned in he wheel-banged Berger's car front and rear to bundle it out of the race. Nothing ventured nothing gained, I suppose, but that's exactly what Gerhard gained — nothing! And he lost two points.

So Nannini was third, the determined Boutsen fourth, Patrese fifth (and, for the third time in 1990, he set the fastest lap — 1m 24.513s on lap 53, a record 111.644 mph). And an excellent sixth was Aguri Suzuki (Lola). "I'm not just happy about winning," said Alain. "I'm happy about the way we won. The car was magnificent, we planned a strategy which involved me passing Ayrton in the pits and Nigel helped me a lot. The championship is still very difficult but it can be done." It was a great Spanish Grand Prix, but sadly it will long be remembered as the meeting at which the unfortunate Martin Donnelly so very nearly lost his life.

As a postscript though, and to end on a more cheerful note, there were cheers all round when, on the Monday after the race, the long-running "What is Nigel Mansell going to do in 1991?" saga came to an end. He made the very welcome announcement that he had decided not to retire and that he would be driving for Williams-Renault. Hooray!

Crunchpoint. As Prost swings in to the first turn, Senna refuses to give way on his right. Seconds later both were embedded in the gravel trap, out of the race. Prost was unamused, Senna was the new World Champion and animosity between the two was sharply rekindled.

With the benefit of hindsight, it's easy to see that the Japanese Grand Prix was an accident waiting to happen, just as it had been in 1989. At both events the sport's top two men, Ayrton Senna and Alain Prost, were the only ones in contention for the World Championship. In 1989, as bitter rivals in the McLaren team, they resolved the battle by driving into each other, leaving Prost with the title while Senna was disqualified after winning the race. In 1990 they were in different teams, and they shared a warmer relationship following their reconciliation at Monza. But the stakes and the tension were very high indeed.

With six wins to his credit, the second title that Senna craved would be his if he won at Suzuka. The track is owned by Honda, McLaren's engine supplier. They were equally anxious to succeed — especially as they'd powered only one of Suzuka's three Japanese GP winners. But, once again, the opposition was Prost. With five victories, he needed to win in both Japan and Australia to gain his fourth championship. Everything was going to depend on grid positions, because Suzuka has a major problem. There's only one place to pass — the ludicrous chicane at the end of the convoluted 3.64-mile lap. That's where Alain and Ayrton had interlocked in 1989. Clearly, both of them needed to be on the front row.

But if a repeat collision featuring a McLaren and a Ferrari seemed likely at Suzuka, Benetton had already had their accident. For the personable Alessandro Nannini was in hospital after a nine-hour operation to replace his right forearm, severed in a helicopter crash near his Siena home. Amazingly, Sandro seemed set to recover. Sadly, it appeared doubtful that he would ever race again. His place at the Japanese Grand Prix (where, ironically, he had inherited victory in 1989) was to be taken by Grand Prix racing's Mr Nice Guy, Roberto Moreno, a close friend and protégé of Nelson Piquet. Roberto would thus be number two to his hero for his first drive in a competitive car. In Japan, this all-Brazilian partnership was to be unimaginably successful.

The drama at Suzuka started early. With the more than reasonable expectation of being the fastest man in practice, Senna, as he had successfully done three times before, asked for pole position to be switched from the right-hand side of the grid, where the grip was inferior, to the left. So when he duly got his 51st pole position, with a stupefying lap in the closing seconds of the last qualifying session, he was outraged to find that his request had been refused. He was thus to be penalised at the most important time of the race — the start. "It negates all the hard work you do to get there," he said. His concern was compounded by the knowledge that the main beneficiary was Alain Prost. Because, with a smooth and flowing lap that was just as impressive as Senna's, Prost had been second fastest.

Obviously, both Honda and Ferrari were making a very special effort at Suzuka. Honda had produced another evolution of their V10 engine for McLaren, while Ferrari had modified their V12's induction system in the name of extra power and better throttle response. Sunday's 20-minute pre-race practice showed that, in race trim, the Ferraris had the edge. Mansell was fastest with Prost next, half a second faster than Senna. Half a second multiplied by 53 laps equals nearly half a minute. With a better

Gianni Morbidelli replaced Paolo Barilla at Minardi,
prior to a full season with the team in 1991.

chassis than the McLaren, Prost was confident. Always providing, of course, that he could exploit his superior grip and get to the first corner in front of Senna from his left-side grid slot.

He did. After a magnificent start, which began with his Ferrari a full car's length behind Senna, he was cleanly ahead of the McLaren when he turned in to the first right-hander. Only to be rammed by Senna's McLaren ... He spun off into a wide, soft gravel trap from which there was no escape. Senna was there too. It was 1989 revisited, except that this time neither of them was going anywhere except back to the pits on foot. Senna was now the 1990 World Champion, without so much as completing one race lap in Japan.

Now it's easy to pontificate about a collision, but Senna was wildly optimistic in trying to pass where he did. Prost was ahead, on the racing line, and clearly would not yield. Nor should Ayrton have tried to get by, in the opinion of most experts. ''But maybe he didn't care. All he had to do was to take Prost out to win the championship. He had nothing to lose, but Prost did. Alain should have given him room and fought back later.'' A contentious viewpoint, but right or wrong it was irrelevant. Both championship contenders were out. The enormous crowd had been denied what they'd come to see, and the recently resolved bitterness between them had been violently rekindled. It was every bit as bad publicity for Formula One as their similar coming-together the previous year had been.

But the Japanese Grand Prix wasn't just a race for two people. It was a race for 25 (for the third time running the grid was one short, Jean Alesi non-starting having strained neck muscles in a practice crash). Gerhard Berger was in the lead, after a meteoric start which took him past Mansell's Ferrari and well clear of his pursuers. With a clear track in front of him, this was Gerhard's chance to score his first win in a McLaren after a very disappointing season. But, almost unbelievably, he blew it at the start of the

There was plenty of pre-race razzamatazz, but the huge crowd's hopes of a gripping contest were marred by the first corner accident which took the sheen off the championship crown.

TEAM ANALYSIS

FERRARI

Bitter disappointment over way championship hopes dashed. With revised engine (butterfly induction for greater power and cleaner throttle response), Prost and Mansell second and third on grid and impressive first (Mansell) and second in pre-race warm-up. From left-hand side of grid, Prost exploits grip advantage and leads Senna into first corner only to be rammed during Ayrton's contentiously aggressive passing attempt. Alain walks in with championship hopes destroyed. Mansell takes lead after Berger spins off on lap two. In for tyres with eight-second lead on lap 27. After superb 5.2-second stop, driveshaft universal joint breaks as he accelerates out of pit lane. Retires, angrily frustrated, for ninth time in 15 races. FISA chief Jean-Marie Balestre and Ferrari team manager Cesare Fiorio both castigate Senna, but no protest made or action taken. Prost and Ferrari must now settle for second place in their championships, with the recently-healed Prost/Senna feud vividly renewed.

TYRRELL

Alesi sixth fastest in Friday qualifying despite massive ''off'' which severely wrenches neck muscles and causes withdrawal from event. Satoru Nakajima drives great race on home track. From 14th on grid (eighth in Sunday warm-up) to ninth on lap two. After long battles with Herbert and Warwick (and 6.3s lap 25 tyre stop), into points by lap 35. Stays there to end of race to take third sixth place of season.

WILLIAMS

A very disappointing race. Both drivers again complain of understeer when qualifying fifth (Boutsen) and eighth (Patrese). On Goodyear C compound tyres, Boutsen races fine until long tyre stop (13.1s, sticking left rear wheel) from which he resumes tenth. Up to fifth, lap 27, and stays there to finish. Another cracking race by Patrese. On harder compound B tyres, races fifth behind Thierry laps 2-20. Profiting from tyre stops, runs third laps 27-36 but then obliged to stop for new rubber. Rejoins fourth and makes fastest lap of race (fourth time in 1990 and third in succession) on lap 40 (1m 44.233s, 126.63 mph). Finishes fourth. Williams drop to fourth in constructors' contest as result of fine Benetton one-two.

BRABHAM

Unimpressive meeting in front of Japanese owners, following welcome announcement that Martin Brundle to rejoin team in 1991. Modena qualifies 22nd and Brabham 23rd. Stefano out at first corner after being ''pushed off by Alliot.'' David out on lap three with major clutch problem.

ARROWS

Alboreto and Caffi re-sign for 1991 when team is to be renamed Footwork-Porsche. Both drivers break gearbox mainshafts on Friday but qualify 24th (Caffi) and 25th in

front of Japanese management. They collide with each other at first corner, leaving Alboreto with damaged front suspension. Caffi has another reliable run to finish ninth (one lap down), but Alboreto retires from 11th, lap 29 (engine).

LOTUS

With Martin Donnelly making slow progress from his severe injuries, Lotus reserve driver Johnny Herbert joins team and qualifies well (15th) for first GP since Belgium 1989 (Tyrrell). Warwick, having resignedly ageed to drive for Jaguar in Group C in 1991, starts 12th. Both then drive excellent races. Derek superbly in points (sixth, laps 2-6), until passed by fired-up Suzuki. Resumes tenth after lap 21 tyre stop, but retires from seventh, lap 39 (gearbox). Inspired Herbert re-establishes his reputation by chasing Warwick and taking sixth place in difficult car (lap 22) before retiring from eighth (lap 32, engine) after lap 26 tyre stop.

OSELLA

No pre-qualifying. Grouillard 27th fastest and does not qualify.

LEYTON HOUSE

Another team which disappoints its Japanese patrons. Capelli and Gugelmin start 13th and 16th. Ivan goes off avoiding Suzuki at first corner, then has to pit twice with electrical problem before retiring, lap 17. Mauricio retires from 12th, lap six, when ''engine just stopped.''

AGS

No pre-qualification necessary, but neither Tarquini (28th) nor Dalmas (29th) qualifies.

BENETTON

With Nannini in hospital after having severed forearm replaced, following post-Spain helicopter crash, saddened team recruits Roberto Moreno (available after Eurobrun's withdrawal). Piquet qualifies sixth and Roberto a superb ninth in his first top-team car. Both drivers make inspired choice to start on harder B compound Goodyear tyres for planned non-stop race. Piquet takes lead, lap 27, after Prost, Senna, Berger and Mansell retirements. Stays there, nursing tyres, to win his 21st GP (and first since Monza 1987). Up to fourth in championship and earns bonus of some £450,000! Moreno achievement equally creditable. From ninth on grid, having had to change to spare car (set up for Nelson) after parade lap problem, moves up to amazing third behind Piquet, lap two. Calmly stays there, making no mistakes, and moves up to second following lap 27 Mansell retirement. Having failed even to pre-qualify ten times in 14 races with Eurobrun, finishes second to his friend and mentor Nelson Piquet to give Benetton their first ever one-two.

DALLARA

Lacklustre meeting. Pirro starts 19th with cracked finger bone after Friday shunt and retires from 12th, lap 25 (engine). De Cesaris qualifies 26th and spins out of race from last but one, lap 14.

Johnny Herbert substituted for the injured Martin Donnelly. As the Ulsterman continued his slow recovery in a London hospital, Herbert climbed as high as fifth before retiring. The following Satoru Nakajima delighted the crowd by claiming the final championship point.

MINARDI
Ferrari test driver Gianni Morbidelli replaces Paolo Barilla and starts 20th before spinning out of 13th place and into retirement, lap 19. Pier-Luigi Martini qualifies well (11th) and races to reliable eighth (one lap down).

LIGIER
Once again, slow but reliable. Larini qualifies 18th and finishes seventh (one lap down). Alliot starts 21st after going off twice on Friday. Collides with Modena at first corner but finishes tenth (one lap adrift).

McLAREN
Two championships won in undistinguished circumstances. Using further revised Honda engine, and benefiting from McLaren's exclusive testing access to Honda-owned Suzuka, Senna takes inspired 51st pole position. Berger starts fourth. Ayrton vigorously complains about rejection of his request for pole position to be moved from "dirty" right side of track to "clean" left. "It negates all the hard work done to earn it." (True, and precedents existed to justify changing it.) Later walks out of Sunday drivers' briefing meeting in emotional state. Outdragged by Prost to first corner (proving his point about grid). Tries to pass Alain on inside but takes both himself and his World Championship rival out of race with early repeat of their 1989 collision. Walks back to pit as tarnished 1990 World Champion. FISA boss Jean-Marie Balestre roundly condemns Senna, but no action taken or protest made by Ferrari despite fierce contention by outraged team manager Cesare Fiorio that race ought to have been stopped. Senna unmoved by criticism. "No regrets. It was a result of the incorrect pole position decision and just one of those things." Berger, now in lead, makes complete porridge of McLaren's race by sliding into sand trap at same corner on second lap. Second successive "no points" race for team, but Senna and McLaren now unbeatable in their 1990 World

Championships. Not, however, admired for the way they finally achieved them.

LOLA
Another Japanese-owned team, but this one finishes with head held very high. On home circuit, which he knows well, Aguri Suzuki tenth on grid but more significantly sixth in Sunday warm-up. Then drives absolute blinder of race. In points (sixth) by lap seven. After lap 25 tyre stop, up to fourth with series of fastest laps. To third when Patrese makes tyre stop, lap 37, and finishes there, with second fastest lap of race, to become first-ever Japanese driver to finish on podium. Well done! Eric Bernard starts 17th before retiring from 11th, lap 25 (oil leak/engine fire).

COLONI
Bertrand Gachot, 30th, fails to qualify after heavy off on Friday.

EUROBRUN and **LIFE** teams, impoverished and virtually certain not to qualify, withdraw from last two races, thereby cancelling need for pre-qualification for Osella, AGS and Coloni drivers.

It was announced in Japan that the Arrows team was to be renamed Footwork-Porsche in 1991. The German company's new V12 was unveiled in Japan. Alex Caffi and Michele Alboreto joined in the celebration with good reason; both had been retained by the team for the following season.

Nigel Mansell looked to have the race in the bag, until his transmission gave out as he left the pits following a tyre stop. Here, he contemplates his future prospects in the company of 1991 employer Frank Williams.

Roberto Moreno proved to be an inspired choice for Benetton. At the helm of a competitive F1 car for the first time in his career, the brilliant Brazilian came home second. His thoughts, however, were very much with Sandro Nannini (inset). The Italian lost his right forearm in a helicopter accident 10 days before the race, placing his driving career in serious jeopardy.

second lap when he slewed off into the same gravel trap that had claimed Prost and Senna. For the second Grand Prix in succession, McLaren were to score no points. Team supremo Ron Dennis, anxious to do well in Honda country, must have been considerably less than delighted with his two drivers. The drivers' and, later, constructors' championships may well have been McLaren's, but the way they were finally achieved was certainly not to be admired.

Prost out. Senna out. Berger out. Mansell leads! Piquet was close behind him, followed by Roberto Moreno! From eighth on the grid, the little Brazilian had passed Patrese and Boutsen and was now headed only by his team leader and Mansell. Benetton's main objective before the race was to take third place from Williams in the constructors' championship. They'd decided to use Goodyear's harder B compound tyres in an effort to go through non-stop, and their cars were set up with plenty of downforce to maximise adhesion. Now, with both their drivers ahead of Boutsen and Patrese, running fourth and fifth, they were in a position to do so — assuming Moreno, unused even to pre-qualifying his Eurobrun let alone completing a whole gruelling race, could go the distance. Not only did he do so, but he calmly sat just behind Piquet, showing no sign of fatigue or susceptibility to the Williams-Renaults.

Just as Moreno wasn't pushing Piquet, nor was Nelson pressing Mansell. ''I knew that I couldn't pass him with my set-up, so I just concentrated on driving smoothly and saving my tyres.'' So Nigel raced away to build up a lead of over eight seconds. Nothing but the reliability of his Ferrari lay between him and a second victory of the year. Behind him, there was no change amongst the first six (Piquet, Moreno, Boutsen, Patrese and an inspired Aguri Suzuki battling with Derek Warwick) until Boutsen came in for tyres. That put Johnny Herbert, substituting for the injured Martin Donnelly in the Lotus team, into an excellent sixth place in his first GP since Belgium 1989. Something extra for British fans to cheer in addition to Nigel's commanding drive and Derek's habitual perseverance.

On lap 27, Mansell rolled up to his Ferrari mechanics for a new set of Goodyear Cs knowing that he'd drop to at least third behind the non-stop Benettons — and maybe lower. It was a superb stop, taking only 5.82 seconds, and Nigel had got the power well and truly on before his wheels even hit the deck. And that was what broke a universal joint — something which had never happened to the 641 before. Exit Mansell along with any chance that Ferrari had of winning the constructors' championship in Australia. At half-distance, the top four in the championship were all out of the Japanese

Local hero. Aguri Suzuki heads Warwick, Herbert, Nakajima and Bernard on the way to an excellent third place. The Larrousse Lola driver became the first Japanese ever to mount a Grand Prix podium.

Grand Prix and Nelson Piquet was leading. More astounding was the fact that Moreno was second ahead of Patrese (also hoping to race non-stop on Bs), Suzuki, Boutsen and Derek Warwick. The latter was driving in his last but one GP, having signed to drive for Jaguar's Group C team in 1991.

To Nelson's surprise, the Williams-Renaults that he'd so feared were no threat to him or Roberto. Or, amazingly, to Aguri Suzuki. In his Lola-Lamborghini, on a home track which ''I know like the back of my hand'', Aguri was flying. He recorded a series of fastest laps to pull away from Patrese, Boutsen and, with the sad demise of Derek Warwick, his countryman Satoru Nakajima, who was driving a similarly inspired home race in his Tyrrell-Ford. Unlike the Benettons, Riccardo had to stop for new tyres, but he regained his fourth place from Boutsen and, for the third race in succession, set the fastest lap (1m 44.233s, 126.63 mph).

So ended the Japanese Grand Prix. To be honest, it hadn't been exciting beyond half-distance, but it had certainly been interesting and unusual, with Benetton's maiden one-two and Piquet's first win in 52 races. There was a heart-warming second for the charming, though consistently overlooked, Roberto Moreno. He made the most of this opportunity quite brilliantly. Understandably, he was in tears as he dedicated his place to Alessandro Nannini. A staggering third place went to Aguri Suzuki — the first Japanese driver to mount a Grand Prix podium. There was deserved success too for Japan's other Formula One driver, Satoru Nakajima finishing sixth. The championships were decided in favour of Senna and McLaren, and it was a great day for Brazil with first and second places and a new World Champion. But there was frustrated misery for Prost, Mansell and Ferrari, whose reward for mammoth effort was failure. For every winner there's always a loser. All that Maranello could hope for was to round off the season with a rousing victory at the 500th World Championship Grand Prix, in Australia.

Jubilation! Piquet's first victory since 1987 gave the Benetton team a welcome fillip.

Nelson Piquet leads Berger and Prost during his magnificent early charge. His 22nd GP victory was fully deserved.

The Senna/Prost collision in Japan had resolved the 1990 World Championship. Although a lot of people were very unhappy about the way Senna had won his second title, everyone went to Australia in high spirits. The last Grand Prix is certainly the most enjoyable of the season. The 2.34-mile track on the outskirts of Adelaide is everything a street circuit should be, with plenty of room to pass, spectacular corners, a superfast straight and magnificent facilities. The organisation and administration are superb, the Australians make their foreign visitors very much at home, the food and wines are legendary and this year the weather was hot, sunny and welcoming. What more could you want? Nothing, actually, but despite that there was a big added bonus in 1990. The sixth Australian Grand Prix was the 500th Formula One World Championship race, and Adelaide seized the promotional opportunity like a drowning man grasps a rope. I'd been immensely impressed by Australia's enthusiasm for its Grand Prix in previous years, but 1990 was very special indeed. The whole city seemed to have devoted itself to following, and enjoying, everything to do with the meeting. The hotels, the restaurants, the shops, television, radio — everyone was bubbling with the pure enjoyment of it all.

Just one thing threatened to blunt the edge of a great occasion — the rekindled Senna/Prost feud. The Brazilian delivered a searing verbal attack on his French rival at a special press conference, eloquently declaring his belief that the Japanese collision was Prost's fault, rather than his, and reiterating that he had no regrets. Prost, the injured party in the eyes of most people, kept his head down and refused to comment further than saying: "If I speak to no one about it, I won't get misquoted." In the meantime, FISA had set up a special safety commission to enquire into all the recent accidents and to make recommendations covering revised regulations and their implementation.

So, with Australia's very considerable media machine gleefully exploiting the possibility of another confrontation, there was an electric atmosphere in Adelaide. The championship may have been resolved, but wasn't that, paradoxically, going to make the prospects for a great race even better? Senna would be determined to show that he was a worthy champion by winning 1990's last, and landmark, race. Prost would be resolved to show that he was the better man by doing the same thing. Nigel Mansell, relieved of the need to support his team-mate's efforts to carry number one in '91, would be gung-ho to win his last race for Ferrari. Gerhard Berger (winner at

Adelaide in 1987) would be equally keen to win his first race in a McLaren. Weren't Benetton in with a chance too, after their victory in Japan? Not forgetting Williams, for whom Boutsen had won in 1989's notorious rain-lashed race. The ticket sales soared almost as much as the temperature, and that was in the mid-30s! And with just cause, for the 1990 Grand Prix was destined to be Australia's most eventful and exciting yet, and one of the best of a vintage year.

The Adelaide circuit, incorporating public roads in daily use, is bumpy. Its tarmac surface is low on grip, and its combination of high-speed curves and straights, allied to two hairpin bends and three right-angled corners, is a killer on brakes. But that didn't make any difference to Ayrton Senna. He was fastest in every practice session on Friday and Saturday, and his 52nd pole position time of 1m 15.671s (111.74 mph) knocked a full second off his own 1989 benchmark. "I race for pleasure — nothing else," he said, but his achievement

Hopes dashed. Senna had built up a huge lead when gear selection bothers caused him to crash.

Olivier Grouillard notched up a rare, though welcome, finish, taking his Osella to 13th.

certainly didn't please anyone else! Ayrton was, as he had so often been in the past, in a class of his own, 0.6s faster than the next man on the grid. But, unlike Monaco, Monza, Spain and Japan, that next man wasn't Alain Prost — it was Senna's team-mate Gerhard Berger, making Adelaide the scene of the sixth all-McLaren front row of 1990. Bad news for Ferrari, who were desperately anxious to win more Grands Prix in the season than McLaren, the constructors' championship victors. (They'd each won six so far.)

It wasn't *too* bad though, for Maranello's men, Mansell and Prost, were third and fourth on the grid at a circuit where, unlike Spain and Japan, there was room to pass. However, a highly-motivated Senna, with a clear track in front of him and a chilling ability on street circuits (he'd won both Phoenix and Monaco in 1990), was a daunting rival. With Jean Alesi a fine fifth, Patrese sixth, the Benettons of Piquet and Moreno seventh and eighth and Boutsen's

Williams ninth, there was an excited air of expectancy for a race which is *so* tough and demanding that no more than 11 of the 26 starters had finished in previous seasons.

In the Sunday morning warm-up the Ferraris of Prost and Mansell sandwiched the McLarens of Senna and Berger, a mere 0.2s covering all four of them — evenly matched indeed! With his highly-polished McLaren gleaming in the sunny brightness of Adelaide's incredibly clear atmosphere, Senna catapulted into the lead ahead of Berger, Mansell and Prost, while Piquet rocketed past Patrese and Alesi up to fifth. At the end of the lap Senna led by 1.7 seconds, but, behind him, third-placed Mansell was contemplating Berger's gearbox closely.

At Stag Hotel corner on lap two, Berger faltered — having inadvertently killed his ignition — and in a scarlet flash Mansell was up to second. But that wasn't all, for Piquet was well and truly on the move. Fourth past Prost on lap three and then third past Berger six laps

TEAM ANALYSIS

FERRARI
Satisfying end to excellent season, despite political problems. Prost, demoralised and depressed as a result of media pressure following Japan collision, fourth on grid with Friday time. Fastest in Sunday warm-up before being reprimanded by FISA for walking out of drivers' briefing. Down to fifth laps 3-46. Second laps 62-72 (Senna out, Mansell tyre stop and past Berger). With brake and tyre problems yields to Mansell, lap 73, to finish third. Second in championship. Mansell drives magnificent last race for Ferrari after qualifying third fastest. Past Berger to second, lap two. Chases Senna hard for 45 laps but drops back with tyre wear. Makes 7.72-second stop for tyres, lap 46. Rejoins fifth for inspired charge. Passes Berger to fourth, lap 57. Third laps 62-72 (Senna retirement). Second past Prost, lap 73. Then, with series of four record laps, closes on Piquet. Tries for first at last hairpin but fails. Finishes 3.1 seconds behind Nelson with record lap 50 (1m 18.203s, 108.75 mph). A glorious finale to *Il leone's* Ferrari career.

TYRRELL
Alesi, fully recovered from Suzuka accident neck strain, qualifies excellent fifth for his last race with Tyrrell, after overcoming major practice braking problem. Drives well in "the hardest race of my career" but, with flu, suffers from the heat and demanding circuit. Stops twice for tyres and finishes eighth (one lap down) in "fantastic car", despite agony from cramp in right foot. Nakajima, no lover of street circuits, starts 13th. Up to 11th, lap 44, despite fading brakes, but retires, lap 54 when, exhausted, misses braking point and slams into tyre wall at Paddock Turn. Rejuvenated team now looks forward to 1991 with Honda V10 engines.

WILLIAMS
Team continues recent off-pace form with disappointing result by Williams' standards. Using Evolution 3 low-friction Renault V10 engines, Patrese and Boutsen qualify sixth and ninth. Thierry, first in 1989, races sixth, laps 22-61. Finishes fifth after qualifying "happy to have been in the points in my last race for Williams." Riccardo sixth until lap 22, when spins to avoid Morbidelli's Minardi blow-up. Rejoins ninth with new tyres and races hard to finish sixth (one lap down) with fading brakes. With new chassis and Nigel Mansell, team confident of 1991 improvement.

BRABHAM
Team reverts to longitudinal gearbox for last race with Judd V8 engine. David Brabham happy and relieved to qualify (25th) for his home GP, only the second Australian to do so after Alan Jones. Spins twice under braking in unstable car and disappointed to retire from 25th and last, lap 19. Stefano Modena starts his last Brabham race from 17th on grid. Down to 22nd after lap 20 tyre stop. Interim 1991 car now being tested with Yamaha V12 engine.

ARROWS
In outclassed car, both Michele Alboreto and Alex Caffi fail to qualify for last race with Arrows (as opposed to Footwork-Porsche) team. "Good balance but no grip," says Michele. "We are well advanced with the new project," says team boss Jack Oliver "and we can only look forward ..."

LOTUS
Fighting for survival, Lotus finish an awful 1990 season on a low note. Derek Warwick starts his last GP (before joining Jaguar) 11th on the grid. Up to eighth, laps 22-27, but then has gear selection problems. loses second gear and retires from tenth, lap 44, jammed in third. A sad way to finish an outstanding GP career. Johnny Herbert qualifies 18th with strong oversteer. Up to praiseworthy tenth, laps 44-57. Stops for tyres but retires when clutch breaks as he tries to leave pits. With no sponsor, no engine supplier and no contracted drivers, future sadly looks grim for once-great team.

OSELLA
Handy 22nd place on the grid for Olivier Grouillard, who races to finish relieved 13th (seven laps down) after the usual vilification from other drivers, especially Nigel Mansell, about his blocking tactics. Team delighted to finish, however.

LEYTON HOUSE
A disappointing finish to a poor year. Ivan Capelli and Mauricio Gugelmin start 14th and 16th. Ivan up to 11th laps 1-39 before tyre stop. Rejoins 13th and then retires, lap 47, with throttle jammed shut. Mauricio, overcome by brake problems, retires from 13th in gravel trap, lap 27. New car with Ilmor engine for 1991 well advanced.

AGS
Gabriele Tarquini starts 26th. Lapped by lap 15. Races at tail of field until lap 59 engine blow-up and accompanying fire causes retirement. Yannick Dalmas fails to qualify.

BENETTON
Absolutely stunning finish to team's well-deserved, best-ever year. Piquet and Moreno qualify seventh and eighth with Nelson alarming opposition by being fastest on straight (177.1 mph) in Sunday warm-up. In beautifully balanced car with good grip, Piquet passes Alesi and Patrese to fifth, lap one. Then fourth past Prost, lap three. To third past Berger (lap nine) and second past Mansell (tyre stop), lap 46. Into lead, lap 62, when Senna goes off. Stays there, just ahead of charging Mansell, for second successive and 22nd overall GP victory. Fine race too from Roberto, who finishes excellent seventh (one lap down) to underline his right to second team seat in 1991. Piquet catches up with Berger to finish joint third in championship, whilst team consolidates third place ahead of Williams in constructors' championship. Benetton cover geatest racing distance in 1990 (5,185 miles), well pleased with their (and Ford engines') reliability.

DALLARA
No success in last race with Ford DFR engine. De Cesaris starts 15th before retiring lap 24 (electrics). Pirro, 21st on

Fatherly interest. Sir Jack Brabham was on hand to advise David, but the thrice World Champion's son was to be an early retirement.

grid, retires from 12th out of 14, lap 69 (electrics). With no points from dismal season, team hopes for better 1991 with Judd V10 engine.

MINARDI

Team happy with last 1990 race before switching to Ferrari power for '91. Pier-Luigi Martini content with tenth on grid and very content with ninth in race after trouble-free run. Gianni Morbidelli qualifies 20th for second Minardi race before retiring from 21st, lap 21, when engine blows (nearly taking Patrese off).

LIGIER

Two more finishes underline team's reliability (fifth highest racing mileage in 1990), but slowness depresses results. Larini and Alliot 12th and 19th on grid. Nicola finishes tenth (for fifth time), two laps down, and Philippe 11th, three laps down. With new drivers (Boutsen and Comas) and new Lamborghini V12 engine, team hopefully looks forward to better 1991.

McLAREN

Flat finish to another very successful (but considerably less dominant) year. Highly motivated Ayrton Senna, yet to win in Australia, takes 52nd pole position in crushing style. Builds commanding half-minute lead by lap 60, despite brake problems from the start. Fails to select second gear at fast Paddock Turn, lap 62, and smashes into fifth retirement of season. Berger, second on grid, down to third lap two (Mansell) and fourth lap nine (Piquet). Apart from tyre stop, stays there to end, and shares third place with Piquet in championship. Gerhard's first year without win since 1985. Senna and McLaren victorious in drivers' and constructors' championships but, for first time since 1987, team loses more races than it wins.

LOLA

A very unhappy last meeting with Lamborghini power. After multitude of problems, Bernard qualifies 23rd and Suzuki 24th. Aguri up to 21st, lap seven, but retires with broken transmission. Eric retires from 16th, lap 22, with same problem.

COLONI

Only 30th fastest, Bertrand Gachot fails to qualify.

Andrea de Cesaris was one of many to clout the unyielding kerbs. An electrical failure eventually put him out.

later, with Mansell ahead of him closing on Senna! ''Our choice of Goodyear's D compound tyres was good,'' said Nelson. ''I was able to outbrake Prost and Berger.'' That was significant, for when the race had started McLaren were already worried about their brakes, which had given trouble in the warm-up, whereas Benetton were totally relaxed about theirs.

The battle for the lead was enthralling. On lap 11 (of 81), Mansell had closed the gap to Senna to under a second. But Piquet, in third

Smile please. Most of the present-day F1 crop posed for an end-of-term shot with former Grand Prix greats, Hunt, Hulme, Fangio, Moss and Brabham. One notable absentee was Prost, the Frenchman in a despondent mood all weekend.

Mansell's Ferrari career ended on a high note, after a tremendous recovery drive to second place.

place, was faster than both of them, and gaining. As early as lap 16, Senna was bearing down on backmarkers Tarquini and Grouillard. Using his fabled ability to scythe his way through traffic, he extended his lead over Mansell to three seconds, only for Nigel to fight back. Lap 25 saw him just 0.7s behind the McLaren. Prost was on a charge too, closing fast on Gerhard Berger.

On lap 28, Senna increased the pressure and the gap to 2.4 seconds, with Mansell second, Piquet third, Berger fourth, Prost fifth and Boutsen sixth ahead of Moreno and Patrese. And then came the event that seemed at the time to have won Senna his 27th, Jackie Stewart-equalling Grand Prix. Mansell, on fading tyres, went up an escape road. With a tyre-smoking, 360-degree spin he regained the track undamaged, but now Ayrton led by 16 seconds and Nelson Piquet was tucked under Mansell's rear wing. Then, to a gigantic roar from the crowd, Piquet was past a slithering Mansell to second, with the latter's Ferrari now only just ahead of Berger and Prost. Magic!

Into the pits shot Nigel for the only tyre stop the first four made. Some 7.72 seconds later, with no repetition of his Japanese débâcle, he was on the move again — down to fifth behind Senna (leading now by over 20 seconds), Piquet, Berger and Prost. Goodbye Nigel, and tough luck after a fighting drive. But we were so wrong!

There were no worries for Senna as he extended his lead over Piquet to 24 seconds, but team-mate Berger was down to fourth behind Prost as Gerhard harmlessly leapt over one of Adelaide's high, rounded kerbs.

With Senna pacing himself to victory, the man to watch was Nigel Mansell. He may not be going to win his last race for Ferrari, but it wasn't for lack of trying. On lap 57, he took Berger and fourth place. On lap 61 he broke the lap record (1m 19.060s) and on lap 62 he was third — because Senna was out! "I couldn't get second at that left-hander (Paddock Turn) and went straight in to the tyre barrier." And as Ayrton, destined not to win in Australia once again, legged it back to the pits, it was his countryman Nelson Piquet in the lead, seven seconds ahead of Prost with Mansell closing fast on the Frenchman. What a race!

Nigel was nothing short of sensational in his charge to the front. Lap 70: lap record (1m 18.876s). Lap 71: lap record (1m 18.454s). Past Prost to second on lap 73 and now, with eight laps still to go, only 6.9 seconds behind Piquet.

But Nelson knew the score and coolly stepped up his pace. Too much though! On lap 77, he slid wide into the run-off area outside the superfast Brewery Bend. By the time he'd gathered it all up, Mansell was right behind him thanks to a final record lap in 1m 18.203s (108.75 mph). The most exciting Australian GP of all was going to thrill right to the chequered flag.

As Piquet and Mansell raced together down the 185 mph Jack Brabham Straight on the last lap, they closed on Stefano Modena's Brabham. ''I could see Piquet coming up behind me and a red car much further back. I let Piquet through under braking, then I could hear this screaming engine coming by and it was Mansell. He must have braked at least a hundred metres later than me and he missed Piquet by a fraction.''

Back in the swing of things. Piquet savours his second consecutive victory.

''I left my braking as late as I could,'' said Nelson, ''and just made it. A fantastic win for me and everyone who had faith in me in the team.''

Fantastic indeed, with Mansell just 3.1 seconds adrift after sorting himself and the Ferrari out. With Prost third and Berger fourth, none of the Big Four had achieved their ambition to win, but Piquet's second successive victory couldn't have been more popular. And, after his breathtaking drive, Nigel was now the hero of Australia as well as Britain and Italy.

Australia 1990 had been a truly worthy 500th World Championship Grand Prix, and it ended a wonderful year of Formula One that was going to be very hard to beat in 1991. But Grand Prix racing seems to get better every year. As they sadly left Adelaide, the teams were already looking forward to Phoenix!

As hosts of the 500th World Championship GP, the Australians rightfully made a song and dance about it. But would they swap a XXXX for one of these?

REVIEW OF 1990

1990 will be remembered as an outstanding year of Grand Prix racing, albeit sadly marred by the dreadful injuries suffered by Martin Donnelly and Alessandro Nannini. The fact that Sandro's accident (in a helicopter) was unconnected with racing makes it no less distressing. We can only hope that these two brave, likeable men make complete recoveries.

That apart, the World Championship's 40th year, which saw its 500th race in Australia, was very good indeed. McLaren may have won their third successive constructors' championship (their fifth in seven years), but they did so by a much slimmer margin.

In truth, two men dominated the year. Ayrton Senna made history in Spain with his 50th pole position from what was then 108 starts — an incredible achievement. His 25th win in Belgium took him past Fangio, to become the most successful South American driver in terms of wins (albeit a long way behind the great Argentinian in terms of championships), and in Japan he won his second World Championship in controversial fashion, literally driving Prost off the circuit. Prost's season was also outstanding though. He took five wins in his first year with the Prancing Horse, of which the one in France was Ferrari's 100th. There was a hat-trick of victories in Mexico, France and Britain, a fighting win against the odds in Spain that kept alive his hopes of being number one in '91 and he increased his career record totals to 44 wins and 665.5 World Championship points. It was right that one of them should win the title, for both deserved to do so.

They weren't the only ones who deserved praise for their driving in 1990. Jean Alesi more than established himself as a top man, even if his lack of humility failed to endear him to his Tyrrell team. Nelson Piquet repeatedly showed that, if he has a decent car, he is still amongst the best. His victories at Suzuka and Adelaide underlined his continuing ability. Sandro Nannini drove well everywhere, leading convincingly in Germany, whilst Roberto Moreno took the Italian's place in Japan and drove brilliantly to finish second. Nannini's grievous injuries seem likely to end an

Every picture tells a story. Although he won at Estoril, Nigel Mansell's second season with Ferrari was largely one of despair.

outstanding career. Sadly, the same must be said of Martin Donnelly, who had demonstrated great ability and potential in a second-class car.

Which leads me to the two great disappointments of 1990. Nigel Mansell never seems to get the luck. It was a burst tyre that deprived him of the World Championship in 1986. In 1990, his hopes were dashed by repeated failures to finish in his Ferrari. So, better luck in '91 in a Williams-Renault Nigel! But what about Gerhard Berger? When he signed for McLaren, people confidently forecast that he would be the equal of Senna. But it didn't turn out that way. Pole positions, yes. Race leadership and fastest laps too, but no wins.

Grand Prix racing is about men, machinery and teamwork, and they all have to be good. So there are a lot of truly talented drivers who fail to realise their potential because of the cars they drive. In 1990, Ivan Capelli, Stefano Modena, Derek Warwick, Martin Donnelly and Pier-Luigi Martini were five examples of that. In Formula One, everything has to be right.

Polemeister. Ayrton Senna could usually afford to take a relaxed view of his opposition's progress during qualifying. The Brazilian became the first man to notch up 50 pole positions, and there are plenty more to come...

So what about the machinery? Well, what a super year Tyrrell had! Written off as rather pathetic has-beens after their distant years of greatness with Jackie Stewart, the Ockham team made a magnificent comeback in 1990. The mercurial Jean Alesi worked wonders with the 019. His second places in Phoenix (with 1989's 018 chassis) and Monaco were amazing. Next season, with Honda V10 power and the equally talented but more amenable Stefano Modena, Tyrrell could be right back at the top. Williams, like Berger, were a disappointment. Despite two convincing wins, the team wasn't nearly as successful as McLaren, Ferrari or Benetton. The car, with its impressive Renault V10 engine, was undoubtedly very good, but was it good enough? Benetton sparkled with two brilliant end-of-season victories. In 1991, there'll be the new John Barnard-designed car. John's the man who was responsible for both the all-conquering McLaren MP4 and the Ferrari 640, so we can expect something very special.

It was an absolutely disastrous year for the once-great Lotus organisation. The car didn't work, both original drivers had horrific crashes and the team lost both its Lamborghini engines and its very substantial Camel sponsorship. Future prospects look bleak. If it was disastrous for Lotus, though, what was it for the underfunded and constantly struggling AGS, Coloni, Eurobrun and Life teams? For race after race, they would turn up with the desperate hope that they could just get through the daunting Friday morning hour of pre-qualifying. Tarquini and Dalmas (for AGS) and Roberto Moreno (for Eurobrun) did so occasionally, and even went on to qualify for the race itself. The others never did, and in the money-motivated Formula One world that can be terminal.

But the Grand Prix scene is eternally optimistic. I, for one, have no doubt that, as ever, next year is going to be even better. And here's why! Just visualise a grid containing Senna and Berger in McLaren-Honda V12s plus Prost and Alesi in even better Ferraris, backed by a team that has sharpened up its act. Then there will be Nigel Mansell in an improved V10 Williams-Renault, Piquet in the new Benetton, Modena driving a Tyrrell-Honda V10 and returnee Martin Brundle at the wheel of a new Brabham propelled by a Yamaha V12 (they beat Honda in motorcycle Grands Prix so why not in cars?). But there's more! Thierry Boutsen, smarting from his dismissal by Williams, will drive a new Lamborghini-powered Ligier alongside European F3000 champion Erik Comas. Porsche V12 engines will power the Footwork (ex-Arrows) chassis, an all-new Chris Murphy-designed Leyton House gets an equally new Ilmor V10 motor, little Pier-Luigi Martini will be out to prove his worth in a Ferrari-powered Minardi, Dallaras are to be propelled by John Judd's new V10 and new teams come from Eddie Jordan (with Ford V8 power) and Modena with V12 Lamborghini engines.

· The competition is going to be spellbinding and the spectacle riveting. So roll on '91!

Photos: Keith Sutton/Diana Burnett

Neither Claudio Langes (Eurobrun, above left) nor Bruno Giacomelli (Life, above right) ever made it beyond Friday's pre-qualifying session.

1990 FORMULA ONE GRAND PRIX
ROUND ONE

USA

Phoenix, Arizona

March 11, 1990.

Circuit Length: 2.36 mls/3.798 km

Laps: 72

Official Starting Grid

			28 Gerhard Berger	(1.28.664)	
Pier-Luigi Martini	(1.28.731)	23	McLaren-Honda		
Minardi-DFR			22 Andrea de Cesaris	(1.29.019)	
Jean Alesi	(1.29.408)	4	Dallara-DFR		
Tyrrell-DFR			27 Ayrton Senna	(1.29.431)	
Nelson Piquet	(1.29.862)	20	McLaren-Honda		
Benetton-Ford			1 Alain Prost	(1.29.910)	
Olivier Grouillard	(1.29.947)	14	Ferrari		
Osella-DFR			5 Thierry Boutsen	(1.30.059)	
Stefano Modena	(1.30.127)	8	Williams-Renault		
Brabham-Judd			3 Satoru Nakajima	(1.30.130)	
Riccardo Patrese	(1.30.213)	6	Tyrrell-DFR		
Williams-Renault			25 Nicola Larini	(1.30.424)	
Paolo Barilla	(1.31.194)	24	Ligier-DFR		
Minardi-DFR			29 Eric Bernard	(1.31.226)	
Roberto Moreno	(1.31.247)	33	Lola-Lamborghini		
Eurobrun-Judd			2 Nigel Mansell	(1.31.363)	
Aguri Suzuki	(1.31.414)	30	Ferrari		
Lola-Lamborghini			12 Martin Donnelly	(1.31.650)	
Bernd Schneider	(1.31.892)	10	Lotus-Lamborghini		
Arrows-DFR			9 Michele Alboreto	(1.31.948)	
Alessandro Nannini	(1.31.984)	19	Arrows-DFR		
Benetton-Ford			7 Gregor Foitek	(1.32.398)	
Derek Warwick	(1.32.400)	11	Brabham-Judd		
Lotus-Lamborghini			15 Mauricio Gugelmin	(1.32.904)	
Ivan Capelli	(1.33.044)	16	Leyton House-Judd		
Leyton House-Judd					

Race Classification

Pos.	Driver	No.	Nat.	Car	Laps	Time/retirement
1	Ayrton Senna	27	BR	McLaren-Honda	72	1h 52m 32.829s
2	Jean Alesi	4	F	Tyrrell-DFR	72	1h 52m 41.514s
3	Thierry Boutsen	5	B	Williams-Renault	72	1h 53m 26.909s
4	Nelson Piquet	20	BR	Benetton-Ford	72	1h 53m 41.187s
5	Stefano Modena	8	I	Brabham-Judd	72	1h 53m 42.332s
6	Satoru Nakajima	3	JPN	Tyrrell-DFR	71	
7	Pier-Luigi Martini	23	I	Minardi-DFR	71	
8	Eric Bernard	29	F	Lola-Lamborghini	71	
9	Riccardo Patrese	6	I	Williams-Renault	71	
10	Michele Alboreto	9	I	Arrows-DFR	70	
11	Alessandro Nannini	19	I	Benetton-Ford	70	
12	Bernd Schneider	10	D	Arrows-DFR	70	
13	Roberto Moreno	33	BR	Eurobrun-Judd	67	
14	Mauricio Gugelmin	15	BR	Leyton House-Judd	66	
R	Paolo Barilla	24	I	Minardi-DFR	54	Gave up; sore left arm
R	Aguri Suzuki	30	JPN	Lola-Lamborghini	53	Brakes
R	Nigel Mansell	2	GB	Ferrari	49	Engine/clutch
R	Gerhard Berger	28	A	McLaren-Honda	44	Clutch
R	Gregor Foitek	7	CH	Brabham-Judd	39	Collided with Grouillard
R	Olivier Grouillard	14	F	Osella-DFR	39	Front suspension
R	Andrea de Cesaris	22	I	Dallara-DFR	25	Brakes/engine
R	Alain Prost	1	F	Ferrari	21	Engine oil leak
R	Ivan Capelli	16	I	Leyton House-Judd	20	Electrics
R	Derek Warwick	11	GB	Lotus-Lamborghini	6	Rear suspension
R	Nicola Larini	25	I	Ligier-DFR	4	Sticking throttle
DNS	Martin Donnelly	12	GB	Lotus-Lamborghini	0	Gearbox

Fastest lap: Berger, on lap 34, 1m 31.050s, 93.311 mph/150.165 km/h

Drivers' World Championship

Pos.	Driver	Total
1	Ayrton Senna	9
2	Jean Alesi	6
3	Thierry Boutsen	4
4	Nelson Piquet	3
5	Stefano Modena	2
6	Satoru Nakajima	1

Constructors' World Championship

Pos.	Team	Total
1	McLaren	9
2	Tyrrell	7
3	Williams	4
4	Benetton	3
5	Brabham	2

Non Qualifiers

No.	Name	Car
*26	P. Alliot	Ligier-DFR
35	S. Johansson	Onyx-DFR
21	G. Morbidelli	Dallara-DFR
36	J.J. Lehto	Onyx-DFR

* Disqualified for receiving outside assistance during practice.

Non Pre-Qualifiers

No.	Name	Car
17	G. Tarquini	AGS-DFR
18	Y. Dalmas	AGS-DFR
34	C. Langes	Eurobrun-Judd
39	G. Brabham	Life
31	B. Gachot	Subaru-Coloni

1990 FORMULA ONE GRAND PRIX
ROUND TWO

BRAZIL

Autodromo José Carlos Pace,
Interlagos, Sao Paulo

March 25, 1990

Circuit Length: 2.687 mls/4.325 km

Laps: 71

Official Starting Grid

			27 Ayrton Senna	(1.17.277)	
Gerhard Berger	(1.17.888)	28	McLaren-Honda		
McLaren-Honda			5 Thierry Boutsen	(1.18.150)	
Riccardo Patrese	(1.18.288)	6	Williams-Renault		
Williams-Renault			2 Nigel Mansell	(1.18.509)	
Alain Prost	(1.18.631)	1	Ferrari		
Ferrari			4 Jean Alesi	(1.18.923)	
Pier-Luigi Martini	(1.19.039)	23	22 Andrea de Cesaris	(1.19.125)	
Minardi-DFR			Dallara-DFR		
Philippe Alliot	(1.19.309)	26	29 Eric Bernard	(1.19.406)	
Ligier-DFR			Lola-Lamborghini		
Stefano Modena	(1.19.425)	8	20 Nelson Piquet	(1.19.629)	
Brabham-Judd			Benetton-Ford		
Martin Donnelly	(1.20.032)	12	19 Alessandro Nannini	(1.20.055)	
Lotus-Lamborghini			Benetton-Ford		
Gianni Morbidelli	(1.20.164)	21	24 Paolo Barilla	(1.20.282)	
Dallara-DFR			Minardi-DFR		
Aguri Suzuki	(1.20.557)	30	3 Satoru Nakajima	(1.20.568)	
Lola-Lamborghini			Tyrrell-DFR		
Nicola Larini	(1.20.650)	25	14 Olivier Grouillard	(1.20.884)	
Ligier-DFR			Osella-DFR		
Gregor Foitek	(1.20.902)	7	9 Michele Alboreto	(1.20.920)	
Brabham-Judd			Arrows-DFR		
Derek Warwick	(1.20.998)	11	10 AlexCaffi	(1.21.065)	
Lotus-Lamborghini			Arrows-DFR		
Yannick Dalmas	(1.21.087)	18			
AGS-DFR					

Race Classification

Pos.	Driver	No.	Nat.	Car	Laps	Time/retirement
1	Alain Prost	1	F	Ferrari	71	1h 37m 21.258s
2	Gerhard Berger	28	A	McLaren-Honda	71	1h 37m 34.822s
3	Ayrton Senna	27	BR	McLaren-Honda	71	1h 37m 58.980s
4	Nigel Mansell	2	GB	Ferrari	71	1h 38m 08.524s
5	Thierry Boutsen	5	B	Williams-Renault	70	
6	Nelson Piquet	20	BR	Benetton-Ford	70	
7	Jean Alesi	4	F	Tyrrell-DFR	70	
8	Satoru Nakajima	3	JPN	Tyrrell-DFR	70	
9	Pier-Luigi Martini	23	I	Minardi-DFR	69	
10	Alessandro Nannini	19	I	Benetton-Ford	68	In the pits, puncture
11	Nicola Larini	25	I	Ligier-DFR	68	
12	Philippe Alliot	26	F	Ligier-DFR	68	
13	Riccardo Patrese	6	I	Williams-Renault	65	Engine
14	Gianni Morbidelli	21	I	Dallara-DFR	64	
R	Alex Caffi	10	I	Arrows-DFR	49	Driver fatigue
R	Martin Donnelly	12	GB	Lotus-Lamborghini	43	Leg cramp, spun off
R	Stefano Modena	8	I	Brabham-Judd	39	Spun off
R	Paolo Barilla	24	I	Minardi-DFR	38	Engine
R	Yannick Dalmas	18	F	AGS-DFR	28	Front suspension
R	Derek Warwick	11	GB	Lotus-Lamborghini	25	Electrical
R	Aguri Suzuki	30	JPN	Lola-Lamborghini	24	Suspension
R	Michele Alboreto	9	I	Arrows-DFR	24	Suspension
R	Gregor Foitek	7	CH	Brabham-Judd	14	Transmission
R	Eric Bernard	29	F	Lola-Lamborghini	13	Gearbox
R	Olivier Grouillard	14	F	Osella-DFR	8	Collision with Alboreto
R	Andrea de Cesaris	22	I	Dallara-DFR	0	Collision with Alesi

Fastest lap: Berger, on lap 55, 1m 19.899s, 121.086 mph/194.871 km/h

Drivers' World Championship

Pos.	Driver	Total
1	Ayrton Senna	13
2	Alain Prost	9
3=	Jean Alesi	6
3=	Gerhard Berger	6
5	Thierry Boutsen	6
6	Nelson Piquet	4
7	Nigel Mansell	3
8	Stefano Modena	2
9	Satoru Nakajima	1

Constructors' World Championship

Pos.	Team	Total
1	McLaren	19
2	Ferrari	12
3	Tyrrell	7
4	Williams	6
5	Benetton	4
6	Brabham	2

Non Qualifiers

No.	Name	Car
15	M. Gugelmin	Leyton House-Judd
16	I. Capelli	Leyton House-Judd
35	S. Johansson	Onyx-DFR
36	J.J. Lehto	Onyx-DFR

Non Pre-Qualifiers

No.	Name	Car
17	G. Tarquini	AGS-DFR
31	B. Gachot	Subaru-Coloni
33	R. Moreno	Eurobrun-Judd
34	C. Langes	Eurobrun-Judd
39	G. Brabham	Life

1990 FORMULA ONE GRAND PRIX
ROUND THREE

SAN MARINO

Autodromo Enzo & Dino Ferrari
Imola

May 13, 1990

Circuit Length: 3.132 mls/5.040 km

Laps: 61

Official Starting Grid

Ayrton Senna (1.23.220) 27		
McLaren-Honda	28 Gerhard Berger	(1.23.781)
Riccardo Patrese (1.24.444) 6	McLaren-Honda	
Williams-Renault	5 Thierry Boutsen	(1.25.039)
Nigel Mansell (1.25.095) 2	Williams-Renault	
Ferrari	1 Alain Prost	(1.25.179)
Jean Alesi (1.25.230) 4	Ferrari	
Tyrrell-DFR	20 Nelson Piquet	(1.25.761)
Alessandro Nannini (1.26.042) 19	Benetton-Ford	
Benetton-Ford	11 Derek Warwick	(1.26.682)
Martin Donnelly (1.26.714) 12	Lotus-Lamborghini	
Lotus-Lamborghini	15 Mauricio Gugelmin	(1.26.836)
Eric Bernard (1.26.838) 29	Leyton House-Judd	
Lola-Lamborghini	8 Stefano Modena	(1.27.008)
Aguri Suzuki (1.27.068) 30	Brabham-Judd	
Lola-Lamborghini	26 Philippe Alliot	(1.27.214)
Andrea de Cesaris (1.27.217) 22	Ligier-DFR	
Dallara-DFR	16 Ivan Capelli	(1.27.521)
Satoru Nakajima (1.27.532) 3	Leyton House-Judd	
Tyrrell-DFR	25 Nicola Larini	(1.27.564)
Emanuele Pirro (1.27.613) *21	Ligier-DFR	
Dallara-DFR	14 Olivier Grouillard	(1.28.009)
Gregor Foitek (1.28.111) 35	Osella-DFR	
Onyx-DFR	33 Roberto Moreno	(1.28.603)
J.J. Lehto (1.28.625) 36	Eurobrun-Judd	
Onyx-DFR	24 Paolo Barilla	(1.28.667)
*Started from back of grid	Minardi-DFR	

Race Classification

Pos.	Driver	No.	Nat.	Car	Laps	Time/retirement
1	Riccardo Patrese	6	I	Williams-Renault	61	1h 30m 55.478s
2	Gerhard Berger	28	A	McLaren-Honda	61	1h 31m 00.595s
3	Alessandro Nannini	19	I	Benetton-Ford	61	1h 31m 01.718s
4	Alain Prost	1	F	Ferrari	61	1h 31m 02.321s
5	Nelson Piquet	20	BR	Benetton-Ford	61	1h 31m 48.590s
6	Jean Alesi	4	F	Tyrrell-DFR	60	
7	Derek Warwick	11	GB	Lotus-Lamborghini	60	
8	Martin Donnelly	12	GB	Lotus-Lamborghini	60	
9	Philippe Alliot	26	F	Ligier-DFR	60	
10	Nicola Larini	25	I	Ligier-DFR	59	
11	Paolo Barilla	24	I	Minardi-DFR	59	
12	J.J. Lehto	36	SF	Onyx-DFR	59	
13	Eric Bernard	29	F	Lola-Lamborghini	56	Gearbox
R	Olivier Grouillard	14	F	Osella-DFR	52	Wheel bearing
R	Nigel Mansell	2	GB	Ferrari	38	Engine
R	Gregor Foitek	35	CH	Onyx-DFR	35	Engine
R	Stefano Modena	8	I	Brabham-Judd	31	Brakes
R	Andrea de Cesaris	22	I	Dallara-DFR	29	Wheel bearing
R	Mauricio Gugelmin	15	BR	Leyton House-Judd	24	Electrics
R	Thierry Boutsen	5	B	Williams-Renault	17	Engine/missed gear
R	Aguri Suzuki	30	JPN	Lola-Lamborghini	17	Clutch
R	Ayrton Senna	27	BR	McLaren-Honda	3	Cracked wheel rim/spun off
R	Emanuele Pirro	21	I	Dallara-DFR	2	Engine
R	Satoru Nakajima	3	JPN	Tyrrell-DFR	0	Accident with Capelli
R	Ivan Capelli	16	I	Leyton House-Judd	0	Accident with Nakajima
R	Roberto Moreno	33	BR	Eurobrun-Judd	0	Dirt in throttle slides

Fastest lap: Nannini, on lap 60, 1m 27.156s, 129.355 mph/208.178 km/h.

Drivers' World Championship

Pos.	Driver	Total
1	Ayrton Senna	13
2	Alain Prost	12
3	Gerhard Berger	12
4	Riccardo Patrese	9
5	Jean Alesi	7
6	Thierry Boutsen	6
7	Nelson Piquet	6
8	Alessandro Nannini	4
9	Nigel Mansell	3
10	Stefano Modena	2
11	Satoru Nakajima	1

Constructors' World Championship

Pos.	Team	Total
1	McLaren	25
2=	Williams	15
2=	Ferrari	15
4	Benetton	10
5	Tyrrell	8
6	Brabham	2

Non Qualifiers

No.	Name	Car
7	D. Brabham	Brabham-Judd
9	M. Alboreto	Arrows-DFR
10	A. Caffi	Arrows-DFR
*23	P-L. Martini	Minardi-DFR

*Withdrew after practice accident

Non Pre-Qualifiers

No.	Name	Car
17	G. Tarquini	AGS-DFR
31	B. Gachot	Subaru-Coloni
34	C. Langes	Eurobrun-Judd
39	B. Giacomelli	Life
18	Y. Dalmas	AGS-DFR, withdrawn

1990 FORMULA ONE GRAND PRIX
ROUND FOUR

MONACO

May 27, 1990

Circuit Length: 2.068 mls/3.328 km

Laps: 78

Official Starting Grid

Alain Prost *Ferrari*	(1.21.776)	1		27	Ayrton Senna *McLaren-Honda*	(1.21.314)
Riccardo Patrese *Williams-Renault*	(1.22.026)	6		4	Jean Alesi *Tyrrell-DFR*	(1.21.801)
Thierry Boutsen *Williams-Renault*	(1.22.691)	5		28	Gerhard Berger *McLaren-Honda*	(1.22.682)
Pier-Luigi Martini *Minardi-DFR*	(1.23.149)	23		2	Nigel Mansell *Ferrari*	(1.22.733)
Nelson Piquet *Benetton-Ford*	(1.23.566)	20		*21	Emanuele Pirro *Dallara-DFR*	(1.23.494)
Andrea de Cesaris *Dallara-DFR*	(1.23.613)	22		12	Martin Donnelly *Lotus-Lamborghini*	(1.23.600)
Stefano Modena *Brabham-Judd*	(1.23.920)	8		11	Derek Warwick *Lotus-Lamborghini*	(1.23.656)
Alessandro Nannini *Benetton-Ford*	(1.24.139)	19		30	Aguri Suzuki *Lola-Lamborghini*	(1.24.023)
Philippe Alliot *Ligier-DFR*	(1.24.294)	26		25	Nicola Larini *Ligier-DFR*	(1.24.334)
Gregor Foitek *Onyx-DFR*	(1.24.367)	35		24	Paolo Barilla *Minardi-DFR*	(1.24.334)
Alex Caffi *Arrows-DFR*	(1.25.000)	10		3	Satoru Nakajima *Tyrrell-DFR*	(1.24.371)
Eric Bernard *Lola-Lamborghini*	(1.25.398)	29		16	Ivan Capelli *Leyton House-Judd*	(1.25.020)
J.J. Lehto *Onyx-DFR*	(1.25.508)	36		7	David Brabham *Brabham-Judd*	(1.25.420)

*Failed to start final parade lap

Drivers' World Championship

Pos.	Driver	Total
1	Ayrton Senna	22
2	Gerhard Berger	16
3	Jean Alesi	13
4	Alain Prost	12
5=	Riccardo Patrese	9
5=	Thierry Boutsen	9
7	Nelson Piquet	6
8	Alessandro Nannini	4
9	Nigel Mansell	3
10=	Stefano Modena	2
10=	Alex Caffi	2
12=	Satoru Nakajima	1
12=	Eric Bernard	1

Constructors' World Championship

Pos.	Team	Total
1	McLaren	38
2	Williams	18
3	Ferrari	15
4	Tyrrell	14
5	Benetton	10
6=	Brabham	2
6=	Arrows	2
8	Larrousse	1

Race Classification

Pos.	Driver	No.	Nat.	Car	Laps	Time/retirement
1	Ayrton Senna	27	BR	McLaren-Honda	78	1h 52m 46.982s
2	Jean Alesi	4	F	Tyrrell-DFR	78	1h 52m 48.069s
3	Gerhard Berger	28	A	McLaren-Honda	78	1h 52m 49.055s
4	Thierry Boutsen	5	B	Williams-Renault	77	
5	Alex Caffi	10	I	Arrows-DFR	76	
6	Eric Bernard	29	F	Lola-Lamborghini	76	
7	Gregor Foitek	35	CH	Onyx-DFR	72	Collision with Bernard
R	Derek Warwick	11	GB	Lotus-Lamborghini	66	Brakes/spun and stalled
R	Nigel Mansell	2	GB	Ferrari	63	Electronics
R	Paolo Barilla	24	I	Minardi-DFR	52	Gearbox
R	J.J. Lehto	36	SF	Onyx-DFR	52	Gearbox
R	Philippe Alliot	26	F	Ligier-DFR	47	Gearbox
R	Riccardo Patrese	6	I	Williams-Renault	41	Engine
R	Andrea de Cesaris	22	I	Dallara-DFR	38	Throttle linkage
R	Satoru Nakajima	3	JPN	Tyrrell-DFR	36	Spun off
R	Alain Prost	1	F	Ferrari	30	Electronics
R	Alessandro Nannini	19	I	Benetton-Ford	20	Engine
R	David Brabham	7	AUS	Brabham-Judd	16	CV joint
R	Ivan Capelli	16	I	Leyton House-Judd	13	Brakes
R	Nicola Larini	25	I	Ligier-DFR	12	Differential
R	Aguri Suzuki	30	JPN	Lola-Lamborghini	11	Electrics
R	Pier-Luigi Martini	23	I	Minardi-DFR	7	Electrics
R	Martin Donnelly	12	GB	Lotus-Lamborghini	6	Transmission
R	Stefano Modena	8	I	Brabham-Judd	3	Differential
DNS	Emanuele Pirro	21	I	Dallara-DFR	0	Stalled on grid
DQ	Nelson Piquet	20	BR	Benetton-Ford		34 Disqualified; received push-start after spinning off

Fastest lap: Senna, on lap 59, 1m 24.468s, 88.133 mph/141.838 km/h

Non Qualifiers

No.	Name	Car
9	M. Alboreto	Arrows-DFR
14	O. Grouillard	Osella-DFR
15	M. Gugelmin	Leyton House-Judd
33	R. Moreno	Eurobrun-Judd

Non Pre-Qualifiers

No.	Name	Car
17	G. Tarquini	AGS-DFR
18	Y. Dalmas	AGS-DFR
31	B. Gachot	Subaru-Coloni
34	C. Langes	Eurobrun-Judd
39	B. Giacomelli	Life

1990 FORMULA ONE GRAND PRIX
ROUND FIVE

CANADA
Gilles Villeneuve

June 10, 1990

Circuit Length: 2.728 mls/4.3902 km

Laps: 70

Official Starting Grid

Ayrton Senna	(1.20.399)	27			
McLaren-Honda			28	Gerhard Berger	(1.20.465)
Alain Prost	(1.20.826)	1		McLaren-Honda	
Ferrari			19	Alessandro Nannini	(1.21.302)
Nelson Piquet	(1.21.568)	20		Benetton-Ford	
Benetton-Ford			5	Thierry Boutsen	(1.21.599)
Nigel Mansell	(1.21.641)	2		Williams-Renault	
Ferrari			4	Jean Alesi	(1.21.748)
Riccardo Patrese	(1.22.018)	6		Tyrrell-DFR	
Williams-Renault			8	Stefano Modena	(1.22.660)
Derek Warwick	(1.22.673)	11		Brabham-Judd	
Lotus-Lamborghini			12	Martin Donnelly	(1.22.703)
Satoru Nakajima	(1.23.605)	3		Lotus-Lamborghini	
Tyrrell-DFR			9	Michele Alboreto	(1.23.744)
Olivier Grouillard	(1.23.779)	14		Arrows-DFR	
Osella-DFR			23	Pier-Luigi Martini	(1.23.795)
Philippe Alliot	(1.23.899)	26		Minardi-DFR	
Ligier-DFR			30	Aguri Suzuki	(1.23.915)
Emanuele Pirro	(1.24.269)	21		Lola-Lamborghini	
Dallara-DFR			25	Nicola Larini	(1.24.285)
Gregor Foitek	(1.24.397)	35		Ligier-DFR	
Onyx-DFR			36	J.J. Lehto	(1.24.425)
Eric Bernard	(1.24.451)	29		Onyx-DFR	
Lola-Lamborghini			16	Ivan Capelli	(1.24.554)
Andrea de Cesaris	(1.24.621)	22		Leyton House-Judd	
Dallara-DFR			10	Alex Caffi	(1.25.113)
				Arrows-DFR	

Race Classification

Pos.	Driver	No.	Nat.	Car	Laps	Time/retirement
1	Ayrton Senna	27	BR	McLaren-Honda	70	1h 42m 56.400s
2	Nelson Piquet	20	BR	Benetton-Ford	70	1h 43m 06.897s
3	Nigel Mansell	2	GB	Ferrari	70	1h 43m 09.785s
4	Gerhard Berger	28	A	McLaren-Honda	70	1h 43m 11.254s*
5	Alain Prost	1	F	Ferrari	70	1h 43m 12.220s
6	Derek Warwick	11	GB	Lotus-Lamborghini	68	
7	Stefano Modena	8	I	Brabham-Judd	68	
8	Alex Caffi	10	I	Arrows-DFR	68	
9	Eric Bernard	29	F	Lola-Lamborghini	67	
10	Ivan Capelli	16	I	Leyton House-Judd	67	
11	Satoru Nakajima	3	JPN	Tyrrell-DFR	67	
12	Aguri Suzuki	30	JPN	Lola-Lamborghini	66	
13	Olivier Grouillard	14	F	Osella-DFR	65	
R	Martin Donnelly	12	GB	Lotus-Lamborghini	57	Engine
R	Gregor Foitek	35	CH	Onyx-DFR	53	Over-revved engine
R	Andrea de Cesaris	22	I	Dallara-DFR	50	Gearbox
R	J.J. Lehto	36	SF	Onyx-DFR	46	Misfire
R	Riccardo Patrese	6	I	Williams-Renault	44	Brakes
R	Philippe Alliot	26	F	Ligier-DFR	34	Engine
R	Jean Alesi	4	F	Tyrrell-DFR	26	Spun off/crashed
R	Alessandro Nannini	19	I	Benetton-Ford	21	Spun off/crashed
R	Thierry Boutsen	5	B	Williams-Renault	19	Spun off/crashed
R	Nicola Larini	25	I	Ligier-DFR	18	Hit by Boutsen
R	Emanuele Pirro	21	I	Dallara-DFR	11	Collided with Alboreto
R	Michele Alboreto	9	I	Arrows-DFR	11	Collided with Pirro
R	Pier-Luigi Martini	23	I	Minardi-DFR	0	Spun off

*including one-minute penalty

Fastest lap: Berger, on lap 70, 1m 22.077s, 119.645 mph/192.551 km/h

Drivers' World Championship

Pos.	Driver	Total
1	Ayrton Senna	31
2	Gerhard Berger	19
3	Alain Prost	14
4	Jean Alesi	13
5	Nelson Piquet	12
6=	Riccardo Patrese	9
6=	Thierry Boutsen	9
8	Nigel Mansell	7
9	Alessandro Nannini	7
10=	Stefano Modena	2
10=	Alex Caffi	2
12=	Satoru Nakajima	1
12=	Eric Bernard	1
12=	Derek Warwick	1

Constructors' World Championship

Pos.	Team	Total
1	McLaren	50
2	Ferrari	21
3	Williams	18
4	Benetton	16
5	Tyrrell	14
6=	Brabham	2
6=	Arrows	2
8=	Larrousse	1
8=	Lotus	1

Non Qualifiers

No.	Name	Car
7	D. Brabham	Brabham-Judd
15	M. Gugelmin	Leyton House-Judd
24	P. Barilla	Minardi-DFR
33	R. Moreno	Eurobrun-Judd

Non Pre-Qualifiers

No.	Name	Car
17	G. Tarquini	AGS-DFR
18	Y. Dalmas	AGS-DFR
31	B. Gachot	Subaru-Coloni
34	C. Langes	Eurobrun-Judd
39	B. Giacomelli	Life

**1990 FORMULA ONE GRAND PRIX
ROUND SIX**

MEXICO

**Autodromo Hermanos Rodriguez,
Mexico City**

June 24, 1990

Circuit Length: 2.747 mls/4.421 km

Laps: 69

Official Starting Grid

Gerhard Berger	(1.17.227)	28			
McLaren-Honda			**6** Riccardo Patrese		(1.17.498)
Ayrton Senna	(1.17.670)	27	*Williams-Renault*		
McLaren-Honda			**2** Nigel Mansell		(1.17.732)
Thierry Boutsen	(1.17.883)	5	*Ferrari*		
Williams-Renault			**4** Jean Alesi		(1.18.282)
Pier-Luigi Martini	(1.18.526)	23	*Tyrrell-DFR*		
Minardi-DFR			**20** Nelson Piquet		(1.18.561)
Satoru Nakajima	(1.18.575)	3	*Benetton-Ford*		
Tyrrell-DFR			**8** Stefano Modena		(1.18.592)
Derek Warwick	(1.18.951)	11	*Brabham-Judd*		
Lotus-Lamborghini			**12** Martin Donnelly		(1.18.994)
Alain Prost	(1.19.026)	1	*Lotus-Lamborghini*		
Ferrari			**19** Alessandro Nannini		(1.19.227)
Andrea de Cesaris	(1.19.865)	22	*Benetton-Ford*		
Dallara-DFR			**24** Paolo Barilla		(1.19.897)
Michele Alboreto	(1.19.941)	9	*Minardi-DFR*		
Arrows-DFR			**21** Emanuele Pirro		(1.20.044)
Aguri Suzuki	(1.20.268)	30	*Dallara-DFR*		
Lola-Lamborghini			**14** Olivier Grouillard		(1.20.274)
David Brabham	(1.20.447)	7	*Osella-DFR*		
Brabham-Judd			**26** Philippe Alliot		(1.20.657)
Gregor Foitek	(1.21.012)	35	*Ligier-DFR*		
Onyx-DFR			**25** Nicola Larini		(1.21.116)
Eric Bernard	(1.21.273)	29	*Ligier-DFR*		
Lola-Lamborghini			**36** J.J. Lehto		(1.21.519)
			Onyx-DFR		

Drivers' World Championship

Pos.	Driver	Total
1	Ayrton Senna	31
2=	Gerhard Berger	23
2=	Alain Prost	23
4=	Jean Alesi	13
4=	Nigel Mansell	13
4=	Nelson Piquet	13
7	Thierry Boutsen	11
8	Riccardo Patrese	9
9	Alessandro Nannini	7
10=	Stefano Modena	2
10=	Alex Caffi	2
12=	Satoru Nakajima	1
12=	Eric Bernard	1
12=	Derek Warwick	1

Race Classification

Pos.	Driver	No.	Nat.	Car	Laps	Time/retirement
1	Alain Prost	1	F	Ferrari	69	1h 32m 35.783s
2	Nigel Mansell	2	GB	Ferrari	69	1h 33m 01.134s
3	Gerhard Berger	28	A	McLaren-Honda	69	1h 33m 01.313s
4	Alessandro Nannini	19	I	Benetton-Ford	69	1h 33m 16.882s
5	Thierry Boutsen	5	B	Williams-Renault	69	1h 33m 22.452s
6	Nelson Piquet	20	BR	Benetton-Ford	69	1h 33m 22.726s
7	Jean Alesi	4	F	Tyrrell-DFR	69	1h 33m 24.860s
8	Martin Donnelly	12	GB	Lotus-Lamborghini	69	1h 33m 41.925s
9	Riccardo Patrese	6	I	Williams-Renault	69	1h 33m 45.701s
10	Derek Warwick	11	GB	Lotus-Lamborghini	69	
11	Stefano Modena	8	I	Brabham-Judd	68	
12	Pier-Luigi Martini	23	I	Minardi-DFR	68	
13	Andrea de Cesaris	22	I	Dallara-DFR	68	
14	Paolo Barilla	24	I	Minardi-DFR	67	
15	Gregor Foitek	35	CH	Onyx-DFR	67	
16	Nicola Larini	25	I	Ligier-DFR	67	
17	Michele Alboreto	9	I	Arrows-DFR	66	
18	Philippe Alliot	26	F	Ligier-DFR	66	
19	Olivier Grouillard	14	F	Osella-DFR	65	
20	Ayrton Senna	27	BR	McLaren-Honda	63	Puncture
R	J.J. Lehto	36	SF	Onyx-DFR	26	Engine
R	Eric Bernard	29	F	Lola-Lamborghini	12	Brakes
R	Aguri Suzuki	30	JPN	Lola-Lamborghini	11	Accident with Nakajima
R	Satoru Nakajima	3	JPN	Tyrrell-DFR	11	Accident with Suzuki
R	David Brabham	7	AUS	Brabham-Judd	11	Electrics
R	Emanuele Pirro	21	I	Dallara-DFR	10	Engine

Fastest lap: Prost, on lap 58, 1m 17.958s, 126.856 mph/204.156 km/h

Constructors' World Championship

Pos.	Team	Total
1	McLaren	54
2	Ferrari	36
3=	Williams	20
3=	Benetton	20
5	Tyrrell	14
6=	Brabham	2
6=	Arrows	2
8=	Larrousse	1
8=	Lotus	1

Non Qualifiers

No.	Name	Car
10	A. Caffi	Arrows-DFR
15	M. Gugelmin	Leyton House-Judd
16	I. Capelli	Leyton House-Judd
*33	R. Moreno	Eurobrun-Judd

*Excluded from event for receiving a push-start after spinning off.

Non Pre-Qualifiers

No.	Name	Car
17	G. Tarquini	AGS-DFR
18	Y. Dalmas	AGS-DFR
31	B. Gachot	Subaru-Coloni
34	C. Langes	Eurobrun-Judd
39	B. Giacomelli	Life

1990 FORMULA ONE GRAND PRIX
ROUND SEVEN

FRANCE
Paul Ricard

July 8, 1990

Circuit Length: 2.369 mls/3.813 km

Laps: 80

Official Starting Grid

Gerhard Berger *McLaren-Honda*	(1.04.512)	28	27	Nigel Mansell *Ferrari*	(1.04.402)
Alain Prost *Ferrari*	(1.04.781)	1	27	Ayrton Senna *McLaren-Honda*	(1.04.549)
Riccardo Patrese *Williams-Renault*	(1.05.059)	6	19	Alessandro Nannini *Benetton-Ford*	(1.05.009)
Thierry Boutsen *Williams-Renault*	(1.05.446)	5	16	Ivan Capelli *Leyton House-Judd*	(1.05.369)
Mauricio Gugelmin *Leyton House-Judd*	(1.05.818)	15	20	Nelson Piquet *Benetton-Ford*	(1.05.640)
Philippe Alliot *Ligier-DFR*	(1.05.986)	26	29	Eric Bernard *Lola-Lamborghini*	(1.05.852)
Aguri Suzuki *Lola-Lamborghini*	(1.06.100)	30	4	Jean Alesi *Tyrrell-DFR*	(1.06.084)
Derek Warwick *Lotus-Lamborghini*	(1.06.624)	11	3	Satoru Nakajima *Tyrrell-DFR*	(1.06.563)
Michele Alboreto *Arrows-DFR*	(1.06.847)	9	12	Martin Donnelly *Lotus-Lamborghini*	(1.06.647)
Stefano Modena *Brabham-Judd*	(1.06.937)	8	25	Nicola Larini *Ligier-DFR*	(1.06.856)
Alex Caffi *Arrows-DFR*	(1.07.207)	10	22	Andrea de Cesaris *Dallara-DFR*	(1.07.137)
Emanuele Pirro *Dallara-DFR*	(1.07.687)	21	23	Pier-Luigi Martini *Minardi-DFR*	(1.07.315)
Yannick Dalmas *AGS-DFR*	(1.07.926)	18	7	David Brabham *Brabham-Judd*	(1.07.733)

Race Classification

Pos.	Driver	No.	Nat.	Car	Laps	Time/retirement
1	Alain Prost	1	F	Ferrari	80	1h 33m 29.606s
2	Ivan Capelli	16	I	Leyton House-Judd	80	1h 33m 38.232s
3	Ayrton Senna	27	BR	McLaren-Honda	80	1h 33m 41.212s
4	Nelson Piquet	20	BR	Benetton-Ford	80	1h 34m 10.813s
5	Gerhard Berger	28	A	McLaren-Honda	80	1h 34m 11.825s
6	Riccardo Patrese	6	I	Williams-Renault	80	1h 34m 38.957s
7	Aguri Suzuki	30	JPN	Lola-Lamborghini	79	
8	Eric Bernard	29	F	Lola-Lamborghini	79	
9	Philippe Alliot	26	F	Ligier-DFR	79	
10	Michele Alboreto	9	I	Arrows-DFR	79	
11	Derek Warwick	11	GB	Lotus-Lamborghini	79	
12	Martin Donnelly	12	GB	Lotus-Lamborghini	79	
13	Stefano Modena	8	I	Brabham-Judd	78	
14	Nicola Larini	25	I	Ligier-DFR	78	
15	Andrea de Cesaris	22	I	Dallara-DFR	78	
16	David Brabham	7	AUS	Brabham-Judd	77	
17	Alessandro Nannini	19	I	Benetton-Ford	75	Electrics
18	Yannick Dalmas	18	F	AGS-DFR	75	
19	Nigel Mansell	2	GB	Ferrari	72	Engine
R	Satoru Nakajima	3	JPN	Tyrrell-DFR	63	Gear linkage
R	Mauricio Gugelmin	15	BR	Leyton House-Judd	58	Engine
R	Pier-Luigi Martini	23	I	Minardi-DFR	40	Electrics
R	Jean Alesi	4	F	Tyrrell-DFR	23	Differential
R	Alex Caffi	10	I	Arrows-DFR	22	Rear suspension
R	Thierry Boutsen	5	I	Williams-Renault	71	Engine
R	Emanuele Pirro	21	I	Dallara-DFR	7	Brakes/spun off

Fastest lap: Mansell, on lap 64, 1m 08.012s, 125.410 mph/201.829 km/h

Drivers' World Championship

Pos.	Driver	Total
1	Ayrton Senna	35
2	Alain Prost	32
3	Gerhard Berger	25
4	Nelson Piquet	16
5=	Jean Alesi	13
5=	Nigel Mansell	13
7	Thierry Boutsen	11
8	Riccardo Patrese	10
9	Alessandro Nannini	7
10	Ivan Capelli	6
11=	Stefano Modena	2
11=	Alex Caffi	2
13=	Satoru Nakajima	1
13=	Eric Bernard	1
13=	Derek Warwick	1

Constructors' World Championship

Pos.	Team	Total
1	McLaren	60
2	Ferrari	45
3	Benetton	23
4	Williams	21
5	Tyrrell	14
6	Leyton House	6
7=	Brabham	2
7=	Arrows	2
9=	Larrousse	1
9=	Lotus	1

Non Qualifiers

No.	Name	Car
17	G. Tarquini	AGS-DFR
24	P. Barilla	Minardi-DFR
35	G. Foitek	Onyx-DFR
36	J.J. Lehto	Onyx-DFR

Non Pre-Qualifiers

No.	Name	Car
14	O. Grouillard	Osella-DFR
31	B. Gachot	Subaru-Coloni
33	R. Moreno	Eurobrun-Judd
34	C. Langes	Eurobrun-Judd
39	B. Giacomelli	Life

1990 FORMULA ONE GRAND PRIX
ROUND EIGHT

GREAT BRITAIN
Silverstone Circuit

July 15, 1990

Circuit Length: 2.969 mls/4.778 km

Laps 64

Official Starting Grid

			2 Nigel Mansell	(1.07.428)	
Ayrton Senna	(1.08.071)	27	Ferrari		
McLaren-Honda			28 Gerhard Berger	(1.08.246)	
Thierry Boutsen	(1.08.291)	5	McLaren-Honda		
Williams-Renault			1 Alain Prost	(1.08.336)	
Jean Alesi	(1.08.370)	4	Ferrari		
Tyrrell-DFR			6 Riccardo Patrese	(1.08.677)	
Eric Bernard	(1.09.003)	29	Williams-Renault		
Lola-Lamborghini			30 Aguri Suzuki	(1.09.243)	
Ivan Capelli	(1.09.308)	16	Lola-Lamborghini		
Leyton House-Judd			**20 Nelson Piquet	(1.09.407)	
Satoru Nakajima	(1.09.608)	3	Benetton-Ford		
Tyrrell-DFR			19 Alessandro Nannini	(1.09.641)	
Martin Donnelly	(1.09.741)	12	Benetton-Ford		
Lotus-Lamborghini			*15 Mauricio Gugelmin	(1.10.044)	
Derek Warwick	(1.10.092)	11	Leyton House-Judd		
Lotus-Lamborghini			10 Alex Caffi	(1.10.110)	
Pier-Luigi Martini	(1.10.303)	23	Arrows-DFR		
Minardi-DFR			21 Emanuele Pirro	(1.10.847)	
Stefano Modena	(1.11.070)	8	Dallara-DFR		
Brabham-Judd			25 Nicola Larini	(1.11.180)	
Philippe Alliot	(1.11.215)	26	Ligier-DFR		
Ligier-DFR			22 Andrea de Cesaris	(1.11.234)	
Paolo Barilla	(1.11.387)	24	Dallara-DFR		
Minardi-DFR			9 Michele Alboreto	(1.11.562)	
Gabriele Tarquini	(1.11.681)	17	Arrows-DFR		
AGS-DFR					

*Did not start   ** Started from back of grid

Race Classification

Pos.	Driver	No.	Nat.	Car	Laps	Time/retirement
1	Alain Prost	1	F	Ferrari	64	1h 18m 30.999s
2	Thierry Boutsen	5	B	Williams-Renault	64	1h 19m 10.091s
3	Ayrton Senna	27	BR	McLaren-Honda	64	1h 19m 14.087s
4	Eric Bernard	29	F	Lola-Lamborghini	64	1h 19m 46.301s
5	Nelson Piquet	20	BR	Benetton-Ford	64	1h 19m 55.002s
6	Aguri Suzuki	30	JPN	Lola-Lamborghini	63	
7	Alex Caffi	10	I	Arrows-DFR	63	
8	Jean Alesi	4	F	Tyrrell-DFR	63	
9	Stefano Modena	8	I	Brabham-Judd	62	
10	Nicola Larini	25	I	Ligier-DFR	62	
11	Emanuele Pirro	25	I	Dallara-DFR	62	
12	Paolo Barilla	24	I	Minardi-DFR	62	
13	Philippe Alliot	26	F	Ligier-DFR	61	
14	Gerhard Berger	28	A	McLaren-Honda	60	Throttle cable
R	Nigel Mansell	2	GB	Ferrari	55	Gearbox
R	Ivan Capelli	16	I	Leyton House-Judd	48	Fuel pipe
R	Martin Donnelly	12	GB	Lotus-Lamborghini	48	Engine
R	Derek Warwick	11	GB	Lotus-Lamborghini	46	Engine
R	Gabriele Tarquini	17	I	AGS-DFR	41	Engine
R	Michele Alboreto	9	I	Arrows-DFR	37	Engine cut out
R	Riccardo Patrese	6	I	Willliams-Renault	26	Damaged rear undertray
R	Satoru Nakajima	3	JPN	Tyrrell-DFR	20	Electrics
R	Alessandro Nannini	19	I	Benetton-Ford	15	Hit Patrese, spun and stalled
R	Andrea de Cesaris	22	I	Dallara-DFR	12	Gearbox
R	Pier-Luigi Martini	23	I	Minardi-DFR	3	Alternator
DNS	Mauricio Gugelmin	15	BR	Leyton House-Judd	0	Fuel pump drive

Fastest lap: Mansell, on lap 51, 1m 11.291s, 149.977 mph/241.357 km/h

Drivers' World Championship

Pos.	Driver	Total
1	Alain Prost	41
2	Ayrton Senna	39
3	Gerhard Berger	25
4	Nelson Piquet	18
5	Thierry Boutsen	17
6=	Jean Alesi	13
6=	Nigel Mansell	13
8	Riccardo Patrese	10
9	Alessandro Nannini	7
10	Ivan Capelli	6
11	Eric Bernard	4
12=	Stefano Modena	2
12=	Alex Caffi	2
14=	Satoru Nakajima	1
14=	Derek Warwick	1
14=	Aguri Suzuki	1

Constructors' World Championship

Pos.	Team	Total
1	McLaren	64
2	Ferrari	54
3	Williams	27
4	Benetton	25
5	Tyrrell	14
6	Leyton House	6
7	Larrousse	5
8=	Brabham	2
8=	Arrows	2
10	Lotus	1

Non Qualifiers

No.	Name	Car
7	D. Brabham	Brabham-Judd
14	O. Grouillard	Osella-DFR
35	G. Foitek	Onyx-DFR
36	J.J. Lehto	Onyx-DFR

Non Pre-Qualifiers

No.	Name	Car
18	Y. Dalmas	AGS-DFR
31	B. Gachot	Subaru-Coloni
33	R. Moreno	Eurobrun-Judd
34	C. Langes	Eurobrun-Judd
39	B. Giacomelli	Life

1990 FORMULA ONE GRAND PRIX
ROUND NINE

GERMANY
Hockenheim-Ring

July 29, 1990

Circuit Length: 4.2265 mls/6.802 km

Laps: 45

Official Starting Grid

Driver	Time	No.		No.	Driver	Time
Ayrton Senna *McLaren-Honda*	(1.40.198)	27		28	Gerhard Berger *McLaren-Honda*	(1.40.434)
Alain Prost *Ferrari*	(1.41.732)	1		2	Nigel Mansell *Ferrari*	(1.42.057)
Riccardo Patrese *Williams-Renault*	(1.42.195)	6		5	Thierry Boutsen *Williams-Renault*	(1.42.380)
Nelson Piquet *Benetton-Ford*	(1.42.872)	20		4	Jean Alesi *Tyrrell-DFR*	(1.43.255)
Alessandro Nannini *Benetton-Ford*	(1.43.594)	19		16	Ivan Capelli *Leyton House-Judd*	(1.44.349)
Aguri Suzuki *Lola-Lamborghini*	(1.44.363)	30		29	Eric Bernard *Lola-Lamborghini*	(1.44.496)
Satoru Nakajima *Tyrrell-DFR*	(1.44.650)	3		15	Mauricio Gugelmin *Leyton House-Judd*	(1.45.193)
Pier-Luigi Martini *Minardi-DFR*	(1.45.237)	23		11	Derek Warwick *Lotus-Lamborghini*	(1.45.244)
Stefano Modena *Brabham-Judd*	(1.45.547)	8		10	Alex Caffi *Arrows-DFR*	(1.45.604)
Michele Alboreto *Arrows-DFR*	(1.45.755)	9		12	Martin Donnelly *Lotus-Lamborghini*	(1.45.790)
David Brabham *Brabham-Judd*	(1.46.110)	7		25	Nicola Larini *Ligier-DFR*	(1.46.187)
Emanuele Pirro *Dallara-DFR*	(1.46.506)	21		26	Philippe Alliot *Ligier-DFR*	(1.46.596)
J.J. Lehto *Monteverdi-DFR*	(1.46.857)	36		35	Gregor Foitek *Monteverdi-DFR*	(1.47.209)

Drivers' World Championship

Pos.	Driver	Total
1	Ayrton Senna	48
2	Alain Prost	44
3	Gerhard Berger	29
4=	Thierry Boutsen	18
4=	Nelson Piquet	18
6=	Jean Alesi	13
6=	Alessandro Nannini	13
6=	Nigel Mansell	13
9	Riccardo Patrese	12
10	Ivan Capelli	6
11	Eric Bernard	4
12=	Alex Caffi	2
12=	Stefano Modena	2
14=	Aguri Suzuki	1
14=	Derek Warwick	1
14=	Satoru Nakajima	1

Race Classification

Pos.	Driver	No.	Nat.	Car	Laps	Time/retirement
1	Ayrton Senna	27	BR	McLaren-Honda	45	1h 20m 47.164s
2	Alessandro Nannini	19	I	Benetton-Ford	45	1h 20m 53.684s
3	Gerhard Berger	28	A	McLaren-Honda	45	1h 20m 55.717s
4	Alain Prost	1	F	Ferrari	45	1h 21m 32.424s
5	Riccardo Patrese	6	I	Williams-Renault	45	1h 21m 35.192s
6	Thierry Boutsen	5	B	Williams-Renault	45	1h 22m 08.655s
7	Ivan Capelli	16	I	Leyton House-Judd	44	
8	Derek Warwick	11	GB	Lotus-Lamborghini	44	
9	Alex Caffi	10	I	Arrows-DFR	44	
10	Nicola Larini	25	I	Ligier-DFR	43	
11	Jean Alesi	4	F	Tyrrell-DFR	40	CV joint
NC	J.J. Lehto	36	SF	Monteverdi-DFR	39	Running, not classified
R	Eric Bernard	29	F	Lola-Lamborghini	35	Fuel pressure
R	Aguri Suzuki	30	JPN	Lola-Lamborghini	33	Clutch
R	Satoru Nakajima	3	JPN	Tyrrell-DFR	24	Engine
R	Nelson Piquet	20	BR	Benetton-Ford	23	Engine
R	Pier-Luigi Martini	23	I	Minardi-DFR	20	Engine
R	Gregor Foitek	35	CH	Monteverdi-DFR	19	Spun off
R	Nigel Mansell	2	GB	Ferrari	15	Slid off/nose wing damage
R	Mauricio Gugelmin	15	BR	Leyton House-Judd	12	Engine ingested stone
R	David Brabham	7	AUS	Brabham-Judd	12	Engine
R	Michele Alboreto	9	I	Arrows-DFR	10	Engine
R	Martin Donnelly	12	GB	Lotus-Lamborghini	1	Clutch
R	Stefano Modena	8	I	Brabham-Judd	0	Clutch on startline
R	Emanuele Pirro	21	I	Dallara-DFR	0	Collision on startline
DQ	Philippe Alliot	26	F	Ligier-DFR	0	Excluded for receiving push start after startline accident

Fastest lap: Boutsen, on lap 31, 1m 45.602s, 144.084 mph/231.882 km/h

Constructors' World Championship

Pos.	Team	Total
1	McLaren	77
2	Ferrari	57
3	Benetton	31
4	Williams	30
5	Tyrrell	14
6	Leyton House	6
7	Larrousse	5
8=	Arrows	2
8=	Brabham	2
10	Lotus	1

Non Qualifiers

No.	Name	Car
14	O. Grouillard	Osella-DFR
18	Y. Dalmas	AGS-DFR
22	A. de Cesaris	Dallara-DFR
24	P. Barilla	Minardi-DFR

Non Pre-Qualifiers

No.	Name	Car
17	G. Tarquini	AGS-DFR
31	B. Gachot	Coloni-DFR
33	R. Moreno	Eurobrun-Judd
34	C. Langes	Eurobrun-Judd
39	B. Giacomelli	Life

1990 FORMULA ONE GRAND PRIX
ROUND TEN

HUNGARY
Hungaroring

August 12, 1990

Circuit Length: 2.465 mls/3.968 km

Laps: 77

Official Starting Grid

Thierry Boutsen *Williams-Renault*	(1.17.919)	5		6	Riccardo Patrese *Williams-Renault*	(1.17.955)
Gerhard Berger *McLaren-Honda*	(1.18.127)	28		27	Ayrton Senna *McLaren-Honda*	(1.18.162)
Nigel Mansell *Ferrari*	(1.18.719)	2		4	Jean Alesi *Tyrrell-DFR*	(1.18.726)
Alessandro Nannini *Benetton-Ford*	(1.18.901)	19		1	Alain Prost *Ferrari*	(1.19.029)
Nelson Piquet *Benetton-Ford*	(1.19.453)	20		22	Andrea de Cesaris *Dallara-DFR*	(1.19.675)
Derek Warwick *Lotus-Lamborghini*	(1.19.839)	11		29	Eric Bernard *Lola-Lamborghini*	(1.19.963)
Emanuele Pirro *Dallara-DFR*	(1.19.970)	21		23	Pier-Luigi Martini *Minardi-DFR*	(1.20.197)
Satoru Nakajima *Tyrrell-DFR*	(1.20.202)	3		16	Ivan Capelli *Leyton House-Judd*	(1.20.385)
Mauricio Gugelmin *Leyton House-Judd*	(1.20.397)	15		12	Martin Donnelly *Lotus-Lamborghini*	(1.20.602)
Aguri Suzuki *Lola-Lamborghini*	(1.20.619)	30		8	Stefano Modena *Brabham-Judd*	(1.20.715)
Philippe Alliot *Ligier-DFR*	(1.21.003)	26		9	Michele Alboreto *Arrows-DFR*	(1.21.758)
Paolo Barilla *Minardi-DFR*	(1.21.849)	24		17	Gabriele Tarquini *AGS-DFR*	(1.21.964)
Nicola Larini *Ligier-DFR*	(1.22.078)	25		10	Alex Caffi *Arrows-DFR*	(1.22.126)

Drivers' World Championship

Pos.	Driver	Total
1	Ayrton Senna	54
2	Alain Prost	44
3	Gerhard Berger	29
4	Thierry Boutsen	27
5	Nelson Piquet	22
6	Riccardo Patrese	15
7=	Jean Alesi	13
7=	Alessandro Nannini	13
7=	Nigel Mansell	13
10	Ivan Capelli	6
11	Eric Bernard	5
12	Derek Warwick	3
13=	Alex Caffi	2
13=	Stefano Modena	2
15=	Aguri Suzuki	1
15=	Satoru Nakajima	1

Constructors' World Championship

Pos.	Team	Total
1	McLaren	83
2	Ferrari	57
3	Williams	42
4	Benetton	35
5	Tyrrell	14
6=	Leyton House	6
6=	Larrousse	6
8	Lotus	3
9=	Arrows	2
9=	Brabham	2

Race Classification

Pos.	Driver	No.	Nat.	Car	Laps	Time/retirement
1	Thierry Boutsen	5	B	Williams-Renault	77	1h 49m 30.597s
2	Ayrton Senna	27	BR	McLaren-Honda	77	1h 49m 30.885s
3	Nelson Piquet	20	BR	Benetton-Ford	77	1h 49m 58.490s
4	Riccardo Patrese	6	I	Williams-Renault	77	1h 50m 02.430s
5	Derek Warwick	11	GB	Lotus-Lamborghini	77	1h 50m 44.841s
6	Eric Bernard	29	F	Lola-Lamborghini	77	1h 50m 54.905s
7	Martin Donnelly	12	GB	Lotus-Lamborghini	76	
8	Mauricio Gugelmin	15	BR	Leyton House-Judd	76	
9	Alex Caffi	10	I	Arrows-DFR	76	
10	Emanuele Pirro	21	I	Dallara-DFR	76	
11	Nicola Larini	25	I	Ligier-DFR	76	
12	Michele Alboreto	9	I	Arrows-DFR	75	
13	Gabriele Tarquini	17	I	AGS-DFR	74	
14	Philippe Alliot	26	F	Ligier-DFR	74	
15	Paolo Barilla	24	I	Minardi-DFR	74	
16	Gerhard Berger	28	A	McLaren-Honda	72	Accident with Mansell
17	Nigel Mansell	2	GB	Ferrari	71	Accident with Berger
R	Alessandro Nannini	19	I	Benetton-Ford	64	Accident with Senna
R	Ivan Capelli	16	I	Leyton House-Judd	56	Transmission
R	Aguri Suzuki	30	JPN	Lola-Lamborghini	37	Engine
R	Alain Prost	1	F	Ferrari	36	Transmission/spun off
R	Jean Alesi	4	F	Tyrrell-DFR	36	Accident with Martini
R	Stefano Modena	8	I	Brabham-Judd	35	Engine
R	Pier-Luigi Martini	23	I	Minardi-DFR	35	Accident with Alesi
R	Andrea de Cesaris	22	I	Dallara-DFR	22	Engine
R	Satoru Nakajima	3	JPN	Tyrrell-DFR	9	Spun off

Fastest lap: Patrese, on lap 63, 1m 22.058s, 108.169 mph/174.082 km/h

Non Qualifiers

No.	Name	Car
7	D. Brabham	Brabham-Judd
18	Y. Dalmas	AGS-DFR
35	G. Foitek	Monteverdi-DFR
36	J.J. Lehto	Monteverdi-DFR

Non Pre-Qualifiers

No.	Name	Car
14	O. Grouillard	Osella-DFR
31	B. Gachot	Coloni-DFR
33	R. Moreno	Eurobrun-Judd
34	C. Langes	Eurobrun-Judd
39	B. Giacomelli	Life

1990 FORMULA ONE GRAND PRIX
ROUND ELEVEN

BELGIUM

Circuit de Spa-Francorchamps

August 25, 1990

Circuit Length: 4.3123 mls/6.940 km

Laps:44

Official Starting Grid

			27 Ayrton Senna	(1.50.365)
Gerhard Berger	(1.50.948)	28	*McLaren-Honda*	
McLaren-Honda			1 Alain Prost	(1.51.043)
Thierry Boutsen	(1.51.902)	5	*Ferrari*	
Williams-Renault			2 Nigel Mansell	(1.52.267)
Alessandro Nannini	(1.52.648)	19	*Ferrari*	
Benetton-Ford			6 Riccardo Patrese	(1.52.703)
Nelson Piquet	(1.52.853)	20	*Williams-Renault*	
Benetton-Ford			4 Jean Alesi	(1.52.885)
Satoru Nakajima	(1.53.468)	3	*Tyrrell-DFR*	
Tyrrell-DFR			*30 Aguri Suzuki	(1.53.523)
Ivan Capelli	(1.53.783)	16	*Lola-Lamborghini*	
Leyton House-Judd			8 Stefano Modena	(1.53.916)
Mauricio Gugelmin	(1.54.120)	15	*Brabham-Judd*	
Leyton House-Judd			29 Eric Bernard	(1.54.251)
Pier-Luigi Martini	(1.54.312)	23	*Lola-Lamborghini*	
Minardi-DFR			21 Emanuele Pirro	(1.54.595)
Derek Warwick	(1.55.068)	11	*Dallara-DFR*	
Lotus-Lamborghini			10 Alex Caffi	(1.55.199)
Andrea de Cesaris	(1.55.261)	22	*Arrows-DFR*	
Dallara-DFR			25 Nicola Larini	(1.55.278)
Martin Donnelly	(1.55.304)	**12	*Ligier-DFR*	
Lotus-Lamborghini			14 Olivier Grouillard	(1.55.334)
David Brabham	(1.55.668)	7	*Osella-DFR*	
Brabham-Judd			*24 Paolo Barilla	(1.55.859)
Michele Alboreto	(1.56.055)	9	*Minardi-DFR*	
Arrows-DFR				

*Did not take part; cars damaged in accidents before third and final start
**Started from pit lane*

Drivers' World Championship

Pos.	Driver	Total
1	Ayrton Senna	63
2	Alain Prost	50
3	Gerhard Berger	33
4	Thierry Boutsen	27
5	Nelson Piquet	24
6	Alessandro Nannini	16
7	Riccardo Patrese	15
8=	Jean Alesi	13
8=	Nigel Mansell	13
10	Ivan Capelli	6
11	Eric Bernard	5
12	Derek Warwick	3
13=	Alex Caffi	2
13=	Stefano Modena	2
15=	Aguri Suzuki	1
15=	Satoru Nakajima	1
15=	Mauricio Gugelmin	1

Constructors' World Championship

Pos.	Team	Total
1	McLaren	96
2	Ferrari	63
3	Williams	42
4	Benetton	40
5	Tyrrell	14
6	Leyton House	7
7	Larrousse	6
8	Lotus	3
9=	Arrows	2
9=	Brabham	2

Race Classification

Pos.	Driver	No.	Nat.	Car	Laps	Time/retirement
1	Ayrton Senna	27	BR	McLaren-Honda	44	1h 26m 31.997s
2	Alain Prost	1	F	Ferrari	44	1h 26m 35.547s
3	Gerhard Berger	28	A	McLaren-Honda	44	1h 27m 00.459s
4	Alessandro Nannini	19	I	Benetton-Ford	44	1h 27m 21.334s
5	Nelson Piquet	20	BR	Benetton-Ford	44	1h 28m 01.647s
6	Mauricio Gugelmin	15	BR	Leyton House-Judd	44	1h 28m 20.848s
7	Ivan Capelli	16	I	Leyton House-Judd	43	
8	Jean Alesi	4	F	Tyrrell-DFR	43	
9	Eric Bernard	29	F	Lola-Lamborghini	43	
10	Alex Caffi	10	I	Arrows-DFR	43	
11	Derek Warwick	11	GB	Lotus-Lamborghini	43	
12	Martin Donnelly	12	GB	Lotus-Lamborghini	43	
13	Michele Alboreto	9	I	Arrows-DFR	43	
14	Nicola Larini	25	I	Ligier-DFR	42	
15	Pier-Luigi Martini	23	I	Minardi DFR	42	
16	Olivier Grouillard	14	F	Osella-DFR	42	
17	Stefano Modena	8	I	Brabham-Judd	39	Engine
R	David Brabham	7	AUS	Brabham-Judd	36	Electrics
R	Andrea de Cesaris	22	I	Dallara-DFR	27	Engine
R	Thierry Boutsen	5	B	Williams-Renault	21	Driveshaft
R	Nigel Mansell	2	GB	Ferrari	19	Handling
R	Riccardo Patrese	6	I	Williams-Renault	18	Gearbox
R	Emanuele Pirro	21	I	Dallara-DFR	5	Cracked water pipe
R	Satoru Nakajima	3	JPN	Tyrrell-DFR	4	Engine
R	Aguri Suzuki	30	JPN	Lola-Lamborghini	0	Accident at first start
R	Paolo Barilla	24	I	Minardi-DFR	0	Accident after second start

Fastest lap: Prost, on lap 38, 1m 55.087s 134.891 mph/217.088 km/h

Non Qualifiers

No.	Name	Car
17	G. Tarquini	AGS-DFR
18	Y. Dalmas	AGS-DFR
26	P. Alliot	Ligier-DFR
31	B. Gachot	Coloni-DFR

Non Pre-Qualifiers

No.	Name	Car
33	R. Moreno	Eurobrun-Judd
34	C. Langes	Eurobrun-Judd
39	B. Giacomelli	Life

1990 FORMULA ONE GRAND PRIX
ROUND TWELVE

ITALY

Autodromo Nazionale di Monza

September 9, 1990

Circuit Length: 3.6039 mls/5.80 km

Laps: 53

Official Starting Grid

Ayrton Senna	(1.22.533)	27			
McLaren-Honda			1	Alain Prost	(1.22.935)
Gerhard Berger	(1.22.936)	28		Ferrari	
McLaren-Honda			2	Nigel Mansell	(1.23.141)
Jean Alesi	(1.23.526)	4		Ferrari	
Tyrrell-DFR			5	Thierry Boutsen	(1.23.984)
Riccardo Patrese	(1.24.253)	6		Williams-Renault	
Williams-Renault			19	Alessandro Nannini	(1.24.583)
Nelson Piquet	(1.24.699)	20		Benetton-Ford	
Benetton-Ford			15	Mauricio Gugelmin	(1.25.556)
Martin Donnelly	(1.25.629)	12		Leyton House-Judd	
Lotus-Lamborghini			11	Derek Warwick	(1.25.677)
Eric Bernard	(1.25.927)	29		Lotus-Lamborghini	
Lola-Lamborghini			3	Satoru Nakajima	(1.26.081)
Pier-Luigi Martini	(1.26.330)	23		Tyrrell-DFR	
Minardi-DFR			16	Ivan Capelli	(1.26.712)
Stefano Modena	(1.26.950)	8		Leyton House-Judd	
Brabham-Judd			30	Aguri Suzuki	(1.26.962)
Emanuele Pirro	(1.26.964)	21		Lola-Lamborghini	
Dallara-DFR			26	Philippe Alliot	(1.27.043)
Alex Caffi	(1.27.410)	10		Ligier-DFR	
Arrows-DFR			9	Michele Alboreto	(1.27.448)
Olivier Grouillard	(1.27.541)	14		Arrows-DFR	
Osella-DFR			18	Yannick Dalmas	(1.27.673)
Andrea de Cesaris	(1.27.749)	22		AGS-DFR	
Dallara-DFR			25	Nicola Larini	(1.27.937)
				Ligier-DFR	

Drivers' World Championship

Pos.	Driver	Total
1	Ayrton Senna	72
2	Alain Prost	56
3	Gerhard Berger	37
4	Thierry Boutsen	27
5	Nelson Piquet	24
6	Riccardo Patrese	17
7=	Alessandro Nannini	16
7=	Nigel Mansell	16
9	Jean Alesi	13
10	Ivan Capelli	6
11	Eric Bernard	5
12	Derek Warwick	3
13=	Alex Caffi	2
13=	Stefano Modena	2
13=	Satoru Nakajima	2
16=	Aguri Suzuki	1
16=	Mauricio Gugelmin	1

Constructors' World Championship

Pos.	Team	Total
1	McLaren	109
2	Ferrari	72
3	Williams	44
4	Benetton	40
5	Tyrrell	15
6	Leyton House	7
7	Larrousse	6
8	Lotus	3
9=	Arrows	2
9=	Brabham	2

Race Classification

Pos.	Driver	No.	Nat.	Car	Laps	Time/retirement
1	Ayrton Senna	27	BR	McLaren-Honda	53	1h 17m 57.878s
2	Alain Prost	1	F	Ferrari	53	1h 18m 03.932s
3	Gerhard Berger	28	A	McLaren-Honda	53	1h 18m 05.282s
4	Nigel Mansell	2	GB	Ferrari	53	1h 18m 54.097s
5	Riccardo Patrese	6	I	Williams-Renault	53	1h 19m 23.152s
6	Satoru Nakajima	3	JPN	Tyrrell-DFR	52	
7	Nelson Piquet	20	BR	Benetton-Ford	52	
8	Alessandro Nannini	19	I	Benetton-Ford	52	
9	Alex Caffi	10	I	Arrows-DFR	51	
10	Andrea de Cesaris	22	I	Dallara-DFR	51	
11	Nicola Larini	25	I	Ligier-DFR	51	
12	Michele Alboreto	9	I	Arrows-DFR	50	Spun off
13	Philippe Alliot	26	F	Ligier-DFR	50	
NC	Yannick Dalmas	18	F	AGS-DFR	45	Running, not classified
R	Ivan Capelli	16	I	Leyton House-Judd	36	Engine cut out
R	Aguri Suzuki	30	JPN	Lola-Lamborghini	36	Electrics
R	Olivier Grouillard	14	F	Osella-DFR	27	Wheel bearing
R	Mauricio Gugelmin	15	BR	Leyton House-Judd	24	Engine
R	Stefano Modena	8	I	Brabham-Judd	21	Engine
R	Thierry Boutsen	5	B	Williams-Renault	18	Suspension
R	Derek Warwick	11	GB	Lotus-Lamborghini	15	Clutch
R	Emanuele Pirro	21	I	Dallara-DFR	14	Gearbox/spun off
R	Martin Donnelly	12	GB	Lotus-Lamborghini	13	Engine
R	Eric Bernard	29	F	Lola-Lamborghini	10	Clutch
R	Pier-Luigi Martini	23	I	Minardi-DFR	7	Suspension
R	Jean Alesi	4	F	Tyrrell-DFR	4	Spun off

Fastest lap: Senna, on lap 46, 1m 26.254s, 150.418 mph/242.076 km/h

Non Qualifiers

No.	Name	Car
7	D. Brabham	Brabham-Judd
17	G. Tarquini	AGS-DFR
24	P. Barilla	Minardi-DFR
31	B. Gachot	Coloni-DFR

Non Pre-Qualifiers

No.	Name	Car
33	R. Moreno	Eurobrun-Judd
34	C. Langes	Eurobrun-Judd
39	B. Giacomelli	Life

**1990 FORMULA ONE GRAND PRIX
ROUND THIRTEEN**

PORTUGAL

Autodromo do Estoril

September 23, 1990

Circuit Length: 2.703 mls/4.350 km

Laps: 61 (reduced from 71 laps)

Official Starting Grid

Driver	Time	No.		No.	Driver	Time
Nigel Mansell *Ferrari*	(1.13.557)	2		1	Alain Prost *Ferrari*	(1.13.595)
Ayrton Senna *McLaren-Honda*	(1.13.601)	27		28	Gerhard Berger *McLaren-Honda*	(1.14.292)
Riccardo Patrese *Williams-Renault*	(1.14.723)	6		20	Nelson Piquet *Benetton-Ford*	(1.14.728)
Thierry Boutsen *Williams-Renault*	(1.14.934)	5		4	Jean Alesi *Tyrrell-DFR*	(1.15.122)
Alessandro Nannini *Benetton-Ford*	(1.15.411)	19		29	Eric Bernard *Lola-Lamborghini*	(1.15.673)
Aguri Suzuki *Lola-Lamborghini*	(1.16.012)	30		16	Ivan Capelli *Leyton House-Judd*	(1.16.284)
Emanuele Pirro *Dallara-DFR*	(1.16.290)	21		15	Mauricio Gugelmin *Leyton House-Judd*	(1.16.296)
Martin Donnelly *Lotus-Lamborghini*	(1.16.762)	10		23	Pier-Luigi Martini *Minardi DFR*	(1.16.795)
Alex Caffi *Arrows-DFR*	(1.16.946)	10		22	Andrea de Cesaris *Dallara-DFR*	(1.17.066)
Michele Alboreto *Arrows-DFR*	(1.17.081)	9		26	Philippe Alliot *Ligier-DFR*	(1.17.120)
Derek Warwick *Lotus-Lamborghini*	(1.17.259)	11		25	Nicola Larini *Ligier-DFR*	(1.17.269)
Stefano Modena *Brabham-Judd*	(1.17.341)	8		18	Yannick Dalmas *AGS-DFR*	(1.17.621)
David Brabham *Brabham-Judd*	(1.17.715)	7				

Drivers' World Championship

Pos.	Driver	Total
1	Ayrton Senna	78
2	Alain Prost	60
3	Gerhard Berger	40
4	Thierry Boutsen	27
5	Nelson Piquet	26
6	Nigel Mansell	25
7=	Riccardo Patrese	17
7=	Alessandro Nannini	17
9	Jean Alesi	13
10	Ivan Capelli	6
11	Eric Bernard	5
12	Derek Warwick	3
13=	Alex Caffi	2
13=	Stefano Modena	2
13=	Satoru Nakajima	2
16=	Aguri Suzuki	1
16=	Mauricio Gugelmin	1

Constructors' World Championship

Pos.	Team	Total
1	McLaren	118
2	Ferrari	85
3	Williams	44
4	Benetton	43
5	Tyrrell	15
6	Leyton House	7
7	Larrousse	6
8	Lotus	3
9=	Arrows	2
9=	Brabham	2

Race Classification

Pos.	Driver	No.	Nat.	Car	Laps	Time/retirement
1	Nigel Mansell	2	GB	Ferrari	61	1h 22m 11.014s
2	Ayrton Senna	27	BR	McLaren-Honda	61	1h 22m 13.822s
3	Alain Prost	1	F	Ferrari	61	1h 22m 15.203s
4	Gerhard Berger	28	A	McLaren-Honda	61	1h 22m 16.910s
5	Nelson Piquet	20	BR	Benetton-Ford	61	1h 23m 08.432s
6	Alessandro Nannini	19	I	Benetton-Ford	61	1h 23m 09.263s
7	Riccardo Patrese	6	I	Williams-Renault	60	
8	Jean Alesi	4	F	Tyrrell-DFR	60	
9	Michele Alboreto	9	I	Arrows-DFR	60	
10	Nicola Larini	25	I	Ligier-DFR	59	
11	Pier-Luigi Martini	23	I	Minardi-DFR	59	
12	Mauricio Gugelmin	15	BR	Leyton House-Judd	59	
13	Alex Caffi	10	I	Arrows-DFR	58	Collision with Suzuki
14	Aguri Suzuki	30	JPN	Lola-Lamborghini	58	Collision with Caffi
15	Emanuele Pirro	21	I	Dallara-DFR	58	
R	Philippe Alliot	26	F	Ligier-DFR	52	Collision with Mansell
R	David Brabham	7	AUS	Brabham-Judd	52	Gearbox
R	Ivan Capelli	16	I	Leyton House-Judd	51	Engine
R	Thierry Boutsen	5	B	Williams-Renault	30	Gearbox
R	Eric Bernard	29	F	Lola-Lamborghini	24	Gearbox
R	Stefano Modena	8	I	Brabham-Judd	21	Gearbox
R	Martin Donnelly	12	GB	Lotus-Lamborghini	14	Alternator
R	Derek Warwick	11	GB	Lotus-Lamborghini	5	Throttle
R	Yannick Dalmas	18	F	AGS-DFR	3	Driveshaft
R	Andrea de Cesaris	22	I	Dallara-DFR	0	Stuck throttle

Fastest lap: Patrese, on lap 56, 1m 18.306s, 124.264 mph/199.985 km/h

Non Qualifiers

No.	Name	Car
* 3	S. Nakajima	Tyrrell-DFR
7	D. Brabham	Brabham-Judd
14	O. Grouillard	Osella-DFR
24	P. Barilla	Minardi-DFR
31	B. Gachot	Coloni-DFR

*Withdrawn from race, driver unwell

Non Pre-Qualifiers

No.	Name	Car
33	R. Moreno	Eurobrun-Judd
34	C. Langes	Eurobrun-Judd
39	B. Giacomelli	Life-Judd

1990 FORMULA ONE GRAND PRIX
ROUND FOURTEEN

SPAIN

Circuito de Jerez

September 30, 1990

Circuit Length: 2.6209 mls/4.218 km

Laps: 73

Official Starting Grid

				27	Ayrton Senna	(1.18.387)
Alain Prost	(1.18.824)	1			McLaren-Honda	
Ferrari				2	Nigel Mansell	(1.19.106)
Jean Alesi	(1.19.604)	4			Ferrari	
Tyrrell-DFR				28	Gerhard Berger	(1.19.618)
Riccardo Patrese	(1.19.647)	6			McLaren-Honda	
Williams-Renault				5	Thierry Boutsen	(1.19.689)
Nelson Piquet	(1.19.700)	20			Williams-Renault	
Benetton-Ford				19	Alessandro Nannini	(1.20.367)
Derek Warwick	(1.20.610)	11			Benetton-Ford	
Lotus-Lamborghini				23	Pier-Luigi Martini	(1.21.060)
Mauricio Gugelmin	(1.21.167)	15			Minardi-DFR	
Leyton House-Judd				26	Philippe Alliot	(1.21.170)
Satoru Nakajima	(1.21.215)	3			Ligier-DFR	
Tyrrell-DFR				30	Aguri Suzuki	(1.21.244)
Emanuele Pirro	(1.21.277)	21			Lola-Lamborghini	
Dallara-DFR				22	Andrea de Cesaris	(1.21.467)
Eric Bernard	(1.21.551)	29			Dallara-DFR	
Lola-Lamborghini				16	Ivan Capelli	(1.21.910)
Nicola Larini	(1.21.996)	25			Leyton House-Judd	
Ligier-DFR				14	Olivier Grouillard	(1.22.288)
Gabriele Tarquini	(1.22.466)	17			Osella-DFR	
AGS-DFR				18	Yannick Dalmas	(1.22.716)
Stefano Modena	(1.23.133)	8			AGS-DFR	
Brabham-Judd				9	Michele Alboreto	(1.23.161)
					Arrows-DFR	

Drivers' World Championship

Pos.	Driver	Total
1	Ayrton Senna	78
2	Alain Prost	69
3	Gerhard Berger	40
4	Nigel Mansell	31
5	Thierry Boutsen	30
6	Nelson Piquet	26
7	Alessandro Nannini	21
8	Riccardo Patrese	19
9	Jean Alesi	13
10	Ivan Capelli	6
11	Eric Bernard	5
12	Derek Warwick	3
13=	Alex Caffi	2
13=	Stefano Modena	2
13=	Satoru Nakajima	2
13=	Aguri Suzuki	2
17	Mauricio Gugelmin	1

Constructors' World Championship

Pos.	Team	Total
1	McLaren	118
2	Ferrari	100
3	Williams	49
4	Benetton	47
5	Tyrrell	15
6=	Leyton House	7
6=	Larrousse	7
8	Lotus	3
9=	Arrows	2
9=	Brabham	2

Race Classification

Pos.	Driver	No.	Nat.	Car	Laps	Time/retirement
1	Alain Prost	1	F	Ferrari	73	1h 48m 01.461s
2	Nigel Mansell	2	BR	Ferrari	73	1h 48m 23.525s
3	Alessandro Nannini	19	I	Benetton-Ford	73	1h 48m 36.335s
4	Thierry Boutsen	5	B	Williams-Renault	73	1h 48m 44.757s
5	Riccardo Patrese	6	I	Williams-Renault	73	1h 48m 58.991s
6	Aguri Suzuki	30	JPN	Lola-Lamborghini	73	1h 49m 05.189s
7	Nicola Larini	25	I	Ligier-DFR	72	
8	Mauricio Gugelmin	15	BR	Leyton House-Judd	72	
9	Yannick Dalmas	18	F	AGS-DFR	72	
10	Michele Alboreto	9	I	Arrows-DFR	71	
R	Derek Warwick	11	GB	Lotus-Lamborghini	63	Gearbox
R	Ivan Capelli	16	I	Leyton House-Judd	59	Leg cramp
R	Gerhard Berger	28	A	McLaren-Honda	56	Collided with Boutsen
R	Ayrton Senna	27	BR	McLaren-Honda	53	Punctured radiator
R	Nelson Piquet	20	BR	Benetton-Ford	47	Battery
R	Andrea de Cesaris	22	I	Dallara-DFR	47	Engine
R	Olivier Grouillard	14	F	Osella-DFR	45	Wheel bearing
R	Pier-Luigi Martini	23	I	Minardi-DFR	41	Loose wheel
R	Philippe Alliot	26	F	Ligier-DFR	22	Spun off
R	Eric Bernard	29	F	Lola-Lamborghini	20	Gearbox
R	Satoru Nakajima	3	JPN	Tyrrell-DFR	13	Spun off
R	Gabriele Tarquini	17	I	AGS-DFR	5	Collided with Modena
R	Stefano Modena	8	I	Brabham-Judd	5	Collided with Tarquini
R	Jean Alesi	4	F	Tyrrell-DFR	0	Punctured tyre/collision — Berger/Patrese
R	Emanuele Pirro	21	I	Dallara-DFR	0	Spun off

Fastest lap: Patrese, on lap 53, 1m 24.513s, 111.644 mph/179.674 km/h (record)

Non Qualifiers

No.	Name	Car
7	D. Brabham	Brabham-Judd
10	B. Schneider	Arrows-DFR
*12	M. Donnelly	Lotus-Lamborghini
24	P. Barilla	Minardi-DFR
31	B. Gachot	Coloni-DFR

*Accident during practice

Non Pre-Qualifiers

No.	Name	Car
33	R. Moreno	Eurobrun-Judd
34	C. Langes	Eurobrun-Judd
39	B. Giacomelli	Life-Judd

1990 FORMULA ONE GRAND PRIX
ROUND FIFTEEN

JAPAN

Suzuka International Racing Course

October 21, 1990

Circuit Length: 3.641 mls/5.859 km

Laps: 53

Official Starting Grid

			27 Ayrton Senna	(1.36.996)	
Alain Prost	(1.37.228)	1	McLaren-Honda		
Ferrari			2 Nigel Mansell	(1.37.719)	
Gerhard Berger	(1.38.118)	28	Ferrari		
McLaren-Honda			5 Thierry Boutsen	(1.39.324)	
Nelson Piquet	(1.40.049)	20	Williams-Renault		
Benetton-Ford			*4 Jean Alesi	(1.40.052)	
Riccardo Patrese	(1.40.355)	6	Tyrrell-DFR		
Williams-Renault			19 Roberto Moreno	(1.40.579)	
Aguri Suzuki	(1.40.888)	30	Benetton-Ford		
Lola-Lamborghini			23 Pier-Luigi Martini	(1.40.899)	
Derek Warwick	(1.41.024)	11	Minardi-DFR		
Lotus-Lamborghini			16 Ivan Capelli	(1.41.033)	
Satoru Nakajima	(1.41.078)	3	Leyton House-Judd		
Tyrrell-DFR			12 Johnny Herbert	(1.41.558)	
Mauricio Gugelmin	(1.41.698)	15	Lotus-Lamborghini		
Leyton House-Judd			29 Eric Bernard	(1.41.709)	
Nicola Larini	(1.42.339)	25	Lola-Lamborghini		
Ligier-DFR			21 Emanuele Pirro	(1.42.361)	
Gianni Morbidelli	(1.42.364)	24	Dallara-DFR		
Minardi-DFR			26 Philippe Alliot	(1.42.593)	
Stefano Modena	(1.42.617)	8	Ligier-DFR		
Brabham-Judd			7 David Brabham	(1.43.156)	
Alex Caffi	(1.43.270)	10	Brabham-Judd		
Arrows-DFR			9 Michele Alboreto	(1.43.304)	
Andrea de Cesaris	(1.43.601)	22	Arrows-DFR		
Dallara-DFR					

*Alesi withdrawn because of neck injury caused by crash during practice on Friday

Drivers' World Championship

Pos.	Driver	Total
1	Ayrton Senna	78
2	Alain Prost	69
3	Gerhard Berger	40
4	Nelson Piquet	35
5	Thierry Boutsen	32
6	Nigel Mansell	31
7	Riccardo Patrese	22
8	Alessandro Nannini	21
9	Jean Alesi	13
10=	Ivan Capelli	6
10=	Roberto Moreno	6
10=	Aguri Suzuki	6
13	Eric Bernard	5
14=	Derek Warwick	3
14=	Satoru Nakajima	3
16=	Alex Caffi	2
16=	Stefano Modena	2
18	Mauricio Gugelmin	1

Constructors' World Championship

Pos.	Team	Total
1	McLaren	118
2	Ferrari	100
3	Benetton	62
4	Williams	54
5	Tyrrell	16
6	Larrousse	11
7	Leyton House	7
8	Lotus	3
9=	Arrows	2
9=	Brabham	2

Race Classification

Pos.	Driver	No.	Nat.	Car	Laps	Time/retirement
1	Nelson Piquet	20	BR	Benetton-Ford	53	1h 34m 36.824s
2	Roberto Moreno	19	BR	Benetton-Ford	53	1h 34m 44.047s
3	Aguri Suzuki	30	JPN	Lola-Lamborghini	53	1h 34m 59.293s
4	Riccardo Patrese	6	I	Williams-Renault	53	1h 35m 13.082s
5	Thierry Boutsen	5	B	Williams-Renault	53	1h 35m 23.708s
6	Satoru Nakajima	3	JPN	Tyrrell-DFR	53	1h 35m 49.147s
7	Nicola Larini	25	I	Ligier-DFR	52	
8	Pier-Luigi Martini	23	I	Minardi-DFR	52	
9	Alex Caffi	10	I	Arrows-DFR	52	
10	Philippe Alliot	26	F	Ligier-DFR	52	
R	Derek Warwick	11	GB	Lotus-Lamborghini	38	Gearbox
R	Johnny Herbert	12	GB	Lotus-Lamborghini	31	Engine
R	Michele Alboreto	9	I	Arrows-DFR	28	Engine
R	Nigel Mansell	2	GB	Ferrari	26	Transmission
R	Emanuele Pirro	21	I	Dallara-DFR	24	Engine
R	Eric Bernard	29	F	Lola-Lamborghini	24	Engine
R	Gianni Morbidelli	24	I	Minardi-DFR	18	Spun off
R	Ivan Capelli	16	I	Leyton House-Judd	16	Misfire
R	Andrea de Cesaris	22	I	Dallara-DFR	13	Spun off
R	Mauricio Gugelmin	15	BR	Leyton House-Judd	5	Engine cut out
R	David Brabham	7	AUS	Brabham-Judd	2	Clutch
R	Gerhard Berger	28	A	McLaren-Honda	1	Spun off
R	Alain Prost	1	F	Ferrari	0	Collision with Senna
R	Ayrton Senna	27	BR	McLaren-Honda	0	Collision with Prost
R	Stefano Modena	8	I	Brabham-Judd	0	Spun off

Fastest lap: Patrese, on lap 40, 1m 44.233s, 125.739 mph/202.358 km/h

Non Qualifiers

No.	Name	Car
14	O. Grouillard	Osella-DFR
17	G. Tarquini	AGS-DFR
18	Y. Dalmas	AGS-DFR
31	B. Gachot	Coloni-DFR

Non Pre-Qualifiers

With only 30 cars present, following the withdrawals of Eurobrun and Life, no pre-qualifying session was required.

1990 FORMULA ONE GRAND PRIX
ROUND SIXTEEN

AUSTRALIA
Adelaide

November 4, 1990

Circuit Length: 2.347 mls/3.778 km

Laps: 81

Official Starting Grid

Driver	Time	No.		No.	Driver	Time
Ayrton Senna	(1.15.671)	27				
McLaren-Honda				28	Gerhard Berger	(1.16.244)
Nigel Mansell	(1.16.352)	2			*McLaren-Honda*	
Ferrari				1	Alain Prost	(1.16.365)
Jean Alesi	(1.16.837)	4			*Ferrari*	
Tyrrell-DFR				6	Riccardo Patrese	(1.17.156)
Nelson Piquet	(1.17.173)	20			*Williams-Renault*	
Benetton-Ford				19	Roberto Moreno	(1.17.437)
Thierry Boutsen	(1.17.596)	5			*Benetton-Ford*	
Williams-Renault				23	Pier-Luigi Martini	(1.17.827)
Derek Warwick	(1.18.351)	11			*Minardi-DFR*	
Lotus-Lamborghini				25	Nicola Larini	(1.18.730)
Satoru Nakajima	(1.18.738)	3			*Ligier-DFR*	
Tyrrell-DFR				16	Ivan Capelli	(1.18.843)
Andrea de Cesaris	(1.18.858)	22			*Leyton House-Judd*	
Dallara-DFR				15	Mauricio Gugelmin	(1.18.860)
Stefano Modena	(1.18.886)	8			*Leyton House-Judd*	
Brabham-Judd				12	Johnny Herbert	(1.19.091)
Philippe Alliot	(1.19.202)	26			*Lotus-Lamborghini*	
Ligier-DFR				24	Gianni Morbidelli	(1.19.347)
Emanuele Pirro	(1.19.476)	21			*Minardi-DFR*	
Dallara-DFR				14	Olivier Grouillard	(1.19.722)
Eric Bernard	(1.19.858)	29			*Osella-DFR*	
Lola-Lamborghini				30	Aguri Suzuki	(1.19.970)
David Brabham	(1.20.218)	7			*Lola-Lamborghini*	
Brabham-Judd				17	Gabriele Tarquini	(1.20.296)
					AGS-DFR	

Drivers' World Championship

Pos.	Driver	Total
1	Ayrton Senna	78
2	Alain Prost	(73)* 71
3=	Nelson Piquet	(44)* 43
3=	Gerhard Berger	43
5	Nigel Mansell	37
6	Thierry Boutsen	34
7	Riccardo Patrese	23
8	Alessandro Nannini	21
9	Jean Alesi	13
10=	Ivan Capelli	6
10=	Roberto Moreno	6
10=	Aguri Suzuki	6
13	Eric Bernard	5
14=	Derek Warwick	3
14=	Satoru Nakajima	3
16=	Alex Caffi	2
16=	Stefano Modena	2
18	Mauricio Gugelmin	1

*Best 11 results

Constructors' World Championship

Pos.	Team	Total
1	McLaren	121
2	Ferrari	110
3	Benetton	71
4	Williams	57
5	Tyrrell	16
6	Larrousse	11
7	Leyton House	7
8	Lotus	3
9=	Arrows	2
9=	Brabham	2

Race Classification

Pos.	Driver	No.	Nat.	Car	Laps	Time/retirement
1	Nelson Piquet	20	BR	Benetton-Ford	81	1h 49m 44.570s
2	Nigel Mansell	2	GB	Ferrari	81	1h 49m 47.699s
3	Alain Prost	1	F	Ferrari	81	1h 50m 21.829s
4	Gerhard Berger	28	A	McLaren-Honda	81	1h 50m 31.432s
5	Thierry Boutsen	5	B	Williams-Renault	81	1h 51m 35.730s
6	Riccardo Patrese	6	I	Williams-Renault	80	
7	Roberto Moreno	19	BR	Benetton-Ford	80	
8	Jean Alesi	4	F	Tyrrell-DFR	80	
9	Pier-Luigi Martini	23	I	Minardi-DFR	79	
10	Nicola Larini	25	I	Ligier-DFR	79	
11	Philippe Alliot	26	F	Ligier-DFR	78	
12	Stefano Modena	8	I	Brabham-Judd	77	
13	Olivier Grouillard	14	F	Osella-DFR	74	
R	Emanuele Pirro	21	I	Dallara-DFR	68	Engine
R	Ayrton Senna	27	BR	McLaren-Honda	61	Accident
R	Gabriele Tarquini	17	I	AGS-DFR	58	Oil fire
R	Johnny Herbert	12	GB	Lotus-Lamborghini	57	Stalled in pits
R	Satoru Nakajima	3	JPN	Tyrrell-DFR	53	Spun off
R	Ivan Capelli	16	I	Leyton House-Judd	46	Sticking throttle
R	Derek Warwick	11	GB	Lotus-Lamborghini	43	Gearbox
R	Mauricio Gugelmin	15	BR	Leyton House-Judd	27	Rear brakes
R	Andrea de Cesaris	22	I	Dallara-DFR	23	Electrics
R	Eric Bernard	29	F	Lola-Lamborghini	21	Gear selector fork
R	Gianni Morbidelli	24	I	Minardi-DFR	20	Gearbox
R	David Brabham	7	AUS	Brabham-Judd	19	Spun off
R	Aguri Suzuki	30	JPN	Lola-Lamborghini	6	Differential

Fastest lap: Mansell, on lap 75, 1m 18.203, 108.123 mph/174.009 km/h

Non Qualifiers

No.	Name	Car
9	M. Alboreto	Arrows-DFR
10	A. Caffi	Arrows-DFR
18	Y. Dalmas	AGS-DFR
31	B. Gachot	Coloni-DFR

Non Pre-Qualifiers

As in Japan, with only 30 cars present there
was no need for a pre-qualifying session.